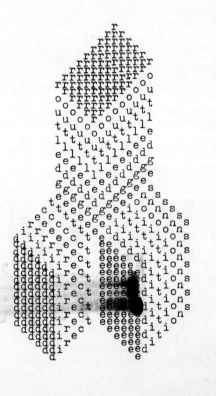

BETWEEN McALPINE AND POLARIS

George Giacinto Giarchi
Lecturer in Community Studies.
Head of Social Work, Health and
Community Studies Department,
Plymouth Polytechnic

ROUTLEDGE DIRECT EDITIONS

Routledge & Kegan Paul
London, Boston, Melbourne and Henley

First published in 1984
by Routledge & Kegan Paul plc

39 Store Street, London WC1E 7DD, England

9 Park Street, Boston, Mass 02108, USA

464 St Kilda Road, Melbourne,
Victoria 3004, Australia and

Broadway House, Newtown Road,
Henley-on-Thames, Oxon RG9 1EN, England

Printed in Great Britain
by Thetford Press Ltd, Thetford, Norfolk

British Library Cataloguing in Publication Data

Giarchi, George Giacinto
  Between McAlpine and Polaris.———
  (Routledge direct editions)
1. Navy-yards and naval stations, American
———Scotland———Holy Loch (Strathclyde)
I. Title
359.7   VA459.H/

ISBN 0-7100-9435-3

For Clare
who
introduced me to the 'inscape' of Hopkins
and
widened my understanding of life

Alienation is the cry of men who feel themselves to be victims of blind economic forces beyond their control, the frustration of ordinary people excluded from the processes of decision-making. (From Jimmy Reid's inaugural address at Glasgow University, 1972)

CONTENTS

ACKNOWLEDGMENTS

The Social Science Research Council financed this study, which otherwise would have been impossible.   I am indebted especially to Professor J.E.T. Eldridge of the University of Glasgow, firstly for introducing me to sociology, secondly for his inspiration, and thirdly for his patient understanding.   I am also grateful for the expert advice given to me throughout this study by Dr Simon Charsley, who read the script several times.   Dr David Dunkerley encouraged me to undertake the project and enabled me to grapple with several research problems.   Geoff Payne and Dr R. Mawby discussed the manuscript and shared with me their views on empirical questions affecting the analysis.

Mike Moore of Glasgow University Computing Centre helped me to cope with the computer programme and facilitated the formidable collation of data.

Without 'Willie' Inglis, late editor of the Dunoon Observer and Argyllshire Standard, I could never have carried out this venture. He not only allowed me access to his records and newspaper files, but also permitted me to use his office, bringing me cups of tea as I scanned and analysed the tabloid columns of the local press, covering the period under study.   Along with many Dunoonites, I remember him with affection and admiration.

Mrs Suzanne Tolan and, particularly, Mrs Dawn Cole typed the manuscript and drew my attention to format and layout requirements. Mrs Isobel Barnes of the Glasgow Herald was also most helpful in tracing some of my press references.

The people of Dunoon and its locality offered me hospitality and generous co-operation.   The administrators and the clergy of Cowal, the staff at the Dunoon Observer office in John Street, and the East Cowal residents gave me so much local information.   They collaborated with me in putting together this story.

I am also indebted to my wife, my daughters and son, who supported me in my venture and who did so with much forbearance and understanding.

The author and publishers would also like to thank the following:
Mrs Marion R. Carmichael of the Dunoon Observer and Argyllshire
Standard, for permission to reproduce various extracts and Map 2.1;
Dunoon and Cowal Tourist Organisation, for permission to reproduce
Maps 1.1 and 2.2 and Tables 7.2, 7.3, 7.4 and 7.5; Robert Hale Ltd,
for permission to reproduce some lines from Clyde Waters by Maurice
Lindsay; Inland and Waterside Planners, for permission to reproduce
Map 4.1; the Scottish Development Department Graphics Group, for
permission to reproduce Map 5.1; Times Newspapers Ltd, for permission to reproduce Map 7.1, which appeared in the Sunday Times on
7 March 1976.   Grateful acknowledgment is made for permission to
reprint verses 1, 3 and 4 of the song 'McAlpine's Fuziliers'
words by Dominic Behan; used by permission of Harmony Music Ltd.

Acknowledgment is also made to Tiparm Music Publishers for permission
to reprint verses 1, 3 and 4 of the song 'McAlpine's Fuziliers' ©
Copyright 1965 Tiparm Music Publishing Inc., as sung by the Clancy
Brothers; words by Dominic Behan.

FOREWORD
by Professor J.E.T. Eldridge

Many people outside Scotland would be hard put to say with any geographical precision where Dunoon is.   Holy Loch perhaps sounds
familiar.   It is the location of a US Polaris base, a product of a
decision taken in 1960 between President Eisenhower and Harold
Macmillan.   It is not the easiest of places for peace demonstrators
to reach.   From time to time, however, the base thrusts itself into
public consciousness.   In November 1981, for example, a Poseidon
ballistic missile was dropped by a ship's crane into the loch.   The
extent of the danger has been disputed but it was not a happy moment
as the New Statesman's indefatigable Duncan Campbell clearly showed.

George Giarchi knows Dunoon.   He was brought up there as a child
and holds its people in respect and affection.   He achieved a long
nourished ambition when, with the support of a post-graduate stu-
dentship at the University of Glasgow, he was able to return and
study the community.   His project was an ambitious one but despite
the cautious words of his academic mentors not to let it get out of
hand, his enthusiasm was unbounded and was matched only by his
energy.   Community studies in Britain are something of a lost art
these days.   For one person to accomplish so much on his own is
even more unusual.   Once he escaped the confines of the Sociology
department there was no stopping him.

What George Giarchi manages to convey is the way in which social
changes occur in the community.   Remote it may be, but Dunoon is
locked into the wider national and international context - not least
the military-political context of the cold war and the economic context of the oil industry.   In the course of his study some of the
mystifications which obscure decision-making are revealed and the
rhetoric with which the powerful seek to justify their actions is
made plain.

Between McAlpine and Polaris does not fit easily into the British
tradition of community studies.   With its concern to uncover the
history that is made behind our backs this is a book which has defi-
nite affinities with the American muckraking tradition.   There is a
sharp awareness of the arbitrary way in which institutional power

can shape the lives and destinies of people not only in the great
metropolitan cities but also in the rural areas.   This makes uncom-
fortable reading not least because much is done in the name of
democracy, the national interest, or even western civilisation that
cannot be readily justified by rational argument.   At least, however, the questions can still be asked and the critical voice heard.
So long as that remains possible the sociologist will have a public
role to perform.   George Giarchi has given us a book which is
stimulating, sometimes humorous, sometimes disturbing and above all
infused with a generous humanism.

John Eldridge

PREAMBLE

In 1974 I set out to explore the impact of the Polaris Base in Scotland upon the local population in the vicinity of Holy Loch in Argyllshire. When I arrived I discovered that this study could not be done without a comparative assessment of the impact of two other current intrusions within the confines of the area. The first was the impact of a newly created North Sea oil platform construction site in the locality. The second was the impact of regionalisation upon the people when the rather remote settlements by the Cowal hills and lochs of Southern Argyllshire were incorporated into the administrative Region of Strathclyde which was centred upon Glasgow. I was fortunate to have been 'on the spot' to compare the effects of these intrusions.

It took me almost nineteen months to become reasonably acquainted with local residents. In that time I arranged 803 interviews at random. 130 persons were questioned in the streets of Dunoon during the autumn general election campaign of 1974. Another 148 were approached during the summer season of 1975 on the Clyde ferry between Dunoon and Gourock. The others were interviewed during the autumn and winter of 1975-6, when I visited 525 homes, which were picked out at random within the locality. The home interviews represented a 6 per cent random sample of the adult population. But the homes visited constituted approximately a quarter of all local residences. This study in a sense is as much the account of 803 local persons as it is mine.

The research demanded more than observation and interviews. 4,800 newspaper issues of the Dunoon Observer were examined and regional accounts and books concerned with the history of the West of Scotland were studied in the Mitchell Library, Glasgow, and at the local library in Dunoon. The more recent issues of the Dunoon Observer published since the coming of the US navy to Holy Loch and the copies also of the national press were studied more closely. It has taken several years to piece together this study. With the passage of time ideas do mature, and, significant changes and events are seen in the perspective of retrospective insights.

Part One

BY WAY OF INTRODUCTION

Chapter 1

SETTING THE SCENE

It is not to be denied that if the point of view from which the
analysis is made were pressed further there would be much more to
be explained.   The extent to which a concept explains something
can never be absolute; it always keeps step with the expansion
and intensification of insight.
(Karl Mannheim 1936) (1)

Extending alongside the fretted shoreline of the Cowal Peninsula,
south Argyll, Scotland, lie tourist resorts which have catered for
work-weary urbanites from the earliest days of the Industrial Revolution.   The peninsula extends out towards the Isle of Bute, washed
on all three sides by the waters of lochs, Kyles and Firth.   It
hangs onto the mainland only by a narrow strip, some six miles
across and is serrated by two glens: Kinglas and Croe.   Most of
the area is mountainous and approximately half is wooded.   Its
settlements lie largely along the shoreline of the Firth of Clyde,
almost all of them facing the densely populated industrial region of
Renfrewshire and Clydebank (see Map 1.1, for location and main communications).

Dunoon, the ancient capital of Cowal, stands at the narrowest
point on the Firth where for centuries travellers have ferried
between Highland and Lowland.   It was known in the thirteenth century as 'the capital castle of the Lordship of Cowal'.   It is
around and within this small town of almost nine and a half thousand people that most of the population of Cowal is clustered in
small villages, most of which lie alongside the Firth or shores of
Loch Striven, the Holy Loch and Loch Long.

In an area that claims to be one of the finest beauty spots in
Britain (and according to many locals: in the world) everything
imaginable is offered to the out-of-door enthusiast on land and on
sea.   Both the yachtsman and the pony-trekker are catered for, as
well as the rock-climber and sea-angler, the sub-acquatist as well
as the bird and wild-life observer.   Cowal lies outside the Highlands, but it offers the tourists its own miniature highland and
heathered peaks and lochs, together with its forest and mountain

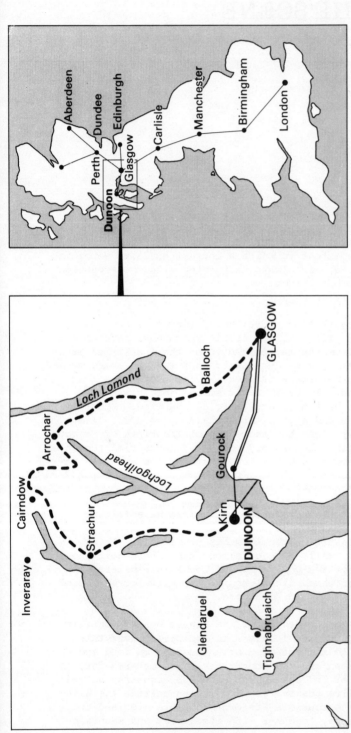

MAP 1.1   Location of Dunoon and communication

Source: Dunoon Information Tourist Office

Communications: When I was in Dunoon between 1974 and 1976, there were two main ferry routes to/from Dunoon and to/from Hunters Quay, linking Cowal with 'the other side'. The Dunoon route carried the main bulk of the passengers. Car ferries sailed from/to both settlements. A local bus service provided by a Dunoon garage owner linked Dunoon with the shore settlements. The public transport service had been discontinued some years before. There has never been a railway line connecting Cowal with Western railway routes.

walks, and its trout streams and salmon rivers.   Over 39 different
bird species, including the heron and the golden eagle, make their
home in Cowal which indicates how wild many parts of the peninsula
are.

It was in this peaceful and semi-isolated area that militarists
established an American naval missile base in 1961.   This was no
ordinary arrangement, because it was Europe's first US Polaris base,
altering the balance of power in the US/Russian confrontation, and
bringing the realities of a nuclear threat more dramatically home to
the local people.   It pushed the semi-rural locality into the very
forefront of a nuclear confrontation.

The element of surprise runs throughout this story from the time
that Macmillan's first announcement that a Polaris Base was to be
sited on the Loch.   Without prior notice Dunoon Town Council
learned by a telegram of the establishment of the base.   The
Polaris set-up was created instantly within the natural harbour.
Unlike other bases, there was here no previous onshore installation,
no building of quays, nor special quarters.

The local newspaper of 4 March 1961 described the arrival at Holy
Loch of the nuclear submarine tendership Proteus on the 3 March:

The vessel entered the loch shortly before 10 o'clock, flying the
stars and stripes at her rear mast.   She was towed stern first
to her mooring by two powerful tug-boats, a third tug being
deployed at the stern to keep her course.   Three planes flew
overhead, while pinnaces of the Royal Navy patrolled the
loch. (2)

The Burgh officials offered the American seamen a civic reception
on Friday 10 March, when the Lady Provost addressed the USN personnel in these terms:

It gives me particular pleasure on behalf of the Town Council and
of the citizens of the Burgh of Dunoon to welcome most warmly the
officers and enlisted men of the USS Proteus, who are to be our
new neighbours at their station in the Holy Loch.   Dunoon and
the Cowal shore may at this moment be unfamiliar to you, but soon
you will get your bearings, and will enjoy with us this lovely
part of Scotland, where we have the hills, the glens, the lochs
and the beautiful Firth of Clyde.   I hope that you will get a
lot of joy and pleasure from the surroundings in which you now
find yourselves.   We are friendly people in Dunoon, and we pride
ourselves that we know how to welcome visitors in our midst.   We
do not, however, look on you as visitors, for you are going to
work and live here, and will, we hope, become one with us. (3)

It was said then that the USN Base would probably remain for
three years in the area.   Today, over twenty years later, people
are wondering if it will ever go.   Many questions must be raised
about the effects that the foreign military has had upon life
locally.   It was to answer some of them that I moved into Dunoon in

1974.   However, I was not fully aware, not knowing until I took up residence in the locality, that another intrusion had added significantly to local pressures.

Hundreds of men had come to build concrete North Sea platforms at Ardyne, to the south of the Burgh of Dunoon.   The influx of outside labourers and technicians from an international labour market were altering the human landscape, in an area already under severe socio-economic pressures.

Hordes of McAlpine navvies excavated the soil and rocks from the banks of Loch Striven and scooped out the sea-bed to create basins offshore.   An altered shoreline dominated by a new hill made up of soil and earth from the site changed the physical landscape.   Here in the quiet countryside where sheep grazed, and where people had retired for the rural solitude, an endless stream of heavy lorries trundled along the narrow roads both day and night.   From daybreak, buses brought in hundreds of navvies.   At least 1,050 men were journeying by ferry from 'the other side', or from Bute to work for McAlpine.   Local contractors watched with dismay as their employees joined them to work for higher wages.

As if to put the final turn on the screw, in May 1975 the district of Cowal was taken out of the region of the Highland and Islands.   The locality was to be contained within the new Region of Strathclyde, with commercial Glasgow as its administrative centre.

The analysis of such impacts, however, cannot be possible unless an appropriate model is devised.   It provides a template against which the mode and outcome of impact can be assessed.   Concepts which are meaningfully built into the model, and which hopefully represent both subjective and objective realities, must also be selected from the existing sociological writings in an attempt to devise suitable heuristic tools.   Having read the more significant British community studies, eleven of which were published in the 1960s, (4) I consulted the leading British and American sociologists who specialised in the study of settlements, (5) but did not find they provided me with any single satisfactory approach, although their insights enabled me to be more aware of the significance of local events which I might otherwise have overlooked.   The more recent Scottish studies and ethnographic accounts of settlements under the impact of modern developments or the North Sea oil boom proved to be more helpful (6) in enabling me to see the invasions I was examining within a context described by many as 'the rape of Scotland'.   But, British studies of local people under the impact of a foreign naval intrusion just did not exist.

The locality therefore came under the three main intrusions of modernity: militarisation, industrialisation and bureaucratisation. All of these created societal pressures.   My study of the Polaris Base's local impact is therefore necessarily comparative.   In what ways did these pressures differ and in what ways were they similar? This study may answer some of these questions.

The concept of impact is often overlooked in the examination of social change.   I have yet to find a sociology study which has 'impact' in its index.   Even Alvin Toffler's (1970) mammoth book Future Shock which attempts to present an overview of what happens to people today overwhelmed by hyper-change, does not really analyse impact, but rather the effects, which is another matter, as we shall see. (7)

Obviously, what 'was', is altered by the change which impact has brought about.   I am not solely concerned with the 'before and after' contrasts which impact creates, the analysis of impact also requires a more dynamic assessment of the element of surprise and initial momentum.   The Oxford English Dictionary refers to the act of impinging, or collision in the context of momentum.   Webster's Dictionary describes 'impact' as collision, impingement;   striking against;   onset;   the power of impressing;   the force of impression; a clash, shock, bump, bolt, percussion. (8)   Impact now commonly suggests 'the driving impetus or momentum, in or as if in a collision, or the dynamic force in impressing or compelling change'. (9)

Three things suggest themselves:

1   impact refers to the instance of percussion/momentum which has outside origin(s) which constitutes a social blitz in terms of an initial effect on collectivities or neighbourhoods;

2   it refers to the impression and perceptions created and has inside repercussions;

3   it also has spin-offs and/or outcomes which are the sum of the percussion of both inside and outside forces.

It is the second point which requires more observations.   Certain people will know what is happening, others will not, some impressions will be created from outside, others from inside.   The impact will result therefore in a three-way percussion reaction:

1   those who know what is happening will react passively or actively;

2   those who are not aware of what is happening will not react, but will continue to act as before;

3   those who think they know what is happening, will react passively or actively in accordance with their own impressions.

The interplay will be mediated by their diverse perceptions, or the lack of it.   Lags in awareness will therefore abound.   The different reasons why impact and changes it creates may bring about lags in awareness and in people's reactions are summed up by W.F. Ogburn (1922).   His ideas help explain why there are cultural differences between one place and another, but also can show why there is a lag between groups or persons in perception, in the effects felt by them and their response to change under impact. (10)

Ogburn identifies isolation, climate and the absence of natural resources, as barriers to cultural development or impact, creating lags between remoter peripheral areas and the mainstream of the dominant culture at the centres. He also cites seven barriers to change, which are immediately relevant to the effects which impact(s) may initiate. These are:

1 the power of a particular economic group or class to resist change because their vested interests might be threatened;

2 the traditional hostility inherent in attachment to particular ways of living which therefore resist the new order;

3 the fear of the unknown attached to the new order, especially when hazards accompany it or any risks;

4 the force of habit, with the attendant conservatism it engenders, especially where innovations have been rare in the past;

5 the social pressure through fear of local ostracism or punishment, because of the preference for security in orderliness or definiteness;

6 the nostalgia for the past and a tendency to glorify and forget the unpleasant when presented with the choice of the new ('selective forgetting'); and

7 the anxiety created because of the uncertainty which is attached to the unknown, the superior utility of well-tried modes of action being the deciding factor. (11)

But, besides the factor of lag, change brought about by impact is also punctuated by surprises. In this study, the element of surprise (almost totally absent from community studies) is a central factor. This will now be elaborated within the episode of impact. Impact is described as an episode. It has three discernible phases: a beginning, a middle, and an end. Firstly, there is the instance of impact or percussion, which is accompanied by initial surprise. It is customary to regard impact as essentially the unwelcome crisis because it is a departure from optimum conditions, whereas the initial unexpected event may be the welcome harbinger of boom not doom which in turn may create unanticipated stress. (12) People may be surprised therefore by joy as well as by tragedy. Indeed, events may bring joy to some and misery to others. There are not enough 'in the wake of prosperity' studies to extend our knowledge of stressful impacts which counterbalance the 'in the wake of disaster' studies. What is important to note at the initial stage of impact is the immediate jolt which may be accompanied by welcome surprise. Often impact is reached when there is a conjuncture of stressful events which pile up, creating overload. (13)

Secondly, there is a period of spin-offs which are accompanied by secondary surprises, when former routines are disrupted locally, or shattered, or challenged. Once again, this could be for the better

(for some), or for the worse (for others).   Moreover, what began as
a pleasant experience may later turn out to be otherwise or 'vice
versa'.   Seldom does impact come in single isolated events, because
it is often part of a constellation of circumstances - hence the episodic nature of impact.   The spin-offs are accompanied by secondary
surprise which, as has been suggested already, may mark a change in
reaction when joy turns into sorrow and hope into disappointment.

Thirdly, there is the period when new routines are adopted or old
ones resumed.   There may even be a more entrenched return to the
older ways of acting.   This return, however, does not mark the end
of the episode, because repercussions from the initial and secondary
percussions may emerge spasmodically.   These will diminish in time,
but may escalate again to the point of re-activating the whole
pleasant or unpleasant experience.   In addition, throughout this
period of new or resumed routines, when a new pace of life, or a
return to the old, have taken place, some lags may occur.   These
may create an uneven reaction, especially where some people, or some
sectors of the population may be suffering from delayed shock.

It is during this third phase that tertiary surprises occur.
With the rise and fall of reaction, with the delayed action for some
and not for others, with the wish to settle down to either a new
order or an old, or older one, there will be the 'not again' or the
'in luck again' response, depending upon who are the beneficiaries
or not.

It would be simple if impacts occurred one at a time.   Settlements and organisations undergo impact cumulatively in a frenetic
modern world noted for transience. (14)   One impact will follow
upon another, and when this occurs reactions to the second or further impacts will overlap with the repercussions from another or
other impacts, which have not yet run their course.   At this point
fatalism may set in, and a sense of helplessness or confusion as
spin-off effects pile up, adding to the other effects resulting from
the first impact.   The results are frustration and bewilderment
which may erupt into violence and sometimes bring about a rise in
crime.

Figure 1.1 indicates the phases of a single impact.   The procession of phases and the overload endured when a locality or neighbourhood is under more than one impact will be described in the
course of this study.   René Thom attempts to describe discontinuous
change mathematically with his 'Catastrophe Theory' which E.C.
Zeeman has described so well. (15)   However, what is discussed at
length by Zeeman and Thom, using the language of mathematics and
geometric shapes, I prefer to describe more directly within the con-
ceptualisation of the social sciences, and, as will be demonstrated
later, through the insightful experience of the poet as well.

In examining change effected by impact, one has to focus upon the
object of such impact.   This being a study of a locality under
impact, one must be clear as to what a locality comprises.   Should
we be talking about the 'community' under impact?   Margaret Stacey

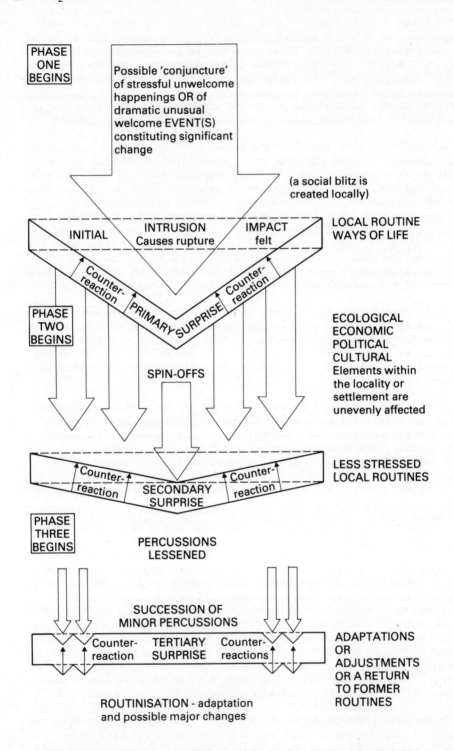

FIGURE 1.1   The phases of impact

has shown that 'community' is a nebulous concept. (16)   J.R. Gusfield has also alerted us to the ideological, existential, systemic,
and utopian biases that have become entwined around the concept of
community. (17)   In using the concept one might create considerable
confusion.   It might in turn be suggested that the locality might
best be regarded as a social system in a state of disequilibrium
under shock.   However, a social system approach does not take the
subjective view of people sufficiently into account.

Moreover, just as the term 'community' has caused confusion both
etymologically and conceptually, so too does the term 'system'.   In
fact, systemic writers have generally to start off their studies by
stating what variants of systems thinking they adopt and those which
they exclude.   Indeed, as authors such as Sztompka have demonstrated, there are at least five conceptual systems models, with a possible total of at least thirteen general assumptions and seventeen
particular assumptions, sometimes included or excluded. (18)   G.A.
Hillery jnr is often cited as having listed over 90 diverse definitions of community, (19) but what is overlooked is the fact that
variant systemic ideas have also caused a sociological babel.

However, systems thinking does rightly emphasise the context of
life or situations, a matter well discussed by Ernest Gellner. (20)

Clearly, the contextual provides the backdrop to the study of
settlements and localities, which, as shall be seen, was central to
R.L. Warren's vertical axes of co-ordination and communication
between the locality and the institutions of the wider world beyond
local confines. (21)   For impact studies the import of this
approach is obvious, as it was to J. Bensman and A.J. Vidich, (22)
and which prompted Stacey to say at the end of her appraisal of the
concept of community: 'In any locality study some of the social
processes we shall want to consider will take us outside the
locality.' (23)

But are there maps of life inside people which represent both the
immediate world and that of the remote world beyond?   This area of
discussion and analysis has been inspired by the phenomenologist
rather than by the systemic thinkers who are more concerned with
structure than form and more with externalities rather than with
internalities, (24) so that their contextual foci may reify.   Concepts as heuristic tools should account for the internal world of
the actor's mind and the external parameters of action.   We require
words that provide counterparts to 'objective' and 'subjective',
'external' and 'internal', but which at the same time have a sharp
precise edge.

But, how can one dovetail the subjective with the objective, the
internal with the external?   It so happens that Peter and Bridgitte
Berger allude to the fact that poets may have much to say that is
highly relevant concerning the effect of externalities on people
'alongside the sea', 'atop high mountains'. (25)   One of the most
insightful poets, who in self-examination described the interplay
between setting and feeling, between the scene and insightful

perception, was Gerard Manley Hopkins.   His poetry conveyed the
concreteness of settings and at the same time captured in his encounter with them the specific individual experience.   He called
this reactive process: 'inscape'.   It contained both the outside
and inside of his experience, based upon the ('haecceitas') particularity or 'thisness' of both the world as experienced and the encounter itself. (26)

    As a sociologist, I am not concerned with the process of percep-
tion or cognition 'per se' (this pertains to psychology), but rather
with their social ramifications in a collective or group setting.
Thus, I am not attempting in this study to explore the 'inscape' of
people as such, but rather to take into account the social processes
in which perceptions were both shared and formed with regard to the
navy and navvy invasions.   Any converging perceptual assessments
will matter in the analysis about the military and industrial
impacts.   The individual perceptions do not necessarily remain a
closed book, people may share views with neighbours, and there is a
consequent intra-subjective experience, in which the purely individual and particular becomes the plural and the shared social
opinion.   So one can say that at that stage the inscape of the
solitary becomes a 'social inscape' experience, wherein people share
and add to each other's perceptions and levels of awareness.   So
although I will adopt Hopkin's basic ideas, I must stress this is
not an 'inscape' study, focused on a singular psychological experience, but rather it is a 'social inscape' study, which is focused on
plural experiences involving the sedimentation of views created particularly by acculturation processes institutionally, and by local
networks of communication whereby the singular becomes the plural,
not through the 'fiat' of the aggregate tallied by counters or by
the computer, but through human interaction at a hundred and one
levels locally.

    The social inscape approach will require further elaboration.
The suffix 'scape', which in 'bar-formation' is used with land and
sea (so that one has sea-scape and landscape) and so associated with
settings, could be highly useful in designating some externalities
in sociology.   As shall be seen, this is not an exercise in seman-
tics.   'Scape', as indicated in the Oxford English Dictionary
(1961) is related to the Dutch word 'schap' meaning creation, constitution or condition, but it also includes as a connotation the
meaning of the Latin 'cappa' - cape or cloak.   This latter sense of
the word conveys the idea of an outer world in which man finds himself and which envelops him.   In much the same way as sociologists
speak of people within 'structures', with these factors in mind, one
might speak of them living within 'scapes'.   The immediate physical
context of a person's life is referred to as her/his 'local scape'
in this approach and the remote world beyond is termed the 'outscape'.

    The 'local scape', therefore, refers to the man-made and natural
environment as physical externalities.   The 'local scape' is identifiable by certain boundaries and landmarks.   The boundaries will
not always be clear: these will be defined by its residents, depen-

dent upon the folk images as described by Suttles. (27)   Suttles
states that territory 'depends on a mental template of its structure
and the way some natural and man-made features of the environment
help determine that structure'. (28)

The 'outscape' is the beyond, but as MacIver observed, there are
social worlds beyond the local scene 'circling us round, grade
beyond grade'. (29)   So one may refer to 'nearer and wider outscapes', according to the degree in remoteness in communication
terms, rather than merely in mileage.   Taking these factors into
consideration, change in this study will be considered in transcape
terms.

Taking up the factor of distance in communication in transcape
terms, and further applying the inscape images, one can identify
'nearer and wider outscapes', whose boundaries, although necessarily
vague, will be relative to the local scape usually in terms of
access and familiarity.   The wider outscape is not observable from
the local scape; often not directly accessible and least experienced by the people of the 'local scape'.

This point is crucial to an impact study, because centres of
influence are often in the outscape where the hidden agenda and
vital decision-making take place in the beyond, in the unknown,
that perplex people, as this study will confirm.   Also, an 'outscape' which is more distant than others in mileage terms may be
regarded as nearer, because of more direct communication, thus
presenting a more dynamic internal/external assessment.   The more
impact, therefore, a place in the outscape exercises upon the local
scape, the more it moves into a position of nearer and nearer influence.   As it draws closer in its influence, people within the local
scape get to know more about it, and its man-made and physical boundaries take on more meaningful forms.   Whether people resent, or
welcome its outside influence, knowledge of this place has locally
become more intense.   If outsiders from its confines come into the
local scape, that knowledge will grow, often taking on various
biases, as my interviews with locals in the Dunoon area will show.

The particular physical and man-made structures such as roads,
buildings, etc. of the local scape create certain effects.   Ecology
is the study of such effects, which shows that the man-made and the
natural may constitute hazards or threat, liberation or progress.
I propose that there is an 'ecological scape' which is the emergent
inhibiting or liberating factors of the environment which create the
quality of a setting for living as well as people's perception of it
as safe or hazardous.

The quality of life is not only determined ecologically, but also
by the impress of the past on the present.   Local custom, traditional codes, galas or pageants or Highland Games, certain buildings
and local landmarks are part of an endogenous historical local
growth which, taken together, impart a local transgenerational quality of life which is expressed to a large extent by communal events
or monuments build up over time.   This transgenerational quality

encapsulates the past and is an enveloping factor kept in being not only by buildings and other localised factors, but also by the written and spoken word about the past. It may also change over time when folk-lore or historical research alters it. People locally regard the past as they see it or have known it as a context or 'scape' in which the present is acted out. This localised trans-generational quality constitutes a 'historical scape'.

One cannot deal with impact from outside upon a locality, unless change in the economic, political, and cultural spheres are assessed. Anthony Smith describes these as 'regions of change'. (30) N.J. Smelser speaks of these as structural processes. (31) These are unevenly affected under impact. The differential impact is dealt with in the economic, the political and the cultural context by sociologists, which are described in this study as 'scapes'. Taking Ogburn's concept of lag, there will be lag in some and not in others when a locality suffers from impact. Which scapes are affected and how will be important to any assessment of the overall change in local conditions.

The economic, the political and the cultural are viewed in other studies as systems, structures or regions of change. In this study they constitute scapes which is preferred, firstly, because systemic concepts 'per se' do not connote the factor of personal envelopment and, secondly, because the realm of subjectivity is not catered for adequately by systemic or structural terms. Impact is ultimately felt and perceived and reported by people within both individual and collective situations. It is the latter which concerns us here and the possible lags sometimes undetected by people but at other times differently felt by groups as impact affects them diversely. Definition may clarify the matter further.

The 'economic scape' is the prevailing resource allocation in the form of goods, services, employment, housing, and the means of production affecting people's life-style, life-chances or standard of living as well as their perception of them, but more particularly their position within a social class.

The 'political scape' is the institutionalised distribution of power and control in public affairs affecting people's freedom of thought and speech as well as their collective perception of freedom, under the influence of party politics, the military, elitist groups, administration, and formal or informal organisations.

The 'cultural scape' is the routinised social pattern of living in the form of acceptable customary behaviour and rituals as affecting people's behaviour and expectations and their leisure pursuits within a social calendar, whose conventions are mediated by local tradition, vernacular values, ethnicity and local institutions: familial, religious, etc., together with people's perception and appreciation of them.

The 'social inscape' approach, as outlined so far, will be utilised when identifying the mode of impact. The episode of impact

will be explored in an attempt to detect any possible processual
pattern(s).   One may then prepare the ground for the study of
effects in scape terms, and also identify possible mediating factors
such as detailed by Ogburn's barriers to change.

The study of impact will involve identifying change within time-
bands.   It is a complex task, because the impacts overlap and require to be traced each to their origin in time, and local lags
between affected groups require to be assessed.   The Ardyne intrusion followed the invasion of the Americans over a decade later.
The initial impact of the McAlpine's invasion came at a time when
the USN Polaris Base had brought about multiple effects over the
years, and, as will be shown, had reached the period of tertiary
surprises by the time the navvies had moved in.   Later, when the
Ardyne events had run into a period of 'spin-offs', at a secondary
surprise level, the new regionalisation scheme hit the locality with
its initial impact.   The identification of those who welcomed and
those who resisted the changes and the diverse effects over time are
not easy to unravel within the overlap between three distinct
impacts.

The American intrusion is the primary focus, but cannot be seen
except in comparative terms.   Examining the changes longitudinally
of all three impacts will go some of the way to presenting a comparative impact study of the American intrusion.

In attempting to present this study the formidable task is only
too apparent.   J. Bensman et al. go so far as to say: 'No one has
yet been able to present a formal methodology for the optimum or
proper method for the scientific study of the community.' (32)
This impact study of local people under outside pressure can hardly
hope to establish one, but it may go some of the way in extending
our appreciation of what people face collectively under the percussions of impact in a world beyond their control, especially what
people endure in peripheral geographic zones.

Chapter 2

THE MAKINGS OF NEW DUNOON

We must break through the walls of the contemporary action, and
go back into the past.   In addition to a descriptive and contemporary analysis and the combination of various statistical inven-
tories taken at various moments of time such as are provided
regularly by the population censuses, we need some insight into
the actual process of these occurrences which have formed the
specific traits of our community.   (R. Konig) (1)

In 1883 the founder and first editor of the local newspaper, which
is now the Dunoon Observer and Argyllshire Standard, wrote and published a small booklet entitled Handy Guide to Dunoon which introduced the reader to the town of Dunoon and its immediate environment
of East Cowal. (2)   Later his son, the second editor, drew a map of
Dunoon District which included the settlements within the eastern
part of the Cowal area.   The first editor's great-grandson, third
editor to the newspaper, hung the map in his office until his recent
death.   The booklet continues to be published.   For four generations the family editors of the local newspaper have written about
life in Dunoon District, always associating the shore settlements
with their capital, Dunoon.   Map 2.1 is based upon the old map,
which was adopted in this research.   I had to be sure that such
confines constituted a meaningful 'whole', before I could be satisfied that for local residents such environs did add up to a 'local
scape'.   We will see later how many locals agreed it did.

The 'local scape' may be anything from a glen with a single homestead to a built-up urban sprawl.   If one is researching the
'social inscape' in terms of its communal sharing and consensus or
its communal disruption and conflict, one must establish the local
field of activity.   Once that field is defined and causally justified, the genesis of life may be historically delineated within it.
Map 2.1 presents the confines of the 'local scape' within which the
genesis of life locally has been generated in interactive and sometimes disruptive terms.

The villages and small town of Dunoon are set within a semi-
remote area which is easily identified as a natural integral

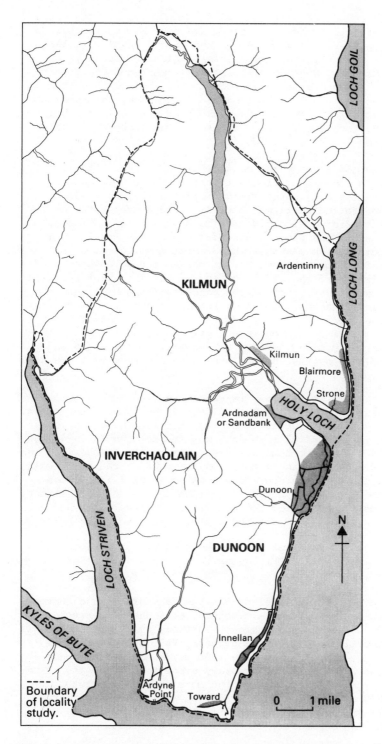

MAP 2.1   Map of Dunoon District showing the boundary of East Cowal

ecological scape.   The physical boundaries are the waterscapes to
the west, the east and the south.   In the north, running inland
from the end of Loch Striven, are the three glens of Tarsan,
Garrachra and Branter, whose enveloping hills surround the area up
to the river Driep, where it flows from the old bridge into Loch
Eck.   Moving southwards along the banks of Loch Eck, one comes to
Whistlefield, a small homestead, then the road cuts over the hills
to Ardentinny by Loch Long, and so one joins the shore road, which
leads through the lochside villages to the town of Dunoon.

Dunoon really comprises three settlements.   Firstly, there is
the old town area converging around the pier and main street.
Secondly, two settlements merge almost imperceptibly into old
Dunoon.   These are the settlements of Kirn and Hunters Quay to the
north-east which stretch alongside the road called the East Bay.
On the other side of the pier is the West Bay (see Map 2.2).   The
shoreline is dotted with mansions which skirt the four miles of
promenade, running from the West Bay to the East Bay.   These dwellings were built around the middle or end of the last century, with
a few blatant exceptions, such as the concrete dance hall near the
pier and some modern shops which look incongruous by the Victorian
buildings.   The sweep of the bays to the left and right of the
pier, with the neat line of houses and gardens alongside the promenade, presents an imposing aspect.   However, the old walls and
grey façades of once prouder hotels and homes indicate that the town
has seen better days.

The town, as shown on Map 2.2, is mainly centred upon Argyll
Street (the chief shopping place), Hillfoot Street, and John Street.
Apart from the hotels and boarding houses skirting the two bays,
Dunoon is mainly residential.   When I was in the town in 1975, the
main street had six public houses, three restaurants, two cafés, two
tea-rooms, four Scottish Banks, three chemist shops, the Burgh Hall,
a Presbyterian church and a Woolworth's store.   In 1975 a closed-
down cinema, the old La Scala, stood boarded up and for sale at the
centre of the main street, and the old Picture House, which had been
also on the main street, had already closed down some years before.

On the hill behind the pier stands the High Kirk, complemented by
the imposing steeples of two Presbyterian churches which overlook
the main street.

A modern indoor swimming pool on the East Bay breaks the contours
of a nineteenth-century watering resort.   Only when one reaches the
inner streets and comes across three relatively small modern council
estates - at the Glebe (off George Street), Valrose Terrace (off
Alexander Street), and at Ardenslate (alongside Ardenslate Road) -
does one come across a more contemporary scene (see Map 2.2).   Running into the Ardenslate scheme are the more modern Waverley Court
flats, where USN enlisted personnel live.   Off the main street,
standing like a warehouse, is the American Commissary.   Both the
naval flats and the Commissary are tucked out of sight.

American cars in the streets with their US number plates, however, stand out from the Scottish scene, American accents betray the presence of hundreds of civilian-clad naval personnel.

The town today is much the same as it was when I was there in 1974-6, the same cannot be said of the road and the scene as one motored from Dunoon to Ardyne along the East Shore in a southerly direction.   When I was in the area between 1974-6, lorries and green McAlpine vans thundered in a continuous flow from morning till night, whilst scores of navvies laboured alongside the shore to widen or straighten it.   On approaching Ardyne, low-flying helicopters patrolled the environs around Toward and Ardyne.   It was a noisy area when once it had been quiet and peaceful.   At Ardyne the gigantic towers of concrete platforms for the North Sea oil-field appeared beyond the trees, rising above dust and hundreds of men at work, amidst the shouting of gangers and the whirr of huge mixers. Each tower was higher than the Post Office Tower in London.

When I journeyed in 1974-6 from Dunoon in the other direction, the scene was much the same as it had been in the 1960s and 1970s, and later in the 1980s.   After leaving Hunters Quay, one confronted at Holy Loch the grey hull of the US Polaris depot ship which loomed up incongruously alongside a gigantic floating dry dock with ballistic nuclear submarines alongside.   The hum of engines, and the busy activity of small craft, coasting to and from the long pier at Ardnadam, presented a discordant picture in an otherwise remote and peaceful loch setting, intruding upon the peaceful villages of Sandbank, Kilmun, and Strone, which together with the line of dwellings known as Rashfield, circled the loch and its noisy vessels.   Around Strone Point the small villages of Blairmore and Ardentinny appeared to be more removed from the US naval intrusion, but a sense of peace was soon shattered when arriving at the naval torpedo range at Loch Long, once noted for its quiet retreat and its herons.

The concrete gravity North Sea structures at Ardyne to the south and the USN Base to the north of Dunoon were out of sight when I visited the area in the mid-1970s, but the casual visitor was reminded by the USN cars, the green McAlpine vans, and the strange accents of incomers, that, however remote, Cowal was at the centre of dynamic changes.

Over the years the villages and the Burgh of Dunoon have shared a common 'economic scape'.   Employment and allied related services have mainly centred upon Dunoon; some locals have worked in the pine woods of Cowal and on the few scattered farms, whilst others have travelled to 'the other side' for work.   The main source of income to the locality, however, over the years, has been tourism.

The villages and the town have also shared a common 'political scape'.   Each has shared the same power-play within the same local political zone and constituency.   Public administration has been related for many years to the same localised needs and issues within the locality, where for centuries the administration boundaries have been those of the historic parish of Dunoon and Kilmun, with Inverchaolain the people's ancient burying place.   T. Dunlop states that

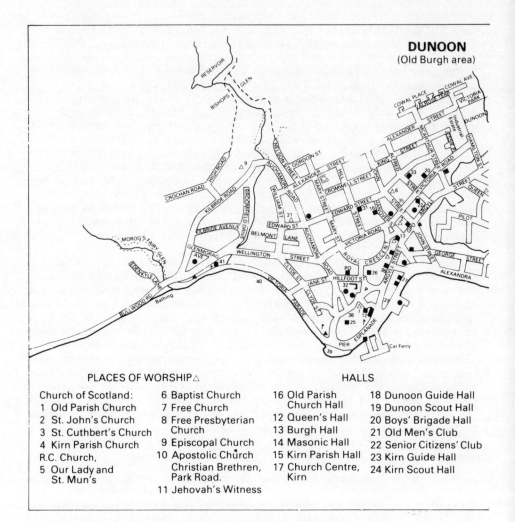

PLACES OF WORSHIP △

Church of Scotland:
1 Old Parish Church
2 St. John's Church
3 St. Cuthbert's Church
4 Kirn Parish Church
R.C. Church,
5 Our Lady and
   St. Mun's

6 Baptist Church
7 Free Church
8 Free Presbyterian
   Church
9 Episcopal Church
10 Apostolic Church
   Christian Brethren,
   Park Road.
11 Jehovah's Witness

HALLS

16 Old Parish
   Church Hall
12 Queen's Hall
13 Burgh Hall
14 Masonic Hall
15 Kirn Parish Hall
17 Church Centre,
   Kirn

18 Dunoon Guide Hall
19 Dunoon Scout Hall
20 Boys' Brigade Hall
21 Old Men's Club
22 Senior Citizens' Club
23 Kirn Guide Hall
24 Kirn Scout Hall

MAP 2.2 Dunoon: its extent and public amenities

Source: Dunoon Information Tourist Office

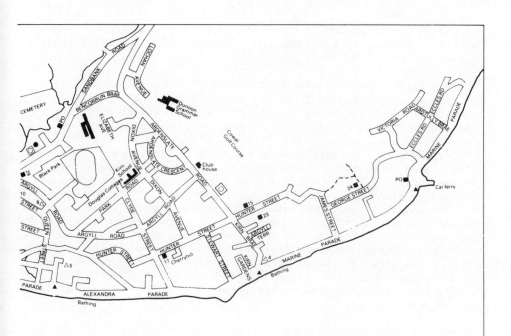

PLACES OF INTEREST.

31 Registrar
   Dunoon Grammar School
32 Dunoon Primary School
   Kirn Primary School
33 St. Mun's Primary School
34 Information Centre
35 'Dunoon Observer'
   Office
36 Cinema (closed down
   in 1970s)

42 Y.M.C.A.
25 Public Library
13 Burgh Hall
26 Milton House
   (Town Clerk)
27 Swimming Pool
28 Sheriff Courthouse
29 Site of New
   Police Station
   Fire Station

OUTDOOR RECREATIONS

37 Argll Gardens
   Dunoon
   Sports Stadium
38 Tennis
39 Crazy Golf
40 Boating
41 Children's Paddling
   Pond and Swing Park

⚑ Putting
○ Bowling Greens
● Parking
▲ Toilets

the parish of Dunoon and Kilmun is 'said to be one of the most ancient in Scotland', (3) which has regulated the life of the local people for centuries 'quoad sacra quoad civilia'.

The villages and small Burgh have also shared a common culture for centuries.   Firstly, Cowal has maintained its distinctive Scottish identity together with an ancient tradition for hospitality. The locality's culture is still centred around Highland music and dance and is proud of its clan lore, all of which have always found a major place in the local holiday brochures.   The Dunoon press has often commented upon the area's clan heritage.   The highlight of the year has always been the Highland Games at Dunoon, which annually attracts almost four times the local population.   To the playing of 1,000 bagpipes the clans continue to parade through the town at the Games under their ancient banners.   Scotsmen compete, testing their prowess as wrestlers and caber throwers.   The nimble steps of hundreds of Highland dancers still raise the applause of visitors and tourists from the UK and overseas.   These Highland festivities, which last two days, are presided over by the clan chiefs.   The locality's Scottish culture is annually reinforced and conserved by these Highland Games.

Secondly, the Scottish Presbyterian church reinforces ties within and between settlements.   Religious belief appears to matter in an area that has been less exposed to the inroads of secularism. Indeed, when Dunoon was Glasgow's prime resort in the last century, the local people blocked the exits at the pier to prevent Sunday holiday-makers from entering the town.   The visitors were 'breaking the Lord's Day'.   Local church-goers called them 'the Sabbath breakers'. (4)   After a hundred years of holiday-making, Dunoonites are much more tolerant, but still devout church people.   There has always been a 'lag' between Cowal and 'the other side' in sacred as well as in secular matters.

Thirdly, associations and clubs draw people together in communal events.   Shinty, an old Scottish sport, bowling, and golf, attract villagers and Dunoonites to share as spectators or participants. Many other pastimes link villagers with Dunoonites, as can simply be shown, although in a cursory fashion, by the list of some of the main local clubs and organised meetings. Their titles indicate their embrace of the area, rather than just of the town.   Most of the clubs or associations are as follows:

Cowal Horticultural Society	Cowal Five-a-side Association
Cowal Badminton Association	Cowal Choral Society
Cowal District Bridge League	Cowal Tennis Association
Cowal Camera Club	Cowal Golf Club
Cowal Panto Group	Cowal Round Table
Cowal Amateurs (Football)	Cowal Floral Art Club
Cowal XV (Rugby)	Cowal Music Club
Dunoon Argyll Curling Club	Upper Cowal Bowling Club
Dunoon & District Angling Club	Cowal Angling Club
Dunoon & District Gun Club	Cowal Athletic Football Club
Dunoon & District Young Farmers' Club	Dunoon Town & Country Club

Dunoon & District Canine Club   Dunoon Argyll Whist Drives
Dunoon Rural Institute

Certainly, these social groups support the claim many local residents made during my interviews, that they were living a very full
life during the winter season.   In such an area one is reminded of
Durkheim's distinction between 'material density' (ratio of people
to the surface) and 'moral density' (intensity of communication).
Although there is a low density of population by urban standards,
there are indications of a high density of participation and shared
experience.

These factors in terms of local scapes will be demonstrated when
assessing changes over time within the locality.   Local 'time' has
its own particularity.   Marx states: 'Men make their own history,
but they do not make it under circumstances chosen by themselves,
but under circumstances directly encountered, given and transmitted
from the past.' (5)

Sociologists have been well aware of the importance of local history when searching for reasons why people act the way they do,
especially within their study of settlements.   Out of the web of
time the strands of local features appear.   The 'historical scape'
gives to a settlement or locality a certain 'particularity' - in a
sense the present is contained in the envelope of the past.

Following R. Konig and the observations of the last chapter, the
history of Dunoon and its locality will be outlined within the
framework of succession, concentration and segregation. (6)   At the
same time, continuities will be taken into account as suggested by
R.M. Stein. (7)

'Dunoon' could possibly be derived from the word 'Dun-nan-
aoidhean' meaning 'place resorted to by strangers or guests'. (8)
Certainly, from the earliest days, going back to the seventh century, a constant stream of outsiders came into the area, often for
pillage. (9)   But, more important, the location of Dunoon afforded
a stepping-stone for travellers to and from the Western Highlands.
The First Statistical Account of Scotland (1791) states that Dunoon
was an important ferry inlet for Argyllshire, especially before the
new road was built by Loch Lomond up to Inveraray. (10)   Thereafter, the size of the population did tend, for a while, to go down,
as Dunoon's ferry facility was used less.   None the less, travellers, especially farmers or drovers, constantly passed to and from
the West Highlands by the ferry across the Firth.   Indeed, we know
from well-established local sources and a collection of maps at
Castle House, Dunoon, that the only road through the village of
Dunoon led to the ferry, a thoroughfare where strangers met and were
welcomed by the locals of Dunoon. (11)

In addition, Dunoon was a well-known centre for smuggling, and
for the illegal distilling of whisky. (12)   Factors which, as shall
be seen, are curiously repeated today when considering the illegal
traffic in drugs within the area since the US Navy Base was created.

In 1755, there were 1,757 people in the district. (13)   Judging
from the 1791 statistical account, they were a resilient people,
anxious at all costs to develop further the ferry service and the
link with the opposite side of the Firth. (14)   Apparently, there
were frequent attempts to build a pier or quay near the castle. (15)
Today, the pier jutting out into the waters of the Firth, facing the
'other side', stands for the linkage of the town and district with
strangers and guests.   But, what of the ruined castle of Dunoon
above the pier?

The castle was probably founded in the sixth century and, if we
are to believe narrators such as MacKay, was the seat of foreign
invaders who successively took over the castle and area. (16)   The
New Statistical Account (1845) makes reference to a turbulent
ancient local history centred around Dunoon. (17)

Further along the Cowal shores stands the ruins of Toward Castle.
It was once the seat of the Lamonts, from which they ruled Cowal.
However, according to historical accounts, the Campbells of Loch Awe
seized the castle at Dunoon, taking complete control of the district. (18)   The two castles therefore represent dual local clan
loyalties and, as is well known, clan loyalties persist today with a
continuing sensitivity to past history.   The Campbells supported
the Crown.   They had 'outside' loyalties, and coercively strove to
subject the wilder West to the crown.   Hitherto Cowal had clung to
its relative independence and resented the intrusion of central control.   This situation repeats itself today, again in curious continuity.   Some gained by the changes as some do today, so a certain
local ambivalence and division of view has always split loyalties.
The relevance of this with regard to Strathclyde regionalisation
will be seen later in this study.   In spite of a great deal of
local feeling, Cowal became known as 'King's Cowal' - the thorn in
the side of an Argyll that had always been set against control from
the centre or south, and proud of its Dalriadic origins.   The
Lamonts represented independence, and the Campbells dependence.

The stay of the Campbells cannot be said to have been a happy
one.   It ended abruptly in 1646 after one of their atrocities.
Taking the cream of the Lamont Clan, numbering thirty-six, 'special
gentlemen' in boats from the Lamont Castle at Toward, the Campbells
hung them or put them to the sword, burying many alive below Dunoon
castle. (19)   To this day a plaque marks the spot of this burial,
and the Lamonts continue to pay homage.   No plaque marks the spot
where the Campbells lodged on the hill.   They left the town almost
immediately after the atrocity. (20)   But they remained the leading
family in Argyll, ruling the whole area, in spite of their deeds,
because of their support of the crown and the imposition of the
English language.   Today, people locally can still recall the
ostracisation of Campbell families as late as the 1930s, and at the
local Highland Games one may still hear a hiss or 'boos' for the
Campbell band as it walks on to the field to compete for a pipe band
trophy.   There is certainly a local cult in support of the Lamont
clan.   Dunoon was never proud of its 'royal' constables on the
hill, and has always played down the Campbell connection.

Returning to the 'outside' interference by the monarchy, one may cite MacKay, who states: 'The extension of the power and rights of the Scottish monarchy evidently operated as a disturbing force on the more ancient order of things in this district', adding that this brought with it the concomitants of conquest and colonisation by outsiders and 'the dislodging of local inhabitants'. (21)   History was to repeat itself in an area accustomed to invasion and outside interference and migration.

In 1791, when the <u>First Statistical Account of Scotland</u> was written, the local historian wrote 'incoming people are very much low-country tenants', and added that English was the common language of the locals, although 'Gaelic is still the natural tongue with them'. (22)   In addition, he noted that the incoming shepherds were wealthy Southlanders, and that one Teviotdale shepherd owned 1,000 local sheep. (23)   Moreover, of the fourteen proprietors, only three were resident. (24)   It is clear that for lengthy periods Dunoon District was infiltrated from the outside and under a cosmopolitan influence.   This must be set against a background of English domination and interference, especially after the Jacobite movement.

Dunoon District was to be subject to successive takeovers, in terms of both power and culture.   English influence made early cultural inroads into the Cowal strip, when the rest of Argyll was Gaelic.   It is significant that the town of Dunoon is the only one in Argyll which has an English motto: 'Forward'.

Certainly, the influence of outsiders and the appeal of novel life-styles and attractive opportunities across the Firth have been a continuing feature in the story of the town and area.   In the 1791 account, the Dunoon narrator writes: 'Our neighbourhood to Greenock leads our young people to be expensive in their attire, and to imitate such as affect the manners and dress of those who rank higher than themselves'. (25)   For many of the young, 'forward' meant looking towards the south for progress, even for their livelihood, so many left the district.   In fact, it could be said that although Cowal faced north-west it looked over its shoulder of hills and shores to the more 'developed' south.   The god-fearing writer of 1791 claimed that the prolonged conviviality at nights and local merrymaking were caused by the 'near neighbourhood of a much frequented seaport town' - namely Greenock across the waters. (26)

For hundreds of years the social and economic interplay between the two sides of the Firth has been a salient feature which has created certain local ambivalences.   This has recently been accentuated with the 'metropolis-satellite' polarisation between Glasgow and Dunoon.   The connection between the district and the economic centre of the West of Scotland has increased, only to be finally heightened in the Strathclyde complex when Argyll was to be annexed to the Glasgow region of Strathclyde.   A complex network of control stretches throughout the Western hemisphere from the very edges of the periphery to centres of power.   More and more, these centres have influence, politically, economically, culturally, and militari-

ly.   The dependence of satellite settlements on the metropolis is a
recurring phenomenon especially in modern times which extends yet
further to more and more complex networks associated with macrometropoles, as shown elsewhere by the writings of André Gunder
Frank. (27)

Progressive changes were sweeping through Scotland in the last
century, emanating from the cities.   As they increased in size, so
too did small towns and villages around them.   The story of industrial Clydeside is linked with widespread technological developments but particularly with the expansion of Glasgow.   After the
upsurge of the Scottish cotton industry, as described by H. Hamilton, metal industries sprang up within the Clyde valley. (28)
Further down the Firth, towns like Dunoon and Rothesay in Bute were
not industrialised, but they became residential watering places for
the more affluent Glasgow businessmen and in turn became resorts for
the labouring masses.   The Clyde steamships carried them 'down the
watter' by the hundreds to shingle beaches and beautiful vistas by
the 'bonnie banks'.

It is evident that the spatial distribution of Dunoon and district is meaningful only within the social and cultural variables
that are associated with the expansion of Glasgow.   In addition,
sociologists such as E. Shevky and W. Bell, B.J. Berry and P.H.
Rees, have rightly stated that a settlement is a product of its
time, and can only be understood in terms of the society into which
it comes into being. (29)

Although Dunoon and the settlements of the Cowal shores developed within their own historical scape, many miles away from the
industrial belt, by the quiet hills and glens, the influence of
Glasgow altered them culturally and in economic terms.   Kilmun by
Holy Loch, for example, was further developed by Napier of Glasgow,
who built much of the present settlement for Glaswegians who
brought to the area their urban values.   Some older locals will
tell you in Kilmun, with some pride, that David Napier in 1820
sailed the world's first iron steamer on nearby Loch Eck.   They
still live in the past.   There seems to be so little to boast of in
current local achievements.   The long-standing contact of Kilmun,
Dunoon and local settlements with Glasgow merchants has been a significant factor.

The first invasions and consequent concentrations in and around
Dunoon in the mid-nineteenth century are easily identified: firstly, came the Glasgow elite, the wealthy, who established the industrialisation of the West of Scotland.   These were followed by successive groups of mainly middle-class, thrifty, and enterprising
small businessmen and shopkeepers.

In 1822 James Ewing, an ex-Provost of Glasgow, who was influential in the Merchants' House of Glasgow and the Glasgow Bank, who
was also founder of the Glasgow Savings Bank, set up his marine
villa near the old Dunoon Castle.   Writing about Ewing, Reverent
MacKay wrote:

We need scarcely inform tourists or travellers frequenting the
Firth of Clyde that Dunoon has since grown up to be now a very
extensive and populous place indeed, having grown beyond the
dimensions of a mere village ... and whatever extension it has
already arrived at, or whatever may yet be its extent and size,
it is all undoubtedly traceable to Mr. Ewing's good taste and
discernment, in having selected it as his summer residence.   He
may well be styled the founder of Dunoon.   The visitors whom he
drew to the place soon began to follow the example he had set
them;   and villa after villa, and house after house began to
rise. (30)

It could be said that new Dunoon was Ewing's creation.

The merchants of Glasgow, whose city boasted 'the tallest
chimney-stacks in the world', seized the opportunities afforded by
steamship travel, not only to develop markets abroad, but also to
set up residence for themselves along the picturesque Clydeside
estuary.   It became the social thing, and the culturally appropriate step for the wealthy Glaswegians to have a castle-like dwelling
or marine villa by the waters of the Firth.   The Glaswegians'
social and cultural connection is thus central to the story of new
Dunoon.

Indeed, the present line of boarding houses and hotels in Dunoon,
running parallel to the water's edge, were for the most part the
summer residences of Glasgow merchants. (31)   But this was made
possible by the expansion of Glasgow's merchant class, together with
the timely development of steamships, rather than the 'good taste'
of Ewing.   None the less, the influence of the merchant banker
cannot be underestimated, because of his personal links with the
business and banking elite of the city.   The significant thing to
note, from the point of view of the origin of the new township, is
that Dunoon was described in 1866 as 'virtually a suburb or amenity
of Glasgow'. (32)   An interesting footnote to the development of
Dunoon and district is that another Glasgow merchant and friend of
Ewing, Mr Kirkham Finlay, set up his castle at Toward ten years
after, in 1832, so that the two traditionally opposed clan sectors
of Cowal associated with two old antagonistic castles, around which
families polarised in fixed animosity, became linked through the
mutual friendship of two Glasgow merchants.   Although thereafter
family clan divisions in part remained locally, they never asserted
themselves quite so fiercely as before.

The concentration of the wealthy Glasgow merchants along the
shore roads of Cowal, brought to the 'clachan' cottages and thatched
farmsteads, a dramatic change of life-style, as carriages and pairs
brought the wealthiest men of Scotland to their castles by the sea.
M. Lindsay says of these 'patriarchal masters': 'they created a
convention - taken up by middle-class and by the proletariat in
their turn, to go "doon the watter"'. (33)

It is significant that Ewing's own bank, the Savings Bank of
Glasgow, was set up in Dunoon as early as 1839 and that wealthy

incomers such as Kirkham Finlay of Castle Toward, together with
James Hunter of Hafton, made possible the extension of Dunoon
Kirk. (34)   Both Douglas of Glenfinart and Kirkham Finlay provided
school house and educational facilities locally. (35)   This incoming 'upper-crust' provided a Victorian patronage of both church and
schoolroom.   Their predominantly middle-class impress upon the
locality is still evident today.

M. Lindsay described the early settlement of the Glasgow entrepreneurs in the area.

By the middle of the century, mansions and 'marine villas' were
sprouting round the fringes of every accessible loch and open
stretch of the Clyde.   Tea, tobacco, soap, coal, iron and
steel, ships and railway engines, these were the things that
lined the pockets of Glasgow's captains of commerce.   Self-made
men, most of them, they had little in the way of taste.   They
wanted the appearance of grandeur and their architects gave it
to them, in neo-baronial turretings and mock gothic gambols. (36)

It became fashionable to follow the Glasgow elite to the Clyde
resorts and enjoy the sea air.   According to J.S. Patterson: 'By
1864 the "coasting season" was a recognised feature of life in the
West of Scotland.' (37)   For the towns of the estuary this meant a
cycle of life in which successive holiday-makers invaded the locality each year.   Already, in 1845, the narrator of the New Statistical Account of Scotland could describe a scene of rapid and seasonal
changes of population in Cowal where local enterprise strove to
satisfy new settlers and the demands of leisure-seekers:

While building and other improvements proceed actively, numerous
families of tradesmen from the towns on the Clyde, and labourers,
reside for a year or two, and again removed.   Families also
sometimes reside during the summer months in villas or houses,
either their own property, or occupied for the time.   The residence of such is made to suit convenience and taste;   and trans-
fers in such kinds of house property are of frequent occurrence;
and altogether, there may be said to be an irregular and varying
condition of the population as to actual amount. ... Perhaps in
no parish in Scotland is the population more variable, comparing
one year with another. (38)

But the merchants left and the poorer classes moved in, to be
given the new delights thought up and devised by incoming Glasgow
and Renfrewshire shopkeepers and hoteliers, who were the grandparents of many of today's locals.   In the 1930s Lindsay describes
the trip to Dunoon, when the 'Eagle' steamer tied up at Dunoon, and
'the day trippers spilled over the pier and dispersed among the
town's crowded narrow streets in search of fish-and-chip shops, junk
stores and other transferred delights of Glasgow'. (39)   Needless
to say, Dunoon 'pubs' were a feature for weary urban workers.   Most
'pubs' were in the main street and the lower roads near the pier.
Drunken behaviour in the main roads or aboard the steamers has
continued to be a topic of complaint locally.   In the 1860s and

1870s the Glasgow Herald published regular accounts of drunken ex-
cursionists 'doon the watter'. (40)   Clyde ships have always carried a licence to sell spirits at any time of day.   Over the years
the profits have encouraged stewards to turn a blind eye to behaviour that might be reprehensible ashore. (41)   For the Glaswegian
who had little to cheer him, drink offered an escape - in 1868 there
were 1,780 pubs in Glasgow alone. (42)   When he got to the ship at
the Broomielaw of Glasgow he could drink 'all the way' down to the
Firth and round the Kyles and back. (43)   However reprehensible the
drunks and the behaviour of the visitors, they made the Clyde
estuary more affluent.

We have here clear evidence of the 'dual ethic' especially in
Dunoon.   In spite of its presbyterianism, the town catered for the
drinking lads from the big city.   The strangers were passing
through and thrifty locals did not miss the opportunity 'to turn a
penny'.

Dunoon had quite a name as a drinking place even in the early
days of the ferry.   It also enjoyed quite a reputation for the distilling of whisky. (44)   Certainly, from 1841-5 down to the
present, the town's pubs and its inns have had a large trade. (45)
There is no indication, however, that the residents of the town and
its locality enjoyed a reputation for heavy drinking.   The busy
summer season could hardly have given the thrifty population much
time for it and in the winter the more transparent nature of life in
the small settlements (46) made overt heavy drinking less acceptable.   Throughout the Accounts one gets the impression that the
Cowal people were law-abiding.   Their stable families and Christian
life-style mattered.

What attractions did these people offer the visitors?   After
all, most visitors were sober.   The sightseers had to have more
than scenery.   Dunoon people erected a bronze statue in 1896 of
'Bonnie Mary of Argyll' in front of Dunoon's ruined castle.   She
was a Dunoon girl who had fallen deeply in love with Burns.   She
still stands today with bronze eyes focused on the Ayrshire coast
where she was said to have 'exchanged bibles with Robert Burns over
running water, and married in the "Scottish style"'. (47)   Glasgow
people have come by their thousands to stand there and relive the
romance.   They still visit the hill, not to see the castle ruins,
but to see 'Bonnie Mary' and be photographed at the base of the
statue.   They search for Auchamore Farm, the spot where she was
born.

Love has been associated with the quaint Cowal countryside where
Sir Harry Lauder, the renowned Scot, who lived in the Dunoon District for years, composed and sang his best songs by the 'bonnie
banks o' Clyde'.   Ageing married Glaswegians still remember courting days and romance by the Cowal hills.   William Cameron wrote a
poem about the romantic air at Dunoon's Morag Fairy Glen, a spot for
lovers along the West Bay:

There's music in the wild cascade,
There's love amang the trees,
There's beauty in ilk bank an' brae
An' balm upon the breeze;
Then meet me, love, by a' unseen
Beside yon mossy den;
O, meet me, love at dewey eve,
In Morag's Fairy Glen. (48)

The town could also stage big events to attract the crowds such
as yachting races, swimming galas and field sports. As far back as
the middle of the last century Dunoon staged a British boxing championship between John Gondie of Scotland and Ned Langlands of
England - with bare kunckles - to which thousands of people journeyed from all over Britain. (49) We have already noted the
attraction of the Cowal Highland Games. The Games were founded in
1894 and became one of the most outstanding Scottish events of the
year: 'recognised as an athletic event of international standing'. (50) Highland Games had been introduced into Scotland as
part of the vogue of 'Balmorality': 'The couthy simulation of old
customs that have long since lost their meaning, for the sake of
gratifying sentimentality.' (51) However, the sports and music
were SCottish in origin and had an immediate appeal for the Scots.
Their culture was revived by the playing of pipes, the toss of caber
and the swirl of the tartan kilts.

M. Lindsay wrote a poem about the Highland Games at Dunoon. It
conveys the festive but nationalist atmosphere of the grand occasion, when pipe bands muster as if on the eve of battle. Bands
have come from every part of the world and as each clan congregates
they follow their band through the town from the pier to the park
for the competition. 30,000 visitors cram the small streets of a
town built to take 10,000. Visitors festooned with tartan banners
and clan shields, outnumber the locals by three to one. Lindsay
writes:

There's tartan tammies and muckle blads
tae show the garb o' the clans;
there's thistl't lassies and kiltit lads
wi the emblems of fitba fans.
The fuss and the jostle, the rankringam din,
the stow and the heat o the day
are sudently naethin for aa are kin
when the thoosand pipes play.
As the skirlin soun drifts up tae the hills
and spreids owre the skinklan sea,
there's nae ae hert but gaes faster and fills
wi whit Scotland jince culd be.
Yet afore the echo has cooled i the bluid
they're wavean their gew-gaws again.
And Scotland's back tae her dotit mood
o snicheran, sneet hauf-men! (52)

We see here the drifting sight-seers with their football scarves waving them to the Scottish emblems.   For a brief spell, under the sway of the playing of the thousand pipes Scottish youths feel victorious over the English.   The Games represent their individuality as Scots.

The locality has also been renowned since the days of Sir Thomas Lipton for its yacht racing.   The Clyde Yacht Club has had its headquarters at the Royal Marine Hotel, Hunters Quay, at the head of Holy Loch for years.   The Clyde Fortnight during the inter-war years launched some of the biggest British yachting events, especially the six-metre yacht race for the coveted Seawanhaka Cup - a race which always attracted the best yachtsmen in the world. Nearby is the well-known Robertson Yard at Sandbank, where a small number of local craftsmen have built some of the world's greatest yachts, some of which represented Great Britain in international races.   Local pride in joint achievement cements local ties, giving the 'social inscape' yet another 'particularity'.

Dunoon was never to have the reputation for the extrovert Blackpool-like attractions, but it did have its summer shows at the summer theatre, called 'the Cosy Corner', on the front, where the best of Scotland's comic turns amused the holiday-makers for years and where old Scottish comics such as Harry Gordon and Alec Findlay told their first jokes.   The character of the seaside shows will have much to do with the story of recent changes in Dunoon, as shall be seen.

In spite of local resources and business acumen Dunoon did depend upon help from 'the other side' at the height of the summer season.   The influx of both visitors and those who served, awaited and amused them, gave Cowal a cosmopolitan character.   G.C. Smith, in his Statistical Account, notes: 'At the beginning of the century it was usual to recruit hotel staffs with employees who came only for the season from outside the area, generally from Glasgow.   So too with the touring coaches and cabs: horses and drivers were brought down from Glasgow.' (53)   According to the same account 'at the height of the season the population is trebled'. (54)   Hotel and catering staff generally came from Greenock or Glasgow.   The economic ties were also maintained in the 'off-season' during the winter, because of the traffic of skilled labour to service machinery, heating systems, etc., or to prepare business premises for the summer trade.

Tourism was certainly the major means of livelihood for the people of Dunoon and the local settlements up to 1961.   The Burghal area contained, by that time, no less than seven licensed hotels, 130 private hotels and boarding houses and a large number of flats or apartments. (55)   The hotels and boarding houses could account for 3,000 holiday-makers, who came mainly for the scenery, the haggis and the whisky.   The crowded summer months and the quiet winter spell created a contrast in patterns of living and in lifestyle.   Dunoon and district lacked any large-scale industry, so that the winters were 'deadly quiet', as one local put it.

Steady local employment had always been hard to find.   The
hoteliers, landlords and shopkeepers of one kind or another could
financially survive a bleak winter.   Many other locals could not.
The young, especially the males, migrated from Cowal year after
year.   A growing number of their parents commuted to the towns on
'the other side' where they managed to obtain employment.   We have
no idea of the number who travelled over by ferry to these jobs each
day, except that C.G. Smith merely notes: 'Apart from the building
trades, there is little opportunity for learning a trade; some
manage to secure an apprenticeship in Greenock, and travel daily,
but others, less fortunate, have to go farther afield.' (56)   A
steady stream of letters from Scots abroad in the columns of the
local newspaper confirm this constant trend over the years.

A marginal number of local people have always found employment in
the agricultural and forestry belts of Argyll.   In 1961 there were
34, 533 acres in cultivation or farm use, and afforestation enter-
prises utilised 11,110 acres. (57)   But the major part of the agricultural usage of land was for grazing, no less than 31,766 acres,
so that the need for manpower was minimal.

Influx, however, cannot be associated solely with the increase in
visitors during the season.   There have been other forms of invasion.   After the resort was well established at the turn of the
century, when the rhythm of life routinised, older people began to
come to Dunoon for retirement in ever greater numbers.   At the same
time, as has already been seen, the young people began to leave the
town and area to seek work on 'the other side'.   According to the
Returns of the Registrar General for Scotland, the Dunoon birthrate
showed a 'crude rate of natural decrease' except in the two immediate periods following the two World Wars, (58) and yet the population was rising, so one can only account for this increase in population by the influx of outsiders, and these were mainly the aged.
In fact, the Census of 1961 pointed out that Dunoon Burgh had by
that time the lowest percentage of young amongst the Burghs of
Argyll.   The County itself had a very low proportion of youth.
The census indicated that the Burgh of Dunoon had at the same time,
the highest proportion of elderly of 65+ - in a county noted for its
high percentage of aged people. (59)   And the narrator of the Third
Statistical Account observed: 'Many old people retire to Dunoon, in
spite of the shortage of houses, and but for this influx the remark-
able growth of population would not have occurred, for many who are
born within the parish have to leave it to seek employment.' (60)

The data supplied by the Registrar General covering the period
1911-61 showed how Dunoon compared with the county and national
rates of births and deaths. (61)   The Dunoon death-rates on the
whole have had a consistently higher rate for many years than the
national and county rates, and inversely a lower birthrate than the
national and county levels.

What of the movement of population during the war years?   Significantly, there had been a naval infiltration during the two World
Wars, when RN vessels anchored in the Holy Loch, and convoy vessels

lay off the Firth within the Clyde estuary.   It is interesting
that the New Statistical Account (1845) stated that the Holy Loch
was an ancient anchorage for foreign ships. (62)   In the Second
World War, submarines were moored to a mother ship almost at the
same anchorage as that of the present USN tender ship.   Ironically,
since the time of St Kentigern, the Loch has been called 'an Loch
Seanta', which means, according to MacKay (1845) 'the charmed
loch'. (63)   When the grey warships' convoy vessels anchored on its
peaceful waters, that charm was not apparent.

Also in the Second World War, Dunoon District, like most more
remote urban-rural areas, had its share of evacuees.   Locals will
tell you that they called them the 'vak-yew-ees'.   Many of them
remained after the war.   G.C. Smith writes: 'Some of the families
that came as evacuees have remained to make their homes.' (64)
Most of them returned once the war was over, but year after year
their children came back for holidays as grown adults.

In addition to the 'vak-yew-ees', Dunoon had a naval influx.
For three to four years naval personnel were based in and around the
town.   They were ship personnel, submariners and naval men attached
to the barrier-boom stretching from Dunoon to the Cloch on the other
side.   The writer of the 1961 Account notes that the influx of
evacuees, plus the wives of servicemen in Dunoon 'gave hotel-keepers
a busy time'. (65)   By all accounts, it was a prosperous period for
the burgh and the area.   Older local people remember the servicemen
who not only brought the adults hope and cheer ('our fighting men'),
but gave the children chocolate and their lads and lasses
cigarettes.   Shops served the men and women of the Royal Navy at
half price.   It was all part of a great joint war effort.   The
shopkeepers, publicans, hoteliers, landlords and landladies of
Dunoon did not lose out, however.   They had trade all the year
round in a town with no room vacancies and more mouths to feed.   In
spite of the 'blackout', late night dancing at the Pavilion on the
front, late cinema shows at the La Scala and the Picture House in
Argyll Street and the late closing of public houses and cafés were a
feature.

It is clear that shopkeepers, publicans, hoteliers, landlords,
and proprietors of one form or another had more to gain, as has
always been the case, in new Dunoon.   They made up the more prosperous locals.   Most of the twenty-five Provosts and town councillors before 1961 were small businessmen.   They were the 'better-
offs', made up of incomers, for the most part, from Paisley, Greenock and Glasgow.   G.C. Smith describes the town as made up of
'dozens of small shops'. (66)   The shopkeepers set up business
shortly after the advent of the big landowners. (67)

In 1845 when there were only thirteen proprietors in the parish
of Dunoon and Kilmun, there were no less than twelve mansions with
extensive parks, and a total of just under 400 local houses in the
whole area, many of which were owned by the rich merchants. (68)
From a reading of the Accounts (1791, 1845, 1961) one gets the
impression, confirmed by the analysis of the available evaluation

rolls, that after a concentration of the top-heavy upper-class
settlers there was a heavier concentration of self-employed comfortable businessmen whose numbers grew with the development of the
local tourist and catering trade.   This was typical of any watering
place, but this initial influx of merchant princes had left its mark
upon the area, not only ecologically, but in terms of local values.
Money mattered so that status and prestige went hand-in-hand with
material prosperity.

As the holiday resort grew, so too did the exodus of the builders, the navvies and tradesmen who built new Dunoon.   These constituted the local working class.   Most of them could not survive nor
could other local poorer families.   The influx of a resilient self-
employed, thrifty class, imbued with the then popular sentiments of
'self-help', soon dominated the town and surrounding countryside
with middle-class values and a pervasive individualism.   The
decrease of the rural life noted in the 1845 Account went on apace,
as did the exodus of the 'farm hands'.   The local small businessmen
and caterers have been fiercely competitive and individualistic from
the very beginning.   In a sense, they helped to create the new
Dunoon.   The local concentration of resourceful vendors and
caterers from the more developed and 'Gesellschaft' (69) urban areas
on 'the other side' brought with them a certain contractual approach
to life which was urban and industrialist in origin.   'Private-
regarding' attitudes were a local feature in the early days, and in
later days were conserved by the absent landlords and landladies.

There were ratepayers who were absent for a major part of the
year in Dunoon and area, as can be shown by an examination of the
Evaluation Rolls. (70)   The common good in this circumstance may be
so easily lost sight of by influential property-owners in the outscape.   The significance of these remarks with regard to the USN
personnel will later be more apparent.

Clearly, the self-interest of the more influential absent landlords militated against the local needs and interests of younger
married people who were either first-time buyers or hunting for
rented accommodation.   Property stood empty for nine months and was
only available for visitors.   Strangers were preferred to the
locals.   Moreover, the council house provision was inadequate for
many years, certainly until the mid-1960s.   G.C. Smith observed
that accommodation in Dunoon was poor for lower classes.   Fewer
council houses had been built in Dunoon than in the smaller towns
of Campbeltown and Oban.   Taking the shire as a whole, Dunoon, the
biggest Argyll burgh, had a poor record compared with other smaller
burghs. (71)

The ideas of Glasgow University's Adam Smith concerning the free
market economy dominated Scottish thought, and the Protestant ethic
of work involved individualistic efforts: each man was to give an
account of his stewardship before God: the individual, not society,
was called to judgment!   Those were the days when Samuel Smiles's
book on 'Self-Help' was read avidly by the self-employed, and was
instrumental in creating their value system.   The new bourgeoisie

were individualists in Dunoon District, as the court proceedings
showed.

   As might be expected, individualism brought with it early antagonisms.   Consequently, litigations locally were heated and prolonged.   The editor of the Dunoon Observer and Argyllshire Standard
describes the new gentlemen in the second half of the nineteenth
century as a 'litigious people', (72) and a local lawyer, Mr A.
McLean, has made a considerable study of the various fierce court-
room battles over the rights of locals to property. (73)   A main
contention seems to have been between the alleged 'rights' of the
established locals to lanes, cart roads, and certain common land,
and that of the incoming property speculators.   The locals resisted.   From the start the Dunoon people showed that they were able
'to put up a good fight'.   The problem was that mobility later
tended to weaken their numbers and their effectiveness as a group,
as did a core of self-interested influentials.

   Today, the protest of local people, in conflict with the alien
interests of incomers, demonstrates such weaknesses, as will be
seen.   However, there has always been a strong local loyalty to
Cowal which transcends class and material interests.   This is well
exemplified by a local historic confrontation between Dunoonites and
Ewing.   In 1834 after Ewing took over his property on the 'front',
which today is called 'Castle Gardens', he built a high wall around
his 'bit' of land.   This included the old Castle property.   The
Dunoonites claimed that the castle property had become common land
after the exodus of the Campbells.   Not daunted by the high-handed
incomer, the local women patiently and obstinately came by night and
took away whole sections of Ewing's wall.   By day Ewing's men came
and bricked in the gaps, by night the women took them out.   It
ended in a court case at Inveraray in which proceedings were taken
against some of the women, but in the end local feeling won the day,
and the castle property has remained open ever since to the people.
After 150 years local people still speak of the episode.

   A Dunoon poet, Duncan MacLean, wrote a poem concerning the incident which describes the successful fight for freedom and right:

AULD WIVES' BATTLE OF CASTLE HILL

We sing of the castle Dunoon,
The hill gemm'd with daisies so bright,
Where our mothers we know in days long ago
Fought proudly for freedom and right.
The beautiful hill we now own
By the landlord was walled all around,
Till our mothers with skill assailed the old hill
And levelled the wall to the ground. (74)

   This first protest indicates that in those days there was a stro
strong corporate feeling about collective rights.   However, after
1868 in the early days of the Burgh, a new hard core of self-interested locals resisted actions by the council which were in the best

interests of the people.   For example, in 1880 it was suggested
that a public park be opened; a plebiscite was taken, and in the
event, only a relative few could vote, so the proposal was rejected
by 424 votes to 170. (75)   In the days of railway expansion it was
proposed that a railway line should come round via Lochgilphead,
with stations planned at intervals from Strachur onwards, passing
Loch Eck, and halting at Sandbank, before terminating at
Dunoon. (76)   This was resisted by influential individuals.   This
railway project would have threatened local property.

Another example will show how a concentrated body of conservative
influential committed ratepayers was able to block innovation or
interference from outside.   It was suggested in 1921 that electricity be introduced, but 'the ratepayers rejected the proposal'
and it was not until 1929 that electricity was supplied. (77)   The
people's ranks did close on public issues when Cowal was threatened,
as was the case when the nationalisation of the British Railways was
to bring about a cut-back in shipping and the closure of several
Clyde-piers.   Public protests 'proved effective in curbing the
official zeal for excessive centralisation'. (78)   When speaking
about concentrations, one must note that there was a nucleus of
residents who came from across the Scottish borders or even from
some European countries.   In Dunoon according to the 1961 Census,
which assesses the situation as it was when the USN Base was first
established, the ratio of residents born outside Scotland in Dunoon
per 1,000 of the population was 80.   This compares with 70 in
Argyll and 66 in the small burghs.   Cowal was largest with 105.

From the fact that Cowal's ratio was over 1 in 10, and considering that many local families had themselves originated from outside
Dunoon District a generation before, it could be said that localism
may have been less marked in the area as a whole than it might
have been, had the area been without a history of cosmopolitanism.
G.C. Smith remarks: 'Neither representation on public bodies, nor
office-holding in the local societies, nor even personal association
is confined to the "natives": the grouping is rather according to
taste and interest rather than according to length of residence.' (79)

Important to the cosmopolitan scene is the fact that for over a
hundred years many strangers have attended church side by side with
local people throughout the summer months.   A communal parochial
spirit did exist in certain congregations, but as one will shortly
see, it hosted and served the stranger.   It could be said perhaps
that the Cowal religious congregations have been accustomed by
reason of the cycle of summer and winter swings of population to
experience 'mechanical solidarity' as a parish or fellowship in the
quiet periods; and 'organic solidarity' (80) in the busier season,
which helped to create an openness in spite of the area's remoteness.   A consequent degree of pliancy and a flexibility has characterised the worshippers, on the whole, and a greater ability to
adapt.

The geographic character of Dunoon and district would appear to create for the local people a certain tendency towards closure, with infrequent boats connecting the locality with 'the other side' during the winter months - there were few boats in the winter season before 1961, just as is so today.   Contact with 'the other side' by road has always been arduous and lengthy and possible only for car owners.   Networks have tended to be 'territorially based' (as described in Barnes's terms), but with the incoming workers and the summer crowds the people's sense of tolerance and adaptation appear to have also been considerable.   Educationally, the very experience of schooling in Dunoon has been instrumental in creating tolerance and knitting together the villages around the shores of Argyllshire.

Dunoon Grammar School has enjoyed an educational reputation throughout Argyll.   For many years pupils have come from all parts of the Western Highlands and boarded at the local hostel serving the Grammar School.   The school has had an unusually widespread appeal and wider intake, because in many parts of the West there are no secondary schools. (81)   Local pupils have been able to mix with boys and girls whose values and outlook have been quite different. This has reinforced the tolerance of local residents.   In addition, all the secondary pupils from the shore settlements around Dunoon merge with the town's youngsters at the Grammar School, which has also helped to unify yet more local ties in Cowal.

Has there been any segregation in the area before 1961?   As has been seen, the people of Cowal have been largely cosmopolitan over the years.   Most could not claim to be real 'natives', certainly, in the early days.   Resistance to strangers appears to have been minimal in a locality known for its hospitality.   Only the old clan divisions seem to have created marginal local biases, as hinted at already, and although individualism was apparent among the earlier settlers, segregation does not appear to have been a dominant feature.

It is apparent that the area was characterised by conservatism. However, it was tempered by a certain tolerance for 'outsiders', because in a sense the area depended so much upon them.   Individualism was also tempered by a strong religious sense of 'fair play' amongst the general population.   Presbyterianism had exercised a dominant local socialisation influence from the beginning.   It propagated the Gospel locally with less emphasis as time passed by upon the exclusiveness of Calvin's predestined, because the openness and tolerance of the cosmopolitans were modifying features.   The service function of the locality as a tourist and holiday centre had softened some of the salient features of a stricter form of Presbyterianism at that time.   Later the impact on the people will be assessed when the religious fabric of life locally was threatened by the more liberal views of the American incomers.   However modified, local Presbyterians closed ranks when it came to Sunday worship and morality.

One example of local religious tolerance is worth identifying. Irish labourers and Roman Catholics from the Isles and the Lowlands helped to build new Dunoon when it almost doubled its population

between 1831 and 1931. (82)   In contrast with 'the other side',
where Catholic and Protestant schools have created religious barriers, second only to the North of Ireland, Catholic and Protestant
children in Dunoon have singularly grown up side-by-side in both
their neighbourhoods and schoolrooms, even in church and kirk in
religious fellowship.   The fact that the Catholic people in the
mid-1920s were able to secure an excellent and prominent plot of
land for their church on the East Bay, opening on to the promenade,
shows how open the locals were to 'outsiders'.

The dominance of Presbyterians, however, cannot be denied.
There were ten presbyterian charges in the Dunoon/Kilmun parish
District by 1961: three in Dunoon, two in Innellan, two in Kirn,
one in Sandbank, one in Kilmun, and one for Strone and Ardentinny,
showing a total of 4,272 officially committed adult members in
the parish. (83)   To the west, linked with Inverchaolain, was the
Presbyterian kirk at Toward.   The Dunoon kirk is the High Kirk.
But, provision was made for outsiders.   Visitors could choose from
a Free Church service, a Baptist, or Scottish Episcopalian, or
'Congregation of Christian Brethren' church service, or they could
attend the meetings of the Jehovah Witnesses, or Mass at the Catholic Church. (84)   English visitors were not fully provided for,
however, but the same has been true of church service provision in
most small English seaside towns regarding places of worship for
Scots.

In addition, political loyalties have tended to cement local
parish ties.   Since 1707 Argyll has had an MP, but between 1707 and
1831 there was a very small number of electors, in all 43 in the
whole of Argyllshire in 1790, which increased to 107 electors by
1831. (85)   C.M. MacDonald (1961) comments: 'The members were
practically always landed proprietors, and of a total of twelve
members before 1832, ten bore the name of Campbell.' (86)   For a
short spell the Liberals held sway, later the Conservatives took
over.   Out of the fifteen MPs before 1961, eleven were Conservative.   The area of Cowal was noted for its Tory loyalties, as was
to be expected in an area largely made up of small businessmen and
white-collar workers.   This did not rule out local divisions over
political issues.   In fact, local politics divided party members.
Over the years local elections were based upon non-party issues.
Candidates did not usually represent any major party.   According to
the various issues of the Dunoon Observer and Argyllshire Standard,
over the past 100 years and more, local interest in politics seems
to have been intense.   The affairs of politics used to be hotly
debated before crowds at the pier, especially prior to the First
World War. (87)   The people of Cowal, judging from the local press,
appeared to have been well informed and involved in wider politics,
more perhaps than folk in peripheral areas of Scotland. (88)   This
may have been so because many Cowal families migrated from the
'other side'.

It is evident from what has been said so far that the local scape
of Dunoon and district has undergone successive changes by reason of
the invasion of populations from the outscape.   The town itself has

indeed been a 'town of strangers'.   The growth and prosperity of
new Dunoon, especially at the time of the industrial revolution,
have been linked with the prosperity of Glasgow.   Such a linkage
between Dunoon and Glasgow has been identified by contemporary
accounts which described Dunoon as a 'suburb' of Glasgow'. (89)

This linkage has been in part economic, and in part social and
cultural.   E. Shevky and W. Bell have stressed that a locality
cannot be understood except in terms of the time into which it comes
into being. (90)   From the time of the locality's ancient Dalriadic
origin to the time of the Glasgow connection, Dunoon and area have
experienced successive cosmopolitan invasions and concentrations of
outsiders and newcomers with their 'non-traditionalist' ways and
novel life-style.   These created a more open society.   But, this
did not rule out a discernible lag between the peninsula's culture
and economy on the one hand and that of the industrial mainland on
the other.

In the long winter season there has always been a more parochial
way of life when 'local-time' has slowed down after the hectic
summer season.   The rural district has then adopted the leisurely
tempo of any remote Scottish area when life becomes 'mechanical',
more traditional, more particularist and more introverted.

In contrast, the short summer season always quickened the tempo
before 1961.   The town and district would swell to three times
their population size.   Other 'scapes' would invade the quiet
streets;   other demands would create a more heterogeneous randomised galaxy of tasks in the quest to please the strangers.   Life
would become more contractual, with the emphasis upon pursuit of
money within a very limited period;   life would become more
'Gesellschaft' in nature.   The interdependence of the summer tended
to be more organic than mechanical, when the instrumental would outweigh the expressive functions of daily living.

Dunoon developed, for well over a century before 1961, a sense of
communal hospitality.   A large core of family businesses, of
hoteliers and caterers, built up an expertise in satisfying and
welcoming the strangers from 'the other side'.   Three-quarters of
the advertised amenities in the Dunoon holiday brochures from 1928
up to 1975 indicate that almost all the prominent hoteliers, caterers and businesses in Cowal bore the same family names throughout
the years.

Their wish to satisfy the visitors dominated a large proportion
of the Town Council meetings and those of various business and
catering associations.   Ambitious schemes often went amiss because
outside demands could be misconstrued and often misguided.   For
example, there was the 'white-elephant project of creating a bathing
lido on the West Bay in 1937.   It was more in keeping with the warm
riviera than with the mild climate of Cowal.   Then, there was the
'pleasure-land' to be built on the 'front', which if it had been
implemented in 1949 would have cost ten times the rateable value of
the burgh. (91)   In a sense these unrealistic schemes were sympto-

matic of the grand dream that Dunoon could still be a major seaside town.   The older and more influential people were in fact living in the 'inscape of yesterday' instead of a contemporary world.

As will now be apparent, folk types do not easily apply. Neither Dunoon nor its satellite villages can be cast into the folk models as put forward by anthropologists and sociologists such as R. Redfield, J.F. Embree, C.P. Loomis and J.A. Beegle, or G. Hillery. (92)   The 'particularity', or specific 'social inscapes' of the Cowal settlements evade the typologies of the above writers and researchers.   The evidence available indicates that Dunoon, in particular before 1961, went through an annual season changeover with contrasting life-styles.   The Cowal settlements presented a cycle of life which may be viewed as a 'social inscape' characterised by 'cyclical solidarity'.   As noted, this was mechanical in the winter;   organic in the summer.   This has affected the township and district territorially, economically, psychologically, religiously, and especially in psycho-social ways, as the area, year by year, mobilised itself by a seasoned decrease/increase in the division of labour in a contrasting summer/winter life-programme.

One cannot, at this distance in time, demonstrate in any conclusive fashion that there was a correlation between the 'cyclical' change-over of solidarity, and the ecological, socioeconomic, and psycho-social stresses, but, as demonstrated, there would appear to be suggestive evidence that the age-old meeting with strangers in a cyclical coming and going of 'outsiders' had a long-term effect upon the social interaction in Dunoon and the surrounding area.   The outcome for the locals, like its history of contact with strangers, appears to have consisted mainly in producing an 'outgoing' populace, whose very livelihood depended upon it, and whose acceptance of strangers demanded a certain high degree of tolerance.

Certainly, the invasion, succession and concentration of people who had in the main come from 'the other side', appears to have had a long-term effect upon the local life-programme.   From the beginning, the people had to interact in an almost 'new town' situation, yet the place was ancient, and had its core of 'established' families.   What was it that enabled the varied influx of people to weld together within the settlements in the integrated manner as described in general by the Accounts?   The joint summer effort of catering for the 'outsider', for a livelihood, or in the shared winter experience of close-living in a semi-remote spot, where a limited ferry service and a wide estuary cut people off from the mainland, may in part explain the apparent although at times uneasy local solidarity.

This description of the township and area before 1961 has dealt with the influence from outside upon the local population as exerted from 'the other side'?   The people have, in effect, enjoyed a rather marginal ecological and social existence between the upper Highlands and the industrial lowlands.   The local people have been apprehensive about events and hypersensitive about attitudes and opinions concerning their locality from outside the area.   In fact, 'communal action' appears over the years to have been hooked to the socioeconomic survival of the township and area as a 'puller of visitors'.   Endless efforts and numerous schemes and expenditure have gone into the commerical venture of attracting more holiday-makers.   For example, in 1960 the local press often commented upon the 'Old-Age Pensions Holiday Scheme', at a time when the number of visitors to the town was dropping.   The press statement of a spokesman for the 'Dunoon Development Association' aroused consider-able local comment at the start of a new season, when he said: 'We want people to go home and tell their children and grand-children that Dunoon is "the" place to spend a holiday.' (93)   But, the same issues of 1960 were also pessimistic about the town's future as a resort, and so too was the Third Statistical Account.   The Glas-wegians and Lowland Scots, who once made their way to the area during the 'Fair', were flying out to distant shores by cheap holi-day packages.   The pier passenger intake was dropping at Dunoon. It had plummetted from 501,783 in 1959 (between June and September) to 455,211 in 1960. (94)

The oft-repeated phrase by the 'Glaswegian Maws and Paws': 'Err fra ferr' ('Here for the Fair') had already lost its significance in 1961 for the Costa Clyde.   But, the people of Dunoon and district never lost their sense of enterprise.   They were proud of the beauty of the locality.   They were adamant that they are second to none for their hospitality and were still inventive in staging the big event like the famous Cowal Games and the international regattas.   They would not accept in 1961, nor have they since, the shift of the holiday-makers to other places.   The sad fact was that only the retired were attracted to Dunoon District in large numbers. And the editor of the Third Statistical Account (1961), wrote un-wittingly on the eve of the Polaris invasion: 'It is hardly likely that there will be a "rush" to Argyll from neighbouring industrial areas in search for sites for new towns or in the hope of finding relief from the danger of nuclear annihilation.' (95)

Little did he realise that secret talks between Macmillan and Eisenhower concerning a Holy Loch Polaris Submarine Base were in progress.   Very soon after his words were written people were seriously discussing a 'rush' from the locality of Eastern Cowal to escape the dangers of nuclear annihilation.   Indeed, for the first time in history, many of the locals would look with fear upon the 'charmed' Loch.   However, there were many other locals who would not share those fears, because for them the housing and hospitality needs of the affluent American incomers would be as welcome as the Glasgow trippers in the Victorian summer of industrial Clydeside.

The historical turn of events surrounding the advent of Polaris will shortly be reviewed, but they will make little sociological sense unless the locality is set within the wider military American 'outscape' as well as within the nearer political 'outscape' of London.

Part Two

THE SOURCE AND MODE OF THE IMPACTS

Chapter 3

THE MILITARY INVASION

> The military institution sets the style and quite rigorously
> dominates all other community institutions.   The military
> organization is the primary referent for community, group, and
> individual existence.   The other institutions whilst not sup-
> planted are ancillary.   (C. Wolf)(1)

The 1960 decision to set up the US Polaris Base and the subsequent
arrangements reached 'in camera' by Macmillan and the president
caught the entire nation by surprise.   Parliamentarians knew
nothing about Macmillan's deliberations which began in discussion
with an American president who was a military veteran. (2)

When Mr Emrys Hughes asked the prime minister on 27 October 1960,
in the Commons, what conversations he had with President Eisenhower
about the establishment of a Polaris Submarine Base in Scotland,
Macmillan replied: 'My conversations with President Eisenhower are
confidential.' (3)   The Commons had to wait till the Queen's speech
on 1 November before the location and the Anglo-American talks could
be discussed.

On 1 November 1960 the Queen told the British public that a US
Polaris Base would be set up in the UK.   She added: 'The anchorage
will be provided in Holy Loch in the Clyde, and the depot ship
should be established there during February of next year, the floating dock will follow later.'   To soften the blow the Queen's statement added: 'stringent safety precautions will be adopted to prevent any risk to health or safety in normal conditions'. (4)   The
people of Cowal were shocked.   The reassurances regarding precaution only served to underline the fears of the people.   What were
normal conditions?   The whole area of Cowal was to become a 'hazard
environment', (5) and the decision was a 'fait accompli'.

The shock news of the establishment of the Base was reported in
the Dunoon Observer after the Queen's Speech on the 5 November under
the headline 'Holy Loch to house Polaris Base'.   It noted:

This statement was made in the House of Commons on Tuesday.   The

US Depot Ship Proteus, (18,500 tons) will anchor in the Loch in
February next year and a floating dock will follow later ...
under an agreement no more than three submarines at a time will
be lying in the Loch.   The US plans to base 1,500 men on
Proteus, and at least 400 of them are expected to bring families.
No special housing will be built for them.   Instead there is a
plan to rent accommodation on both sides of the Firth of
Clyde. (6)

Already the holiday character of the Cowal Strip was threatened, but
the Provost (Miss McPhail) and the Town Clerk emphasised 'that the
Dunoon area landladies and hoteliers could cope with accommodating
the US personnel and their families without their having to go elsewhere'. (7)   It became clear that the 'boom' to an ailing holiday
area mattered to the controlling local authorities, whose influentials were mainly local business people.   But from the start people
were divided in opinion regarding the American newcomers and the
military strategy behind the establishment of the Polaris Base.

The people of Cowal, especially the Dunoonites, could protest
when the need required it.   Jack House (1968) wrote:

Having studied the archives of, first the Police Commissioners,
and then the Town Council of Dunoon, I have become conscious of
the fact that Dunoon is an extremely individual place.   Nothing
is ever accepted at its face value in Dunoon.   It has to be
argued about, denigrated, debated, contradicted and taken to the
vote - not just the vote of the Town Council, but the vote of the
whole community.   I do not know any town which has held so many
plebiscites of the population. (8)

In the face of decisions made beyond the Cowal horizon in the outscape any local protest and debate were futile, and as shall be
seen enjoyed little backing.

Rumours and the half-truths abounded in the months which followed
the Queen's Speech.   Mr Shinwell, MP for Easington, complained in
the Commons to the prime minister on the 3 November that he was not
telling 'the whole truth'. (9)   He echoed the fears of the large
segments of the British people that Britain would have no control
over the weaponry.   Mrs Hart MP pointed out that there were various
versions of the truth regarding control of the weapons; one from
the prime minister, one from the Foreign Secretary, and another from
Washington. (10)   Essentially, the problem was that there had been
no open discussion, and a conspiracy of secrecy had shrouded the
Anglo-American talks.   Mr Ellis Smith MP, on the 3 November, complained in the Commons: 'The Prime Minister's speech was made without any warning ... Parliament knew nothing about it before it was
made.' (11)   And Mr Hale MP referred to 'announcements made in
Washington on which we cannot ask questions'. (12)   Instead of the
Base being discussed at length in the House following these questions, London rents were brought up for extensive debate. (13)

Taken by surprise, in the time-lag between announcement and the

implementation of the decision to set up the Polaris Base, the issue
was surrounded with complexity, so that objections were lost in following side-issues which diverted public attention from the real
issues.   One such 'side-track' was whether the Polaris Base was
really a naval base or just an anchorage.

The Minister of Defence stated on the 8 February 1961 in the
Commons: 'A great many people are creating a misleading impression
by saying that this is a base.   What it is, is a few buoys in a sea
loch to which a depot ship will moor, and nothing could be more
mobile than that.' (14)   Such remarks served to cushion the facts
that ballistic missiles were stacked on the vessels off-shore.
Words were piling up to hide the ugly realities.

Then, there was the rumour that Polaris was not coming after all.
So much so that Mrs Castle asked in the Commons on the 2 March 1961,
what approaches the prime minister had from the president of the USA
for the cancellation of the Base. (15)   Then, there was the emphasis upon the commercial benefits to the boom town of Dunoon, as, for
example, the statements on this in the Commons by Lord Orr-Ewing,
Civil Lord of the Admiralty, on 8 March 1961. (16)   The whole
pattern of twists and turns drew the public along and away from the
real intent and master plan in higher places in truly 'zig-zag'
fashion.   The mystifications and confusions caused were summed up
later by an MP in 1963: 'We were told that it was not a base but a
depot, and that it was not a danger to the West of Scotland because
the real base was in America.' (17)   One can hardly credit that the
Civil Lord of the Admiralty stated, at the height of the debate in
the Commons: 'I do not think that Glasgow would be affected one jot
or tittle by a submarine base staging-post thirty miles away.' (18)

The opinion of the people in the West of Scotland was reflected
in the 'anti-nuke' marches and by a constant flow of letters to the
national and local press throughout the UK protesting over the
Anglo-American decision.   It is significant that, on the date of
the official debate, on 16 December 1960, in the Commons, with
regard to the creation of the Base on Holy Loch, neither the Secretary of State for Scotland, nor one of his joint under-secretaries
were present. (19)   As Tories, they could hardly oppose Macmillan's
line of action, nor as representatives of the Scottish people could
they openly and clearly support the original Macmillan-Eisenhower
decision.

Up to the last there were hopes the Polaris Base might not be
established after all.   The New York Times stated in December 1960:
'Bases abroad, such as the Holy Loch, become more trouble than they
are worth, when the local population is antagonistic.   We might as
well re-consider the scheme, and leave the Holy Loch to its memories
of bells and bell ringing and the murmur of ancient prayers.' (20)
The American press recognised Scottish antagonism, but the statement
only served to make those British readers who were issued with
reports of the New York view, imagine that the Polaris Base might
yet be cancelled.

Whilst the local people were either thunder-struck over the
dramatic events, or unsure as to exactly what was happening, protest
marchers were being organised from outside Cowal.   Already the
anti-Polaris song had been phrased and composed.   Its verses
summed up the mercenary interests of those Dunoonites who welcomed
the opportunity 'to make more money'.   As outsiders marched or sat
before the old Ardnadam pier in protest, the locals heard these
sentiments sung lustily in the following verses.

The Provost o'Dunoon
She wants her half a'croon (repeated three times),
But we dinnae want Polaris

The Yanks they say
Are ge'en subs away   (repeated three times),
But, we dinnae want Polaris

It's suicide tae keep 'er on the Clyde
Tae keep 'er on the Clyde (repeated three times),
But, we dinnae want Polaris. (21)

There were two letters sent to the press at John Street, Dunoon,
the first of many others to come concerning the USN Base.   These
reflected the unease amongst many of the people with regard to the
stress that had been placed locally by some on the 'boom' the Base
would bring.   The first from Kilmun stated: 'I hear earnest people
around me say that the base will be a good thing, but I suspect that
behind these solemn eyes there works a greedy mind which can already
picture the roll of dollars the Monster will have in each
hand.' (22)

The other letter came from Strone; significantly both letters
came from the shores of the Loch.   It stated:

All who love the Clyde coast should support strongly any public
leaders who oppose the establishment of a Polaris Base in the
Holy Loch.   Call a public meeting now.   Don't let another week
elapse without a petition against the violation of our rights to
citizens.   Let no hotelier or shopkeeper be lulled into thinking that trade will benefit.   Shops will be unable to compete
against the American Supermarkets which will mushroom overnight.
If Polaris comes, boarding houses can close their doors perma-
nently.   Visitors will shun the entire Clyde area.... In a very
short space of time, the Clyde coast will be a deserted fortress.
Wake up, Cowal, and into battle. (23)

The economic scape appeared to come first in the consideration of
some locals.   Letters to the local press from 5 November till well
into 1961 were to stress local greed.   It is interesting that protest locally was organised from Sandbank, where at the local
butcher's shop people were asked to sign a message to the prime
minister which read as follows:

People of the village of Sandbank, Holy Loch, herewith protest

vigorously against the setting up of a Polaris Submarine Base in
any part of Britain, and call on the government to stop the manu-
facture of this deadly new weapon.   Saturation point has long
been passed, and the magnitude of destructive power in the continuing arms race is creating a state of uncontrollable tension
among the nations. (24)

The letter was written by Mrs Margaret Robertson, a resident of
Ardnadam, who led the local people who lived by Holy Loch against
the American naval presence and she continued to do so for many
years.   The locals named her 'Aunty Polaris' (a play upon 'anti-
polaris').   The Dunoonites of that time did not provide any anti-
Polaris personality, nor did they organise any anti-USN protests.
They were a divided people with regard to the advent of the USN.
Too many people in the burgh stood to gain by the incomers, especially when one takes into account the ailing summer trade.

No such letter to No. 10 Downing Street was arranged by people of
Dunoon burgh.   There the war years' 'boom' consequent upon the
British Holy Loch Submarine Base and other incoming military personnel was well remembered.   One local observed at the time: 'It
would appear that quite a number who applaud the decision have nostalgic memories of the booming war years, when they certainly never
had it so good.' (25)   In the burgh, the retired were disturbed,
the working class were apprehensive, and the 'better-off' caterers
and small business people were preparing for a bonanza.   The uneven
impact for each group varied according to perception, and there was
enough rumour about a three-year stay of the USN to make it possible
to soften the blow with regard to the impact on the ecological scape
for those who put money first, and enough also about the ecological
dangers to harden the opposition of the protesters.   'Divide and
conquer' is the old adage, and locally, as will be seen more particularly later, there was divided opinion with regard to the USN
presence.   The impact of a novel dramatic event had widened the
class and occupational differences.   Uneven impacts were a necessary consequence.

Glasgow, always linked with new Dunoon, decided to take up the
issue.   By 47 votes to 28 the Glasgow Corporation on Thursday 8
December 1960, had voted to support the local people against the
government. (26)   Meanwhile in Rothesay, Dunoon's old seaside
rival, there appeared an advert describing the new local dahlia:
'Polaris Base'. (27)   Someone had cashed in at once.   To return to
more serious aspects, it was significant that the motion at the
meeting of the Dunoon Town Council on the 13 December 1960, that 'a
great number of townspeople were genuinely perturbed by the possible
hazard to health, especially to children brought about by the advent
of the Polaris Base' was not carried. (28)

Once the depot ship anchored the routine of life was shaken.
Aliens moved in (1,500), and more than doubled the number of those
outsiders residing in the district who were born outside the
locality.   There were 734 'aliens' in Dunoon and Cowal on the eve
of the USN invasion according to the 1961 census.

The main scapes affected by the intrusion of the Polaris Base were:

1 ecological - the area became a hazard environment;

2 political - the area became a USN talking-point in Congress, and a major party concern in the House of Commons;

3 economic - the area became an overseas USN 'boom' centre with a foreign and superior currency altering the relative economic status of the area vis-à-vis surrounding settlements in Scotland, and the relative importance of occupational groups, who were catering in the main for a mainly bachelor 'cosmopolitan' military population;

4 cultural - the area was invaded by a military and foreign culture, whose values, norms, and life-style, were from the wider outscape.

Outside of Dunoon, people throughout the UK were sensitive to the radiation hazards and protested.   Throughout the summer of 1961 the Dunoon Sheriff Court was packed with CND protesters on trial for breach of the peace and obstruction.   Many local people were more concerned with the invasion of their quiet streets by rowdy demonstrators than by that of the USN submarines.   A local resident from the burgh in support of the USN establishment was quoted in the Dunoon Observer as saying: 'One has only to see the beatniks in the anti-Polaris demonstrations to realise that the quality of the opposition is not very high.' (29)   There were those who saw the point of having a deterrent policy and fully supported Macmillan.

The USN personnel had been quick to create social contact with the local residents whom they sought to woo in various ways.   The Captain addressed the Dunoon Rotary Club on the question of Polaris just over a month after arrival, and within the year, in September 1961, the Commander gave a trophy for the Cowal Holy Loch Sailing Club; ever after the Polaris Regatta was to be a Clyde feature. Although USN personnel were beginning to drift into the Sheriff Court many local people continued to be more concerned with the CND demonstrators on trial at the Sheriff Court.   Throughout 1961 disturbed Dunoonites and sandbankers were busy washing anti-Polaris slogans off their walls, as thousands of demonstrators from all over Britain invaded their quiet winter streets singing their 'anti-nuke' songs.

Other locals were pleased to join them.   On Christmas Eve 1961, loud-speakers around the shores of the Loch boomed with the message of a missionary clergyman, speaking to hundreds of youths at the Scottish Youth Peace Campaign March: 'We are going to march and march till the Polaris Base Proposal is cancelled, even as John the Baptist on the banks of the Jordan called on the people of Israel to repent, to do away with this crime against mankind.' (30)   The Polaris issue was bigger than any local issue; for millions it was global.

It is interesting that the spokesman, like many others in the 1960s, was a stranger, that most marchers were strangers, and that even the banks of the Loch and Cowal shore had been appropriated by outsiders: 'On the banks of our Clyde'. The fact was that what had happened locally had repercussions nationally and internationally. Scots identified the terrain as essentially a threatened Scottish domain, and others from across the border regarded it as essentially a UK preserve. Many local Dunoonites felt as if they had been besieged by fanatical 'beatniks' and radicals, whilst others were opposed to a foreign military invasion and were pleased that their shores were manned by committed Christians and by morally outraged citizens who were ready to defend the locality against the social threats and nuclear dangers which darkened their shores. Some of the protest marchers were bizarre in dress and behaviour, but so too were many 'Yankee sailors'.

The military organisation, which was literally thrust upon the West of Scotland, was also culturally alien to the Cowal scene. When the area became a military zone during the two World Wars it did so only for under five years on each occasion, and the intrusion was within the context of the national effort. Local men and women had enlisted to support the military services which had moved into Cowal. After the wars were over, people had wanted to forget submarine encounters and battles at sea and to get on with the real business of life in as peaceful and as safe an environment as possible. Indeed, for many people the Americans were as unwelcome as the warlike Campbells, who had left a blight upon their shores. One cannot appreciate how unwelcome the USN personnel were and the socioeconomic effects of the US military intrusion in East Cowal, unless one also assesses the military ethos and its dominant values. These are alien to those of the civilian sector as epitomised by 'militarism' and the 'military ways', which will be discussed below.

Indeed, the locals who had felt uneasy about the establishment of the Polaris Base might have had every justification for feeling that the initial nationwide protest would surely have some effect upon the powers at Westminster.

The marchers were to increase and the protests were to grow louder for some time. There was hope even then that it might be possible to send the ship back. The many fines of 'sit-down' and 'wade-in' demonstrators totalled more than £2,542. (31) Month by month, strangers by the thousands crowded the Dunoon ferries waving their banners and shouting their political slogans. But, by Christmas 1963 only a few made their way to Holy Loch to protest. Locals who had not accepted the Polaris Base were then left alone to cope with the social stresses created at ecological, political, economic and cultural levels. Whereas the initial shock had been cushioned to a large extent by outside support, the locals later stood in isolation face-to-face with the unknown threats of a hazardous environment and an alien military organisation from the outscape.

The military is largely a composite of 'militarism' and the

'military way' - terms used by Alfred Vagts, which will require some explanation. Vagts defines them as follows:

> The 'military way' is marked by a primary concentration of men and material on winning specific objectives of power with the utmost efficiency.... Militarism, on the other hand, presents a vast array of customs, interests, prestige, actions and thought associated with armies and wars, and yet transcending true military purposes. (32)

He observes that 'civilianism' is the opposite of 'militarism' with regard to values and characteristic forms of behaviour. In the growing rationalisation of the military, 'militarism' presents an anomaly and a vestigal remnant of the feudal military days with the accent upon ritual and symbolism associated with war. 'Militarism' upholds the ancient traditions of warriors. It must be noted that the military are secondarily members of society; whereas other professions are primarily members of society, and secondarily members of their organisation, with the possible exception of the monastic system. In fact, there are similarities between the parochialism and isolationism of religious members in total institutions and of military personnel in their virtually closed cultural world. M.D. Feld says that one cannot deny that the military are a more or less alien body, unwilling and ill-equipped to play the social game as others play it. (33)

The alien culture of the American naval 'militarist' is typified by the training of the US Navy's 'top brass' at the Annapolis Naval Academy. It is significant that the navy has been under admirals whose training has been 'typically' within the Annapolis Naval Academy, and whose experience has been that of 'combat training' rather than that of 'management training' and personnel skills. It is precisely the Academy-trained and the 'combat' experts who are 'par excellence' the militarists, and it is these who set the tone. It is usual to have an Academy-trained Commander at Base on Holy Loch, as may be seen by checking the notices of the 'Change of Command' published over the years in the local newspaper. In 1975 the Academy-trained senior officers were 1 in 6. (34)   M.D. Feld draws attention to the 'intransitive nature' of those who are trained in 'military ways': militarists will not act outside the traditions and values of the organisation in which they have been drilled. (35)

The Annapolis Naval Academy, provides an elitist 8 per cent annual proportion of the naval officers. (36)   These men have been trained for an initial four years in educational and cultural isolation to be the foremost protagonists of 'militarism'. These are the men who reach the top of the naval command. Among their number are the depot ship and submarine captains.

In addition, these are the men who stay longest in the navy. D.R. Segal and M.W. Segal show that whatever the increase in non-Academy officers with extra qualifications added to their rank, it has not had an impact on the proportion of Academy-trained officers

of flag rank from rear-admiral upwards. (37)   These officers are
the pillars of the US Navy whose intellectual, spiritual and physical attributes are in line with the values and naval traditions of
the past 150 years of American military history.   The Academy which
trained them does not accept the university idea of free inquiry.
Indeed, since the student revolts of the 1960s, the Academy and its
alumni have become even more suspicious of the university's own
approaches.   P.H. Partridge cites this latter point. (38)

Paramount to the military is the goal of combat readiness as
K. Lang and S.P. Huntingdon indicate.   The profession of arms requires some discussion because it will help to explain US behaviour
on shore, as also the attitudes of naval personnel to civilians. (39)

B. Abrahamson defines a profession as

an occupation whose members profess a high degree of specialised
theoretical knowledge, plus certain methods and devices for the
application of this knowledge in their daily practice, and who
are expected to carry out their tasks with due attention to certain ethical rules, and are held together by a high degree of
corporateness stemming from the common training and collective
attachment to certain doctrines and methods. (40)

This definition, however, does not apply equally to all ranks of the
US Navy.   It is more directly applicable to the commissioned officers at Holy Loch,but less to the enlisted men.

There are three main elements in military professionalisation
which particularise the military scape: (a) theory, (b) a specific
ethic, and (c) corporateness.   These factors determine much of the
onshore interaction and attitudes of the USN personnel.

Military professional theory is a set of doctrines regarded as
fundamental to the function and practice of military prowess, such
as doctrines of strategy, tactics and logistics.   The theory is the
basis for professional autonomy and the claim to exclusive special-
ism.   Whatever the knowledge of outsiders, their understanding is
'lay' and 'exclusiveness' is generated within the military enclave.
This is particularly so with regard to ballistic warfare.   The USN
personnel at Holy Loch have never responded in public to the nuclear
armament debate.   Ethical rules inculcated in the socialisation of
the military and fostered at the Polaris Base, on ship and on submarines, have established a mode of behaviour peculiar to the profession.   H.L. Willensky observes that the 'professions have norms
which dictate not only that the practitioner do technically compe-
tent, high quality work, but that he adhere to a service ideal -
devotion to the client's interest'. (41)   In this instance the government of the USA is both client and superior.   There is necessarily an unease, therefore, in the services rendered.   Unlike the
client relationship in other professions, the client in this
instance is also the patron who dictates the inputs as well as the
outputs, so there must be a peculiarly ambivalent military attitude
towards the state, which aggravates yet more the opposition of the

militarists to 'civilianism'.   There is an endemic military unease
with regard to civil authorities whether at home or abroad.

   In addition, many military personnel are alienated.   Adopting
Etzioni's concepts of 'coercive compliance' (i.e. people are subject
to enforced regulations), 'utilitarian compliance' (i.e. people are
motivated by money or other calculative factors), and 'normative
compliance' (i.e. people are motivated by moral principles), (42)
the US Navy remains in the last analysis a 'coercive-alienative
structure'.   Whatever the loyalties and normative compliance of
high-minded personnel, all the duties and routines are enforced and
backed by heavy penalties.   C.C. Moskos demonstrates that the command coercive structure ties down the personnel, whatever their culture. (43)   There will be reasons to come back to this coercive
structure, when one researches into the permissive behaviour of many
men on shore and the inept sanctions utilised for disorderly behaviour ashore.   Certainly, the coercive system is geared more to the
injunctions of officers and navy regulations whilst on duty, rather
than to behaviour on shore.   At the same time, the senior command
is obliged to create happy relationships with the local au horities,
so that there be no complaints to HQ.   These are best described as
a 'manufactured relationship'.   When studying the seamen 'hitting
the town', it will be clear that there is one naval ethic within the
Polaris Base, and another within the streets of Cowal.   The alienation of naval personnel stems not only from the emphasis upon discipline at base, but also from the isolation and long periods at sea,
cut off from society.   This is especially applicable to Polaris
crews who are submerged for two months at a stretch without communication with the world outside.   The real world is surely the civilian scape.   The military conserves an almost closed set of values
which constitute an alien 'social scape' and which generates a restricted orientation as is well demonstrated by J. Van Doorn. (44)
Separate club rooms and exclusive facilities at Ardnadam, Holy Loch,
tend to reinforce the restricted mentality of men trained in the
philosophy and practice of effective destruction.

   The naval system maintains the officer-enlisted caste system by a
generous allocation of privileges for officers, which is as evident
in Cowal as elsewhere.   De Tocqueville remarked that Americans
approach the military life with democratic expectations of justice
and fairness, but that the military institution soon shatters the
them. (45)   S.A. Stouffer et al. cite some personal comments which
they judge are fairly typical of enlisted men at the bottom of the
caste structure:

   'All we ask is to be treated like Americans once again.   No "out
   of bounds", no different mess rations and no treating us like
   children.   Why must the enlisted men be confined to camp as
   though they were in a concentration camp, when officers can go
   where they damn well please.   The officers go to town;   the
   officers get the few available women;   there are several social
   affairs given from time to time for officers, but nothing for the
   enlisted men unless it be an exciting bingo party.... The officers are getting American whisky and we are not.... What's the
   matter with us enlisted men, are we dogs?' (46)

These marked differences in privileges are related to a caste
system, which is even more marked in overseas bases than at home in
the USA.   It is the 'extras' that constitute the differential in
the reward system, and it is the caste-like privileges that mark off
the enlisted from the officers, and aggravate the enlisted men. (47)

    The seamen are usually bachelors.   Male chauvinism is prover-
bially rife amongst them.   Much of the difference in life-style and
privilege is determined by the familial status of the men.   There
are no married couples on the anchored vessels at Holy Loch.   Naval
personnel resident ashore have considerably more freedom from routine and most of them are married.   The significant fact is that
many of the married are either commissioned officers or Petty Officers (POs).   Married seamen, as we shall see, cannot often afford
to bring their wives.   The bachelor sailors remain within the daily
curriculum and have 'pass' protocol and navy chores.   Usually the
married do not make 'reveille', but report two hours later.   There
are greater pressures upon the unmarried personnel and the married
seamen who are without their wives, not only because of possible
loneliness, but because they are subject to stricter discipline at
base.

    Being married, however, does not put an enlisted man on a level
with the officers with regard to the privileges which often go with
marriage.   Lower ranking enlisted men have to make their own
arrangements for accommodation locally, whereas quarters are usually
available for officers and NCOs.   The wife of an NCO or officer is
transported free at government expense, together with all their
belongings, to the local overseas base, but a seaman pays for transportation of his wife and belongings. (48)   This often means that
in effect seamen have to be separated from their wives.   Between 15
and 20 per cent of married enlisted men are therefore forced to be
wifeless overseas. (49)

    M.D. Feld speaks of the exclusive character of the military.   He
adds that it is essentially a caste system wherein differentials
affect the particular relationship and liaison between locals and
navy personnel.   One cannot even begin to appreciate the impact of
the US presence at Holy Loch unless one assesses the composition of
the personnel.   Personnel at Polaris Base constitute disparate cultural enclaves composed of heterogenous staff.   These are 'particular' and complex. (50)

    There have been sociological studies of the composition of the
military and those studies of C.C. Moskos and the NORC (National
Opinion Research Center, Chicago University) are worth record-
ing. (51)   From these sources one may sum up the situation as follows: officers are typically graduate married men in their early
thirties with a higher class background, whereas the enlisted men
are typically single high-school products in their early twenties
with a lower class background.   This refers to the military as a
whole, but in the case of the FBM (Fleet Ballistic Missile) system,
certain significant differences must be drawn.   The enlisted men of
the submarines are highly trained and technologically top-grade

personnel, whose status and socioeconomic background in the navy are higher than that of the personnel in the same rank elsewhere in the fleet.   These contrast with the socioeconomic ranking of those aboard the depot ship.   The depot ship is a glorified floating factor where the maintenance of parts and extensive repairs are primary functions.   This latter observation matters, in that the men of the submarines (SSBN) are highly specialist sailors and officers, who contrast with the men of the depot ship at the Polaris Base and other ancillary servicemen, who are less skilled.   As shall be shown, the marked distinction between the submariners and the crews of the depot ship and other ancillary vessels presents organisation tensions which can break out on shore, which might explain why the enlisted naval ballistic crews live apart on the YFMB barge after a tour at sea, and have longer spells back in the States.   The more organisational turbulence is contained at the base, the more it erupts ashore.   Moreover, there are educational differences in training between echelons which are tied to the peculiar character of the cultural values and motivations and commitment of the personnel involved.   The many major pathways identified by D.J. Carrison give some indication of the complex nature of the educational background of the men in the navy and the varied socialisation processes.   But, the men of the FBM system receive extra training in computerisation and the manipulation of the most advanced equipment of the navy, in addition to the twenty listed by Carrison. (52)

But, this is not to say that the gap between the officers and the sailors of the SSBN submarines has narrowed, because the officers have also had additional training.   According to the Department of Defense's Selected Manpower Statistics, 72.3 per cent of all officers have college degrees compared with only 1.3 per cent of enlisted men. (53)   A college degree is a virtual requirement for officers, and a high-school diploma is the 'model' educational requirement for enlisted men. (54)   If this is true of the armed forces as a whole, it is truer of the FBM system officers, who are essentially in the vanguard of military technology.

Clearly, the submariners and the crews aboard the ships will not all be socialised within the military in the same manner, nor will the ranks within each.   The military mind will therefore not be shared to the same degree.   A further significant factor at base must be noted.   A common characteristic of the military scape is conservatism.   This forms a corner-stone of S.P. Huntingdon's theory of civil-military relations, (55) and is an oft-repeated theme in A. Vagt's historical account of militarism, (56) which is also a central element of M. Janowitz's discussion of the identity and ideology of American military leaders. (57)

At the US Polaris Base the conservative and typically Annapolis-trained top command render an account to Washington militarists who are in overall control.   Length of service usually instils in the US personnel a more militarist and conservative set of values, and develops a closed mind, as demonstrated by M. Rokeach, T.W. Adorno, W. Eckhardt and K. Roghmann. (58)   Only approximately 15 per cent of university-trained officers stay on for a second turn in the

military. (59)   As already stated, the Academy graduates mainly
command the submarines and vessels at base, and constitute the dis-
ciplinarians and organisers.   'Militarism' dominates 'civilianism'
at Holy Loch.

J.P. Thomas identified four projections amongst the military:
(a) 'the institutional projection' - i.e. the wish to give one's
life to the military, which can be applied to the Academy graduates,
the combatants and the NCOs at a naval base;   (b) the 'individual
projections' - i.e. the wish to acquire professional expertise, and
identification with professional civil norms rather than with militarism, which can be applied in the main to university graduates,
and others, whose training has been civil for the most part;
(c) the 'community projection' - i.e. the wish to enjoy the corporateness of a unit or the collegiality of an expert group, which can
be applied to technical enclaves and submarine teams;   and lastly,
(d) 'without projection' - i.e. the short-term utilitarianism of
certain 'drifters' who take refuge in the navy for the adventure, or
because it is the best of many evils in a situation of unemployment,
etc. (60)   One can expect this latter group to be found amongst the
enlisted men of the depot ship and supply vessels.

C.C. Moskos has studied the culture of the 'enlisted men' of the
military and identified an 'officer culture' and an 'enlisted culture'. (61)   The majority of the men at the Holy Loch Base are enlisted.   M. De Fleur, in a study of occupation stereotypes as reflected upon TV screens, found that the enlisted ranked last amongst
all occupational types in the USA. (62)   In some respects the situation is one in which the seamen are as serfs in a near-feudal
system, wherein they do all the most menial tasks.   Also, the
studies of R.W. Hodge, P. Siegal and P. Rossi indicate that in the
USA the enlisted career is below that of other skilled occupations. (63)   Indeed, K. Lang goes so far as to state that the enlisted career is one of the last refuges for a genuinely lower-class
culture. (64)   Taking this into consideration, together with the
lower levels in the educational and socioeconomic backgrounds of the
enlisted men, one can appreciate the frustration of the younger
seamen which breaks out when ashore.

With regard to the class situation in the military, C.C. Moskos
says: 'Such an enforced levelling of classes has no parallel in any
other existing institution in American Society.   This is the ele-
mental fact underlying the enlisted culture.' (65)   The connection
between the caste-system aggressiveness and the alienation engendered will help to explain the prevalence of onshore drug habits as
will be seen later.

The racial tensions at the Polaris Base also cause concern.
S.A. Richardson points out that variations in organisations can be
expected to proceed from variations in the cultural background of
members. (66)   The socioeconomic composition of the navy reproduces
the US stratified system. (67)   It also replicates American societal problems such as racism, particularly in the south.   These
issues and the alien American culture invade the local scape from

the wider outscape.   Prior to President Truman's 1948 go-ahead for
racial integration in the US services, blacks were only allowed as
stewards in the messman's branch.   C.C. Moskos made observations
which still apply to the US Navy today: 'Even in the integrated
Navy of today ... black sailors are still over-proportionately concentrated in the messman's branch', and he presents statistical data
to demonstrate the low status and ranking of navy blacks in the
services. (68)   Blacks have been under-represented in the top enlisted ranks.   There is generally an over-representation of blacks
at junior NCO level, whose tasks make them most unpopular, often
creating on-shore white backlash.   They are either accused by the
white seamen as too strict, or by the senior POs as 'chicken'. (69)

Since 1971 there have been more black entrants into the navy, so
that white Commanders have sometimes been haunted by the possibility
that black seamen may show greater loyalty to separatist groups than
to the military. (70)   On the other hand, white servicemen may
still carry their formal social prejudices, which may very well be
latent when on duty, but only assert themselves once ashore. (71)
So, whatever the 'Secretary of the Navy Instruction', official doc.
5350.6, might state about integration, racial attitudes in the American navy remain largely what they were in the American society to
which they belong.   A hierarchic 'fiat' from above is hardly able
to change socialised stances and practices.   The 'black salute',
the symbol of 'black power', has clenched its fists in East Cowal!
Within the locality, a blatant American chauvinism has been much in
evidence as shall be demonstrated.   Many commentators have referred
to this military feature over the years. (72)   The personnel carry
with them the values of the American outscape, which naturally for
them represents the superior life.   The material standards of the
incomers contrast with those of the locals.   The latent ideology of
the men carries with it the outside biases of a well-nourished
incomer whose 'bravado' and arrogance at times have merited the old
tag: 'over-paid, over-sexed, over here'.   Outlooks have clashed
over the years and troubles have been inevitable.   US officers on
Holy Loch have been well aware of the dangers.   From the start in
the early 1960s they hung a large notice above the gangway of the
depot ship which led on to the 'liberty boat' moored alongside.   It
has been there for almost twenty years until the present.   It says:
'You are about to represent your country in Scotland.   Do so with
pride, dignity and honour.'   Above the words are the corssed pen-
nants of Britain and America.

The clash of civil and military orientations is dealt with by the
US Civil Affairs Department. (73)   M.D. Havron comments: 'Inflation brings other problems in tow.   With the influx of a large
military force, people in society normally low on the social ladder,
the cab driver, the pimp, the prostitute, the bartender - suddenly
acquire wealth and affluence.   This is resented.' (74)   The implications were soon to hit Dunoon and its locality.

Having ranged over the characteristics of the monolithic structure of the context of civil-military relations, one ought to take
account of the wider naval organisation before examining what is

happening at the Polaris Base and in 'boom town'.   It enables one
to appreciate the manipulation and exploitation which made the
establishment of the Polaris Base at Holy Loch possible.   Karl von
Clausewitz, in his most influential book On War, emphasises that one
cannot appreciate the military venture unless one sees it in terms
of its power relations to society as a whole, its political intrigue
and its centrality within the economy. (75)   After all, the military has been maintained by the political scape upon which the militarists have always leaned for finance and manpower in competition
with other sectors of the national economy.   They have never done
so as effectively as they have done in the past fifty years.   With
this in mind, Marx and Engels in Anti-Dühring, wrote: 'Nothing is
more dependent on economic pre-conditions than precisely the Army
and the Navy.' (76)   D.B. Bobrow cites the interplay of the military with the civil sector, and cites four central processes at
work: (1) office-holding controls, (2) regulatory controls,
(3) resource allocations, and (4) steering according to goals of
strategy. (77)   But, who is in control?

C.W. Mills develops the theme of control through office-holding,
wherein elites dominate and dictate the socioeconomic inputs of the
military within a circle of influential industrialists, who to a
large extent are military veterans in the civil sector. (78)   The
civilian-dominated Department of Defense, and the predominant civilian bureaucrats in the Department of the Navy itself have always
been sensitive to the military status of America in terms of its
place amongst the world powers.

American nuclear supremacy must be paramount.   In addition, it
must be seen to be 'absolute'.   Public support has had to be
courted to maintain and finance the Polaris, Poseidon and Trident
ventures within the US Navy.   Western eyes have also been fixed
upon the effectiveness of the system, and naval personnel have been
quick to push the argument for greater and greater development.   In
addition, USN political interest, especially in Congress, has been
intense.   Throughout the years the Holy Loch venture has been spot-
lighted politically and naval personnel have 'played' effectively to
the Congressional gallery since 1961.

The role of Congress as a civilian arena of debate is important,
as can be seen from the powers invested in it by the Constitution.
According to Article 1, Section 8, which lays down a broad brief
regarding the military involvement of Congress, the Congress has
power to 'raise and support armies' through taxation, and to 'provide and maintain a navy', also, 'to make rules for the government
and regulation of the land and navy forces'. (79)   However important the civilian controls and the official influence of Congress
over the size of the fleets, the military have successfully convinced Congress that ballistics are more important to the nation
than medicine, education, and welfare.   (Section 412 of Public
Law, 86-149, lays down that armed services must obtain Congressional
permission to procure new ships, aircraft, missiles and commence
development funds.)   Similarly, Congress determines the nature and
composition of personnel through Title 10, US and Officer Grade

Limitation Act.   The control of the military appears to be supreme.
Congress determines the rules for promotion, and moreover, the percentage of officers by rank, and the number of flag officers in the
US Navy. (80)   However, if the US Navy has maintained its major cut
of the nation's budget, it is surely because military veterans have
known how to play upon paranoid politicians, affluent investors and
a dazed public.

The controlling influence and 'watchdog' role regarding Polaris
on the part of the US political machine has been decidedly present,
but so too have been the pressures exerted upon the members of Congress by the electorate who have been made increasingly aware of the
real or imagined threats of the USSR, more recently accentuated by
the Reagan administration.   Every seaman can have recourse to his
Congressman.   Base Commanders have been over-sensitive to issues
which they feared might go over their heads to Washington and foil
the military programme.   The navy therefore attempted to give the
impression over the years that all is well at base.   They have also
conserved a cordial liaison with Congressmen to convince Congress
that the military are effective ambassadors overseas.   Sometimes
special select committees are organised by Congress to investigate
and supervise the activities of military operations or agencies, and
political wars ensue.

Civil-military conflicts are apparent.   Through the National
Security Act of 1947, formal 'official' direct access to Congress by
the Armed forces was closed, which could be interpreted as insulating
the Congressmen from undue pressures.   Contact with Congress had to
be through the Department of Defense.   By 1954 the US armed forces
had both a legislative and a liaison office under the immediate
direction of each departmental secretary. (81)   The US Navy 'militarists' have been well aware that the crucial interface roles have
been civilian and that only the Secretary of Defense in the Department of Defense has cabinet rank.   They have also been acutely
aware of the civilian role of the Secretary of the Navy.

The Secretary of the Navy stands at the boundary between politics
and the military, and must always be a civilian.   He is appointed
by the president and approved by the Senate.   He usually has a
background in management, and an experience in public service.   But
much of his success at the interface depends upon the interaction of
personnel within the Office of Legislative Affairs (OLA).   This
office both assists and advises the Secretary of the Navy in legislative affairs and congressional relations.   The staff of OLA is
made up of 28 military personnel, who are outnumbered by the civilians, who must number 34.   The civilian bias has not always been
easily maintained.   The office supervises the presentation of
statements, and reports answers which go back and forwards between
the navy and the Department of Defense and to Congress, but it also
monitors proceedings on Capitol Hill on the floor of both the Senate
and the House of Representatives, as well as in the Committee Hear-
ings.   Its members know first what is afoot, and have informal
access to Congressmen.   Although the Secretary of the Navy is the
formal head of the US Navy, the relationship between him and the
members of OLA have been crucial to the steering process.

The uneasy civil-military relationship is further compounded. Below the Secretary is the Commandant of the Marine Corps and the Chief of Naval Operations (CNO), but the CNO is also a member of the Joint Chiefs of Staff (JCS).   Together they can exert enormous pressures upon the public and politicians in terms of America's armament position.   The CNO is in charge of naval operations, but subject to the Secretary of Defense as regards these, and is charged with informing the Secretary of the Navy of the actions of the JCS. When he does so, and how, are problematic.   Like the Secretary of the Navy he is outside the political arena, but crucial to any political decision regarding strategy and the development of ballistic weaponry.

The position and role of the Commandant of the Marine Corps need not be discussed here in detail, because at the Polaris Base the Marines are usually under 100 in strength.   Organisationally, they are set apart to guard and monitor secret operations at the Polaris Base.

From this overview of the US Navy, it is clear the civilian political and economic scapes intrude.   The US Navy could be described as a 'cleft organisation' whose civilian and military personnel are often in conflict.   The CNO, in fact, does not always exercise absolute authority over naval personnel and the 'civilianism' of navy personnel around the Secretary of the US Navy badgers the 'top brass'.   In effect, the civil administration constitutes an alien outscape which could often be seen as intruding upon the military programme.   From the first establishment of the base at Holy Loch, Polaris senior officers have been wary of officialdom in the USA and in the UK.

Congressmen make periodic trips to bases overseas.   The US Navy handles 55-60 such trips annually. (82)   D.J. Carrison observes,

All of the armed forces chafe under restrictions imposed on their conduct and resort to diverse and sometimes ingenious ways of establishing informal means of access and influence.... A combination of post-war developments has forced the services to give more and more attention to the cultivation of congressional and public support. (83)

Whatever the civilian nature of top administration, every two years the Navy Department briefs the new Congressmen, and sets up pressures through task forces, which are made up of naval specialists. But, these are of little avail without the influence of military veterans in positions of authority within the civilian sector, and without the backing of the propaganda of the Navy League.

The League serves as a link between the US Navy, the people and the politicians, setting up programmes in which people can bring pressure to bear upon their Congressmen for naval aims and programmes.   Though the navy is not supposed to be involved politically, the League is overtly politically committed.   However, the organisation is not a passive agent for the navy, because it may be

at variance with certain naval projects, so that the US Navy has the
task of convincing the League concerning the viability of certain
projects such as Polaris.   Indeed, mismanagement and misbehaviour
of personnel at US bases can weaken the League's support for the
venture overseas.   The League has necessarily reacted to US events
in East Cowal.

It is clear that there has manifestly been a multiple complexity
in the management of naval affairs over the years.   The heterogeneous structures can therefore create conflicts of expectations, for
example, between the Department of Defense, JCS, OLA, the CNO, the
Material Command, the Secretary of the Navy, the Navy League, the US
public, the Congressmen, and people of the overseas boom town.

It is within this interplay of political, economic and military
scapes that the US Polaris Base was established and maintained.
The economic civil-military interdependence has been a crucial
factor and requires some comment.   Being a consumer rather than a
producer of goods, the military is wholly dependent upon society at
large for its manpower, for educational inputs, and for capital expenses for equipment.

The Polaris Base at Holy Loch has been made possible and has been
kept effective by US industrial agencies.   The military industrial
ties are considerable - over 20,000 US contractors and government
agencies have been continually and currently engaged in creating and
servicing the FBM system. (84)   In addition, the US Polaris Base
for many years had only two other overseas bases: one in Guam and
another at Rota, Spain.   Missile submarines are not welcome in
almost all overseas ports, and so the USA has,therefore, had to hold
on to the Holy Loch anchorage at all costs.

The Polaris investment has also involved seven leading US ship-
yards.   The National Security Industrial Association (NSIA) has
been very much involved in the submarine industry - in 1967 there
were no less than 900 members in its committee from 170 separate
industrial organisations. (85)   A gigantic civil investment for
over twenty years has demanded that the system be maintained.
'Polaris is big money to big Americans' said one of my Dunoon contacts in 1975.   How right he was.   The Holy Loch Base has been an
industrial investment project which at all costs had to be justified, however dubious the deterrent arguments.

The US Navy must justify its colossal expenditure to the American
public to whom in the last analysis it is accountable and also to
the NATO countries.   M. Janowitz writes: 'Rationality in the military profession means that it must, in the contemporary sense,
accept the notion that a successful officer can be one who does not
fight, but contributes to deterrence and the resolution of international conflict.   It is truly unique to perform tasks that one
hopes never to perform.' (86)   The rationality of the naval ballistic system requires considerable justification, especially during a
period of widespread inflation.   K. Lang also stresses that
popular support is always fraught with considerable civilian ambiva-

lence regarding military ventures. (87)   From 1961, when the American depot ship first anchored at Holy Loch, this ambivalence was noticeable.   Often it was replaced by open opposition.

The initial full military impact of the Polaris Base upon the people in East Cowal cannot be fully assessed except in macro/micro terms.   The response of the local people to the American naval invasion of their shores can be partly assessed in its macro and micro implications by following the contemporary account of events in the local press and especially the letters which Cowal residents have sent to the Dunoon Observer from the time the Polaris Base was first announced.   Sociologists, particularly N.E. Long, (88) have stressed the importance of the local press in gauging local policy and assessing the diary of events within small settlements.

The study of the impact of the American militarists and of the Polaris Base personnel upon Dunoon and its locality will rely heavily upon the reports and contemporaneous chronicle of events in the tabloid columns of the Dunoon Observer.   To illustrate the relevance of the Dunoon paper in the context of the local contemporary scene, the Dunoon provost in 1971 referred as follows to the Dunoon Observer, when celebrating its centenary:

A well known Dunoon man, who was noted for his wit, once said that Dunoon folk knew all the news before the paper came out, but they bought it anyway to see if the editor got the story the way they heard it.   Such is life in a small town.   The Dunoon Observer has become part of the community. (89)

With regard to the presentation of events, the Dunoon newspaper was unusual in that it had no banner headlines and presented neither an editorial,nor a journalistic commentary from any particular political angle.   It attempted to be impartial, and to appeal to all, presenting little more than a chronicle of local events.   For example,at the national elections the editor always scrupulously gave each political party exactly the same number of lines.   The readership within the locality has always been extensive, with a circulation of at least 7,500.   Indeed my 6 per cent random sample (to be dealt with in a later chapter) indicated that almost all the persons I interviewed had read the weekly local press.   Ownership and editorship in the hands of the same local family for over a hundred years is a singular phenomenon, and the editor's policy of 'news not views', together with over a century of continuity in conserving this policy, is rare.

There is a 'Safety Valve' section for letters in the Dunoon Observer.   All letters are printed, although sometimes the editor has been known to close the correspondence, giving a week's notice. I examined 2,207 letters to the editor, which were to prove of importance in exploring local feelings about life in Cowal from 1960 onwards.

With the initial shock of Macmillan's decision and the establishment of the Polaris Base came an immediate flow of related letters.

Between 5 November 1960 and 25 March 1961, there were 77 letters
concerning the Polaris Base and/or the Westminster decision.   For
the first time in the local press ever since its establishment in
March 1871, the Dunoon Observer was to be inundated with letters
which linked the locality with the international scene and the
American naval organisation.

Macro factors such as the discussion of nuclear armament policies
of the militarists, the validity of imposing a hazardous environment
upon a free people in the name of national security, and the location of foreign military bases within the UK, were raised in 75
letters out of the 77 letters referring to the USN presence between
5 November 1960 and the end of March 1961.   And there might have
been more such published letters had the editor of the Dunoon newspaper not closed the correspondence between 25 March and 12 August
1961.   The John Street Dunoon Observer editorial office could hardly
cope with the mammoth influx from the locality, and all parts of
Scotland, England and Wales.

The first volume of letters stresses the big impact of the
Polaris Base upon the local people particularly.   Support from
elsewhere served to accentuate the legitimacy of local protest.
Based upon the content and volume of the letters three periods are
discernible within approximate time bands:

1   the initial impact between 5 November 1960 and 31 March 1961
approx.;

2   the spin-off period, between 1 April 1961 and the end of
February 1963 approx.;   and

3   the routinisation period, when an uneasy adaptation and readjust-
ment of life appeared to have occurred, from March 1963 onwards.

The first reactions in letters to the press concerning the
nuclear military intrusion were related to global rather than to
local issues.   These macro issues were precisely the major militarist objectives of nuclear armament supremacy and the sovereignty
of militarism over civilianism.   The first concern of civilians was
about environmental radiation hazards and their right to protest.
They wished to challenge decisions made privately in the White
House, in Westminster, in the lobbies of OLA and Congress, and discussed and agreed to by the CNO in consultation with the Secretary
of the Navy under the American naval flag, rather than after consultation with representatives of the Scottish people under the Lion
Rampant.   Scots became more aware of the unequal Anglo-Scottish
alliance.   Even the elected representatives of the Scottish people
had been kept completely in the dark over the decision to set the
foreign US Polaris Base upon Scottish waters.   People continued to
question yet more the merits of ballistic missiles and the democratic structure of the UK, in debates which have been taken up in
turn not only by the CND movement but by the SNP.   It is not surprising that never had the local press received so many letters concerning any one issue either before 1960 or since.

The first 99 letters which were concerned with macro factors
related to the USN Base were written within the first twelve months
after the USN Base was arranged by Macmillan.   In spite of the CND
marches little could thwart the militarists, so the letters concerned with global military and political issues and environmental
nuclear hazards ceased to flow as regularly after April 1962.

In contrast, letters concerning local issues related to the military invasion became more and more frequent, especially after USN
disorders ashore in the late summer of 1961.   There were 191 such
letters published which discussed the local effects of the USN
presence.   Almost all of these letters cited problems created by
the culture clash between that of the enlisted men and that of the
local scape.   This comes as no surprise.   However, it was significant that out of all the 2,207 letters to the press in the period
under study there were only sixteen letters in the 'Safety Valve'
column written by the American incomers.   This contrasts with the
185 photographs of American senior officers presenting trophies, or
of naval personnel marrying local girls, or of naval captains at a
Burns Supper or local community gathering.   Annapolis-trained officers avoided writing letters to the press, partly because they are
trained to avoid interference in local affairs.   This sensitivity
at micro levels contrasts with their militarist intrusion at macro
levels.   The sensitivity of senior officers, however, became less
apparent when they either avoided or delayed public apology to the
local people when their sailors damaged civil-military relations.

There were 320 letters related to the American intrusion in East
Cowal.   320 letters constituted only 14.5 per cent of the total
number of letters (2,207) sent to the Dunoon Observer within the
period.   However, in the first initial period of approximately five
months (5 November 1960-end of March 1961) as many as 49 letters out
of a total of 120 (64.2 per cent) were concerned with matters related to the USN Base and/or its personnel.   In the second period of
1 year and 11 months (April 1961-end of February 1963) there were 36
such related letters out of a total of 179 (24.4 per cent).   In the
third period of twelve calendar years (from March 1963-end of
February 1976) there were only 192 such letters out of a total of
1,908 (1.9 per cent), but it still represented a ratio of one USN-
related letter in fourteen over the period.

Only 27 letters from local people supported the Americans, or
praised them, in contrast with 127 which openly criticised them.
53 other local letters expressed indifference with regard to the USN
personnel or the American dependents.   There was every evidence of
local unease, and even open opposition to the incomers, at least
amongst a hard local core.   Only seventeen anonymous letters referred to the USN presence.

The content of the 320 letters will reveal the contemporary local
feeling among the civilian population, when discussing the particular effects of the American presence in East Cowal.   Before the
effects of the Polaris Base on the locality are assessed, and before
the full USN story is told, this narrative must shift to the next
larger impact on the locality approximately twelve years later.

Events will show that the story of the Polaris Base at Holy Loch, and its military invasion, were substantially similar to the later episode of the Ardyne industrial intrusion at Loch Striven in terms of the unseen machinations of schemes master-minded in the outscape. Both impacts intruded upon local independence in the name of the common good in terms of the national security.   How they diversely affected the local environmental, economic, political and cultural scapes, will be clarified later in the ethnographic account.

Chapter 4

THE INDUSTRIAL INTRUSION

The term 'development' has always implied a process of economic
and social change for the better.   Few analysts have stopped to
ask themselves if these changes could be for the worse, or if
changes could be better for some sectors of society and worse for
other sectors.   (D.L. Johnson) (1)

During the energy crisis of the mid-1970s the quest for oil preoccupied and dominated industry, politics, and the media.   Just as the
nuclear armament debate in the outscape had been the major polemic
of the day in the 'anti-nuke' days of the 1960s, so was the quest
for oil in the 1970s.   There were socioeconomic reverberations
along remote shores and in peripheral areas of Scotland as onshore
activities were developed to back offshore oil exploration.   East
Cowal was caught up in this swell of change which swept in from the
outscape, threatening to alter the local scape of life yet more in
the locality.

The small town in mass society is ever open to alien intrusions.
A.J. Vidich and J. Bensman, when studying the small town of Spring-
dale within mass society, were able to link local with wider global
events. (2)   They described their study as

an attempt to explore the foundations of social life in a community which lacks the power to control the institutions that regu-
late and determine its existence.... It is in this sense that the
community is viewed as a stage on which major issues and problems
typical of the society are played out. (3)

In addition to militarisation, there were industrialisation
developments associated with oil in the 1970s which shook the Cowal
area.   The Scottish economic scape in which the locality is set
could be described in Cockroft's terms as that

socio-sphere in which all or most of the means of production and
distribution are privately owned and operated for profit, where
there is the accumulation of capital and the progressive rein-
vestment of capital, with a corresponding development of labour

control, salaried classes and regularly paid functionaries, all
of whom inter-relate within a relatively open, competitive market
economy. (4)

The Scottish market is subjected to economic forces in both the
nearer and wider outscape within a banking and industrial system
where there is an increasing polarisation of economic centres into
metropoles and satellites.   Most of what happens in the outscape
beyond the Scottish shores is out of range of locals in peripheries
such as Argyll.   W. Lippman distinguishes between the 'seen' and
'unseen' world in which life is enacted. (5)   The transactional and
commercial machinations within remote centres of power are 'unseen'
and hidden from the eyes of people in the peripheral areas.   In a
sense, taking physical accessability as a variable, it is the periphery which is remote, but taking power as a variable it is the
centre which is inaccessable.

Life locally is not purely determined by the immediate, the felt
and the seen, but also by the remote controls in the 'unseen' corri-
dors of power, because the immediate scape is itself encapsulated
within the pervasive macrocosm.   It will be clear, once substantia-
tion is made, that localities can do little to reverse the decisions
which bind them within scapes.   Macro decisions create consequences
in the local scape.   C.M. Arensberg and S.T. Kimball write:
'Urbanisation, industrialisation and bureaucratisation should be
viewed as consequences, not as process.' (6)   These encroaching
phenomena have impinged on the local scene which is affected by the
metropolis.

The Scottish economy has come more and more under the influence
of London in the newer outscape and of the American macrometropoles
in the wider outscape.   J.P. Scott and M.D. Hughes have demonstrated, with T. Johnson et al., that financially and industrially
Scotland is controlled by the outside economies of England and
America. (7)   Table 4.1 demonstrates the extent of the satellite
state of the Scottish industrial scene:

TABLE 4.1 Foreign ownership in Scottish manufacturing industry
(1966)

Source	No. of firms	Turnover £m	Investment £m	Employment (000s)
North America	85	247	162	61
England	140	219	119	38
Europe	3	7	7	3
Totals	228	473	288	102

Source: The Structure and Growth of the Scottish Economy,
T. Johnson et al., 1971.

The impression that Scotland has become a pawn, a plaything, and
a plundered economy, has grown over the years, and in part explains
the emergence of the SNP.   Scots are very aware of the situation.
During the period when this study was being carried out, the Scottish Daily Record, the popular daily newspaper, with the biggest
daily circulation, published a front-page article on Scotland as a
plundered economy.   The newspaper article was headed: 'The United
States of Scotland'.   The following points were made in large type
on the front page:

> Just over 40 years ago, almost every Scot worked for a Scottish
> firm.   Today only one in five Scots work for a Scottish owned
> firm.   More than 100,000 work for American companies.   One in
> every three Scottish engineers is employed by an American firm.
> ... Only five American firms were here in 1939.... The big ques-
> tion many people now ask ... 'Do we rely too much on decisions
> made on the other side of the Atlantic?' (8)

In 1976 there were 137 American firms in Scotland.   The oil boom in
the mid-1970s had also served to increase the impression of outside
interference.   The SNP made capital propaganda out of it.   There
were the American speculators and the investment of the dollar in
Scottish oil resources, and also in their wake came European and
other overseas investors.   In addition, the English press was
clearly stressing that there was no such thing as 'Scottish oil' -
it was a United Kingdom resource.   The SNP were now advertising
'Oil for the Scots' in press advertisements and on roadside hoard-
ings.   In the midst of this was the nationwide concern, whether
SNP, tory, socialist or other, that oil revenues would solve the
British inflationary problem.   Some Scots felt guilty because it
was made to appear that Scotland was attempting to block the
national effort.

The promise of a solution to British inflation and its run-down
economy was uppermost in the UK, but the extent of the foreign
investment was so alarming that the International Management and
Engineering Group of Great Britain (IMEG) said that Britain would
only obtain between 25-30 per cent of its potential share of the oil
market unless the foreign competition was cut back by more UK offshore activities.   By the time McAlpine had secured Ardyne in Cowal
for the building of concrete North Sea structures, Britain had
missed out badly.   The Department of Energy's Offshore Supplies
Office (OSO) complained that the biggest cut of the returns would
not be coming to Britain.   The race for rig contracts had to be
stepped up.

About the time that McAlpine secured Ardyne in the rush for
orders to oust the Norwegian rig-builders, only £74m out of a total
of £481m invested in service industries was from the UK. (9)   The
Secretary of State for Scotland was so anxious to encourage platform-building ventures that by 1976 there were empty platform yards.
They had been secured in almost a wild and blind stampede for sites.
The point to make is that in the economic hysteria the politicians
and entrepreneurs rode rough-shod over the will of the people in
many a locality and settlement.

The stress was upon the national good and the need to beat inflation.   G. Salaman states that 'the public interest is defined by
the groups with the power to define it'. (10)   It is the preroga-
tive of the privileged in power to define their interests as the
common good, particularly in the media.   On balance, the locality
came second to the national need, and so the people of the urban
areas in the 1970s looked with impatience upon those who complained
that the coastline or the lochs were ruined and the scenic beauty
ravaged.   A labelling stigmatising process was afoot in which the
protesters were represented as 'rustics' or 'ga-ga country gents
and ladies' as one complaining local said to me in Cowal.   Thus it
was that the people 'on the other side' opposite Cowal, could hardly
share in the protest of Toward Civic Trust.   The Firth divided
people because it divided interests.

The 'allocative controllers' who are, according to R.E. Pahl and
J.T. Winkler, those who have day-to-day control of capital, (11)
were all in the outscape.   Aliens with money in mind, they hardly
had the best interests of the localities at heart, or even that of
the nation.   'Self-interest,' said a Dunoon teacher, 'is all
they've had in mind.'

The Scottish American Investment Trust and the American Trust
Company were the major financiers of the Pict Petroleum exploration
of oil in Scotland as also the Edward Bates Group, most of whose
companies are registered in London.   One-third of the British
investment trusts are traditionally committed to North America. (12)
The controlling holdings in the capital of investment companies are
more often held by English insurance companies.   Indeed, Scotland
has been realistically described as an 'internal colony'. (13)
In the 1970s the upsurge of the SNP movement made much of these
factors and won a growing support for its stress on separation.
Whatever the weaknesses of economic independence, there was no doubt
in the 1970s in the minds of millions of Scots that economic control
of their land was in the hands of foreigners beyond the border and
across the Atlantic.

Scott and Hughes speak of a 'financial elite', (14) who operate
from banks, insurance companies and investment trust companies,
which taken together constitute a power scape.   They state 'the
financial elite constitutes the core of Scotland's bourgeoisie:
its numbers are in effective control of local capital, but are tied
by links of multiple dependency to English and American "metropolitan capital".'   Such is the nature of Scotland's satellite economy.
This is the macro-economic scape in which the Ardyne venture has to
be set.

There were myths abroad in the 1970s which clouded the reality.
A. McBarnet, a former energy correspondent of the Glasgow Herald,
shows how big business was successful in using the national press to
present a picture to Scots of the Labour government as a barrier to
exploration.   He stated at the time of this study: 'During the
period the constant quoted refrain from the North Sea operators is
that they can only serve Britain's interests in getting the oil

ashore if the government water down their taxation and nationalisation plans', and added, 'It is now a matter of record that the government did in fact dilute all the policies laid out in the July
1974 White Paper.'   As McBarnet observed: 'Big business was
allowed a soft ride.' (15)

The White Paper had been inspired by state participation in commercial North Sea oil discoveries in an 'oil-for-the-people'
policy, which played upon public concern over fuel shortage.   Inflation was seen as principally due to oil prices fixed abroad, so
that the argument of self-sufficiency in oil appeared to be the
solution to inflation.   The government was scapegoated by financial elites.   McBarnet shows that 'news management' at the press
office took place after information had already been pre-packaged
by the oil companies, so that 'the press investigates nothing.' (16)
The press presented a picture of Britain's prosperity being put in
jeopardy by irresponsible Labour ministers.   It paid off, McBarnet
stated: 'Hints of little or no tax in the North Sea are just beginning to surface now', adding that 'the oil companies hide behind
commercial oil confidentiality and won't comment'. (17)

The possibility of East Cowal being involved in the oil drive
(the rush for black gold) came in September 1972 with a totally unexpected intimation in a letter to the editor reporting:

> that the American firm which took over John Brown's shipyard in
> Clydebank have had a survey made of Ardyne Point opposite
> Rothesay Bay with a view to constructing a yard for the manufac-
> ture of oil rig legs.... A Dunoon Town Councillor has been quoted
> as welcoming the project.... I would ask authority to 'tak-tent'
> before this small county of ours is laid waste by wildcaters and
> speculators who care not what desolation they leave behind so
> long as they make a fast buck. (18)

In fact, McAlpine had already made preliminary plans for the area
with a view to securing a site for the construction of concrete
gravity structures for the North Sea oil complex.   No one locally
had been aware of the moves behind the scenes, they were taken up
with rumour and local concern with regard to the matters mentioned
above, and at that stage were not aware that surveyors had been on
the shore mapping out a possible site for McAlpine and that confidential lucrative offers were made to local farmers by the company.   No one can deny that the whole operation was 'good business'
purely in commercial terms (best described as 'deals').

Sir Robert McAlpine and Sons Limited identified a 90-acre site at
Ardyne for their project sometime early in 1972.   The local press
did not notify the public until November 1972, simply because of the
secrecy surrounding the venture.   Rumour of another interest in the
area was allowed to be spread, whilst behind the local talk real
plans were launched.   On 4 November the local press stated:

> Concrete rigs at Toward: plans for the construction of reinfor-
> ced concrete offshore platforms and submerged tanks, on a site at

Ardyne Point, Toward, are in an advanced stage, announce civil
engineering and building contractors, Sir Robert McAlpine and
Sons Limited.   The work will be carried out to the designs of
the Sea Tank Company of Paris, France.... The choice of site
follows months of investigations. (19)

It is clear that the county had been approached, that the whole
scheme was carefully timed, whilst local residents were not only
kept in the dark but, through rumour of American plans, believed
other schemes were afoot.   The initial impact created surprise, but
somewhat in a low key, as shall be seen.

Later, in the month of December, McAlpine discussed plans at a
three-day conference in the Excelsior Hotel, Glasgow Airport, in
conjunction with Sea Tank Company. (20)   The local report stated:
'subject to planning approval McAlpine intend commencing production
on the first concrete drilling platform at Ardyne Point, Toward,
early in 1973, employing a peak workforce of 400 men in an area
where unemployment is at a "distressingly high level"'. (21)   These
last words must be kept in mind when discussing the actual outcome
of events.   Those plans with regard to the creation of the site
were implemented by March 1973, when the Secretary of State for
Scotland officially allowed the scheme to proceed.   There was no
dramatic local protest, nor immediate debate within the shore
settlements of East Cowal, except at Toward. (22)

In the conjuncture of events and impact from outscape the cumulative implications had not triggered off any debate when Ardyne had
become a focus of attention in 1972.

The fact was that quite apart from McAlpine's low-key operations,
there had been significant events locally, which distracted the
people of Cowal and dulled their awareness of what was happening at
Ardyne.   Some of these will be discussed later, when considering
the effects of both militarisation and regionalisation locally.
Suffice it now to refer to the significant happenings in passing:

1 There were strong indications from 1971 onwards that Cowal would
be annexed administratively with 'the other side' in the new Scottish Regions and that the town of Dunoon would cease to be a burgh.

2 From 1972 onwards drastic cuts of Clyde ferries were proposed.
These were diversely reported, and some anxious locals totally exaggerated them in doomsday terms.

3 From 1972 onwards there was mounting unrest amongst local whites,
who became more and more aware of black USN personnel, whose numbers
appeared to increase dramatically at Holy Loch.

4 Scottish macro issues in 1973 began to win more national attention
up till 1974 when in fact there were two national elections.   The
national SNP revival centred its campaign upon the issues of devolu-
tion and also Scottish independence.

The initial impact of events at ARdyne did not make itself felt at once, because of these four factors which weighed heavily upon the consciousness of the people of Cowal.   It was against these four factors that the low-profile bid of McAlpine's to secure the shore for the Ardyne venture has to be set.   Both the Macmillan and McAlpine schemes had operated on the same programme, and both in the name of the national interest.   The oil tycoons and the UK construction industry had worked very successfully to convince both government officials and MPs as well as the general electorate that McAlpine's Ardyne project was another vital investment in the British oil industry.   McAlpine achieved the contractor's ends fairly easily, because of certain weighty matters:

1 Ardyne lay at the other end of the locality, whilst most people were resident in and around the burgh;

2 also, the county council and not the Burgh Town Council had authority over the area around Toward, which may partly explain the apparent ease with which McAlpine achieved its ends.   Town Council deliberations could slow down contractual procedures locally.   The County Council never missed the opportunity of making arrangements in Cowal without the knowledge of the Dunoon Town Council.   Relations between these Councils had always been strained;

3 the prospect of big money for the local male employees was another possible explanation, in an area where males had usually to leave the area and seek employment 'on the other side'.

It is certain that piles of steel had been collected at the mouth of Ardyne Burn months before Argyll County Council had given formal permission for the McAlpine proposals to be implemented. (23) Photographs of the large piles appeared in the local paper on 3 November 1973.   At this particular time the town and locality were still preoccupied with the USN riots which had taken place the month before in the burgh.   Therefore the movements at Ardyne and the steady influx of engineers and workers had hardly been noticed. It was not until 10 November that people awakened to the full reality.

A letter, signed 'Fugitive from Pollution', stated in the local newspaper of 10 November 1973: 'Make no mistake the oil men and those who follow them are hammering at the door, and unless local people band together to repel the invaders we shall find ourselves in an industrial commune.' (24)   But the burgh people had other things on their minds.   Their Town Council was meeting on Tuesday evenings in the autumn of 1973 to look at the changes that reorganisation would bring, at exactly the same time as the Toward people were beginning to organise their local protest against outside interference with their environment, but not against McAlpine. They had identified the firm of Peter Lynd and Company as an additional threat to that of McAlpine.   On 14 November 1973 a protest meeting at Toward Hall stated:

This public meeting of 90 residents of Toward and surrounding

district all with a common interest in the preservation of Toward
area affirms its strong objections to any further industrial
development at Ardyne Point and resolves that objection be lodged
with the County Council of Argyll and the Secretary of State for
Scotland against the proposed development by Peter Lynd and Company Limited. (25)

The proposed scheme of Lynd and Company had taken attention away
from the McAlpine plans.   Such plans, in fact, had gone through
without opposition whilst Lynd's scheme and the preoccupation of
local residents with the issue of Strathclyde appeared to have been
more immediately important to them.   In any case, what could 90
residents have hoped to achieve, unless backed by others in the
locality and outside?   The lure of work for thousands of unemployed
workers, and the scramble for black gold by hundreds of companies
and entrepreneurs in the outscape could hardly be waived aside by
the protest of the locals.   In any case, North Sea platform-building plans were backed by the Secretary of State in the name of the
national interest.

On 5 January 1974, locals read in the Dunoon newspaper that the
Secretary of State for Scotland had expressed particular pleasure
over the commencement of a £25m concrete platform to be built at
Ardyne, weighing about 275,000 tons and standing 544 feet above the
sea bed.   The pillars of the platform were each to be about the
size of London's Post Office Tower.   Neither the noise nor the
added socioeconomic problems caused by the influx of workers, however, could be fully appreciated either at Ardyne or Toward until
the scheme was fully operational.   But, would not the employment of
local youths outweigh these?

In the beginning, many Cowal men welcomed the employment bulle-
tin's announcement that the work force would be 400 in number.   In
January 1974, McAlpine stated that they 'will require more men than
can be found in Cowal.   The extra contingent will be ferried in,
mainly from Bute.' (26)   The workforce from 'the other side' had
not been mentioned locally.

There had been no allusion to the fact that earth and stones from
the sea basins would need to be piled up ashore.   The tons of earth
excavated were to be landscaped into a man-made hill.   That hill
and the basins were to alter the seascape and landscape.   The
Toward Civic Trust was set up to defend the rights of local people.
But McAlpine's schemes and plans for Ardyne had already been implemented.   The effects upon the local tourist industry and upon the
local way of life were also beginning to tell, but not yet felt,
because people's awareness lagged behind the swift developments.

The Toward Civic Trust recorded:

Cowal enjoys the support and loyalty of a very large section of
the English Midlands population.   When these visitors see the
towers, which are similar to, but much larger than the power
station cooling towers which dominate the Midlands scene, then

these same visitors will turn around and seek more pastoral surroundings, even if it means going back home. (27)

The implications for tourism were to be secondary to the effects
suffered by the local people.

The locals were also to be completely surprised by another turn
of unexpected events, which, like McAlpine's initial plan, was to
have been settled and sealed before they had time to appreciate what
had been happening within their shores.   The villagers of Toward
had been busily engaged in keeping Lynd and Company out.   They had
realised they could not do much to alter McAlpine's scheme as they
had understood it.   They concentrated their efforts in keeping yet
another contractor out.   Locals were against Lynd's plans because
they declared that the spatial confines of local construction work
should go so far and no further.

Suddenly, in the midst of confusing reports and worries concerning other matters such as the nuclear threat at Holy Loch, and the
local fears concerning Strathclyde's administrative powers over
Cowal and Dunoon, McAlpine had secured a lease for the whole area,
comprising lands that Lynd had wished to take over.   Big money had
been offered in private rentals to local farmers for the use of
local land.   Once the news was out, a local beneficiary of Mc-
Alpine's money was reported to have declared, 'Blow the scenery, I'd
be mad to say "no" to the gold they're offering.'   Clearly, in the
midst of the fight against Lynd, negotiations had been in process
and large sums of money had been promised and contracts signed and
sealed.   Comment on McAlpine's achievement was reported as follows
in the local press: 'The news came as a surprise to Mr. Thomas
Jaeger, Chairman of Peter Lynd.' (28)   Lynd's firm had been out-
witted and the big adroit business deal had staggered the villagers
at Toward.

Soon, more and more lorries were trundling along the road from
Dunoon to Toward, and more and more Glaswegian navvies spilled into
the town of Dunoon and the Innellan village.   Advertisements in the
Dunoon Observer for worker accommodation began to appear, such as:
'Houses/Flats (for sale or rent) and homely lodgings for construction staff and workmen employed at Ardyne Point - all replies will
be considered.' (29)   A 'cosmopolitan' workforce invaded the area
on a scale which the area had not known in all its history.

Having extended the lease, McAlpine then began to extend the project further, as is the practice of astute entrepreneurs.   McAlpine
declared that jobs could number 1000 by the end of 1974. (30)   The
first labour force estimate had now more than doubled.   The local
press announced on 16 March that objections to the extension of the
Ardyne complex were to be sent to the Clerk of the Argyll County
Council, Lochgilphead, by 29 March.   Meantime, Toward villagers and
Dunoonites were talking about 'the rape of Ardyne in the national
interest'. (31)   More protests and complaints appeared in the
Dunoon Observer.   One local summed up the contemporary scene well:

Three miles of unspoiled coastline from Port Lamont to Toward
Quay will be under 'their' complete ... control ... 20-30 acres
of valuable farmland would be despoiled ... fleets of mammoth
lorries, trucks, transporters, excavators and juggernauts would
be a danger to travellers and would damage the road.... Life as
they had known it and the future as they had planned it would be
ended for those whose homes lie on the very fringe of this ...
scheme.... With the Polaris Base in the Holy Loch, the NATO Base
in Loch Striven and the two oil rig platforms under construction
at Ardyne Point ... this small area has done for this country and
for its allies more than any community of comparable size in the
UK.... If your readers believe, as I do, ... they will be as
angry as I am and they will write to the County Clerk. (32)

The people were perplexed because they had so much on their minds
in the aftermath of the USN riots and the uncertain position of the
locality within the new regionalisation scheme.   Originally, Mc-
Alpine had obtained permission to build one basin.   Whilst people
were beginning to take this in, McAlpine extended this scheme to
three basins.   A letter from a well-informed local to the Secretary
of State set out the perplexing situation as follows:

This venture was accepted by the people after being given assur-
ances by Messrs McAlpine's lawyers and chief engineer that there
would only be one basin or dock required for their purposes and
that the amenities of the district would be preserved.   This
information they gave us when another group, Messrs Peter Lynd
and Company Limited, applied for permission to work on similar
lines adjacent to them.   We were answered by McAlpine: this was
totally unnecessary, as the number of rigs required would possibly not exceed 10, and the period of use would be something in
the region of 8-10 years.   However, without notice McAlpine have
leased or purchased quite a considerable amount of land and have
proceeded ... to commence digging out a second dock, and are in
process of continuing this venture to a possible third dock. (33)

It was announced on 6 April 1974, in the Dunoon Observer, that
the County was to appoint an Enforcement Officer for the Ardyne
project. (34)

Ironically, the people realised that they could not defend their
shores against outside intrusion without outside help.   The Clyde
Estuary Amenity Council, chaired by Professor Rankin, inspected the
site on 19 April at Ardyne to receive certain guarantees.   These
referred to the possible noise levels and to transport by sea rather
than by road.   Professor Rankin saw the need for the locality to be
screened whilst industrialisation developed.

The final layout of the complex is shown in Map 4.1.   On 28
April, Iain MacCormick MP (SNP) officially visited the site to check
on what was happening.   The MP was satisfied by the assurance that
the 'company would give priority to local labour, once the initial
stages of the operation were over, and the construction of the oil
platforms begun'. (35)

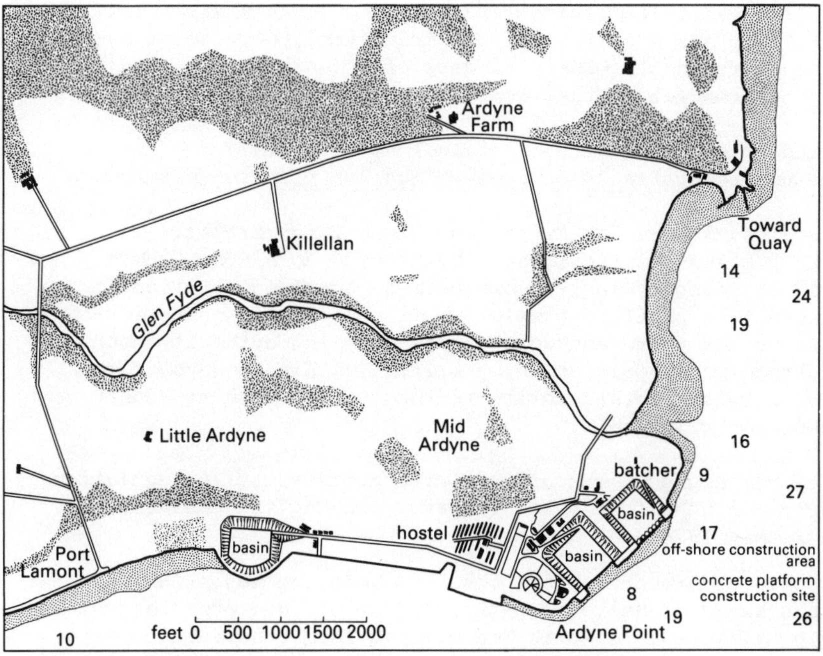

Ardyne Farm

Killellan

Glen Fyde

Toward Quay

14

24

19

Little Ardyne

Mid Ardyne

16

batcher

9

27

basin

hostel

basin

17

off-shore construction area

concrete platform construction site

Port Lamont

basin

8

19

26

Ardyne Point

10

feet 0   500 1000 1500 2000

MAP 4.1

Whilst the people at Toward were shaken by events at Ardyne, people at the other end of Cowal, in Ardentinny, were to be shocked by similar intrusions.   The villagers of Ardentinny received a terse notice from yet another Company which stated:

Town and Country Planning (Scotland) Act, 1972.
Notice under Section 24 of application for planning permission:

Proposed development at Finart Bay, Loch Long, Argyll.
TAKE NOTICE that application is being made to ARGYLL COUNTY COUNCIL by Balfour Beatty Construction (Scotland) Limited for an oil production platform complex.   If you wish to make represen- tations to the above-mentioned local planning authority about the application you should do so by writing within 21 days of the date of service of this notice to the County Clerk at County Offices, Lochgilphead.

The notice was signed in accordance with administrative regulations in Edinburgh on behalf of Balfour Beatty, an English construction firm, on 21 May 1974.

The people of Ardentinny by Loch Long were shocked.   No one locally had heard of Balfour Beatty, and no one had ever thought it remotely possible that a North Sea oil platform construction site would be established in peaceful Ardentinny.   To Dunoonites Arden- tinny has always been the 'back of beyond', but to the villagers it was a refuge from noisy Dunoon, and from the still noisier lowlands on the other side.   When I visited the shores of Loch Long in the summer of 1974, the villagers showed me the notice they had received through their letter boxes.   One after another they told me about the fatal May morning when 'a tremor of fear ran from hoose tae hoose', as one lady put it.   'We thought that in a few days the bulldozers would come and clear awa' oor hames here by the loch.' Another local resident observed: 'Nothing good ever comes fae the Lochgilphead County Clerk, but this wis the warst blow fur us folk here.... A' felt like the Jews, who were telt tae quit their hames under Hitler.'

The Balfour Beatty scheme would have taken over the whole of Glenfinart Bay by Loch Long, immediately affecting the majority of homes in Ardentinny.   Anxiety was inevitable.   A local farmer also added to the general anxiety and confusion when he told the villa- gers that he had received a letter from another construction firm, offering him 'big money' for his land.   The firm built oil drilling rigs.   It must be noted that the County Council was shortly to pass away with the introduction of the new Argyll and Bute Council, whose members were already chosen.   The outgoing administration was bom- barded with requests from industrialists who well knew that the resistance of the dying Council was low, amongst whom were frustra- ted administrators who had not been reappointed under the new Argyll and Bute Council.

A letter of complaint in the local press despaired: 'It seems incredible to me that a whole village and community can be des-

troyed, just as if people were of no consequence.' (36)   The Cowal
Action Group was formed, which was also backed by the local MP.

Eventually, the proposed Ardentinny project fell through, but
the withdrawals were not solely explained by Cowal rallying cry of
'Save Ardentinny'.   It so happened that the Colport British Navy
presence, opposite Ardentinny, was too near for security's sake.
Missiles were stored in nearby caverns, and offshore weapon trials
were carried out on Loch Long.   These had greater priority than the
scheme which would have created lochside problems for the continuance of secret naval operations.

Meanwhile, back at the other end of the locality, where McAlpine
was firmly established, Cowal protest was mounting.   Encouraged by
the apparent success at Ardentinny, local protest against McAlpine's
Ardyne project was taken up in the burgh.

Certainly, within five months, there was more local unrest over
Ardyne.   Some locals were employed at Ardyne, but more and more of
them were being turned away.   Only labourers from 'the other side'
and from south of the border, even from abroad, were securing jobs
at Ardyne.   The (SNP) MP's pledge on his visit to Ardyne 'that the
company would give priority to local labour, once the initial
stages of the operation were over' was thrown back in his face. (37)
The MP was also under pressure to convince McAlpine that taking on
local craftsmen, tradesmen and labourers was ruining their employers, who were losing them without the possibility of any replace-
ments.   Buses had to be taken off the road, because there were not
enough drivers.   They had deserted their buses for the McAlpine
lorries and vans.

Month by month, change after change, and implication after implication, hit the local people.   The third basin at Ardyne was given
the go-ahead in August 1974 by the Secretary of State, who could
over-rule the findings of public inquiries.   The whole exercise of
the local protest movement had been rendered futile by the 'fiat' of
government.   The Ardentinny success had given the locals at Toward
new heart, but there were other reasons for the decisions taken at
Ardentinny, which favoured the local protesters, and which were not
applicable at Ardyne.

Fast upon the official permission of the Secretary of State,
local hotels and guest houses were sold to McAlpine to provide
accommodation for the employees.   Rumours, ill founded and prepos-
terous, however untrue, caused further fears and anxieties.   These
added to local concern over access to suitable accommodation.   The
USN personnel and the summer visitors rented local accommodation so
the McAlpine managers were forced to buy.   The offer of higher
prices tilted the housing market in the direction of McAlpine's
personnel in serval instances.   The USN did not normally buy
houses, but they did often offer high rentals.   The prospect of quick
money for accommodation in an area that was steadily ceasing to be a
holiday attraction appeared to be paramount for many.

Casual workers were moving into the hotels and guest houses in June 1974.   Summer visitors complained that navvies were sharing their holiday accommodation.   In addition, shop assistants, catering and tourist personnel were leaving their jobs and taking short-term employment at Ardyne.   Their weekly wages altered significantly, and sometimes even quadrupled.   For the first time in the history of the locality employers were complaining that local labour was scarce and that men and women who had been loyal employees over the years were leaving burgh jobs for better-paid ones at remote Ardyne. (38)   The movement since the industrial revolution had been from the countryside in to the town, now it was from the town out to the countryside.   One local resident described the industrialisation of the area as 'this industrial octopus spreading its tentacles and ruining amenities and the environment that are so dear to the people.' (39)

By the autumn of 1974 the old routines of work and cycle of life were disrupted.   The effects of this period will be considered in the next section.   Suffice it to say that the conjuncture of events created a veritable maze.   People felt lost in the midst of complex events and twists and turns, which brought bewildering changes. After the American naval invasion, the familiar and customary way of life had been affected and an uneasy routine ensued.   Then came the unexpected Ardyne intrusion.   In the earlier stages of the military invasion, initial shock and subsequent surprises upset the locals, but from one source only at the Holy Loch Base.   With McAlpine's venture in the South-West an additional source of new threats was established.   A sequence of impacts beginning with 'initial surprise' cut across the area, coming in another direction from the North-East.   Pressures from two ends of the locality therefore closed in upon residents of the East Cowal shores.

By 1974 Ardyne was no longer an outlying area where a few farmers lived on remote homesteads, but rather an industrial centre with national and worldwide contracts and with an international work-force serving an international market.   The employer was engaged in building concrete structures which dwarfed the settlements, the town, and the hills of Cowal whose giant shadows cast ominous fear across the local scape.   New social uncertainties suddenly appeared upon the human landscape, whilst at the other end of the locality, the USN Base with its noisy motors, with its crates of missiles, and with its foreign personnel lay incongruously at Holy Loch.   It served distant masters on an international military venture which represented wholesale aggression.

Strangers had always been welcome to the ferry-point and to the locality, but now many locals looked upon the newcomers as 'wreckers'. (40)   In addition, there was a growing sense locally of helplessness coupled with hopelessness.   Jimmy Reid, the well-known West of Scotland defender of people's rights in Clydeside, described the predicament of people in the grips of outside manipulation when speaking as the newly elected Rector at Glasgow University in 1972:

Alienation is the cry of men who feel themselves to be victims of

blind economic forces beyond their control, the frustration of
ordinary people excluded from the processes of decision-making.
Many have not rationalised it.   They may not even understand it,
or may not be able to articulate it, but they feel it.   It
therefore conditions and colours their social attitudes. (41)

The feelings of the local people, when Ardyne was invaded, were
not solely concerned with the fact that decisions had been made from
afar, but that nobody appeared to care south of the Firth about
their fate.   The locals did appreciate the need for a national
effort to take the UK out of the fuel crisis by more and more oil
exploration and production, but they also witnessed the unplanned
siting of too many platform building sites in the UK.   Iain Mac-
Cormick MP, was also accused of changing his hat from developer to
conservationist when it suited him. (42)   A local spokesman spot-
ting the lack of a well-thought-out policy with regard to selection
of sites for platforms in the midst of the rush for locations, remarked in the local press: 'When are we to have government policy
that states what areas should or should not be developed?   At
present the whole set-up in Scotland gives the impression of unco-
ordinated, uninformed bungling', whilst another observed: 'This was
a tourist area and although the people wanted oil they did not want
to lose something they already had.' (43)   Uncertainty was clearly
the dominant feature, but only after a period of delayed shock, at
initial impact.   This appeared to take hold of the people after the
first weeks of confusion, and a general lack of real awareness,
which was almost akin to a state of disbelief.   The uncertainty
locally matches the findings of other contemporary research during
the initial period of the Scottish oil boom. (44)

The most common impact cited in the East of Scotland studies was
the 'imposition of short- and long-term uncertainty', which the
'Report on the North Sea Oil Panel (1977)' makes clear.   This uncertainty underlined in the studies was about: what had been
happening, what was currently happening, and what was going to
happen. (45)   Uncertainty as to what was actually happening, and
what would later happen creates lags in perception and in awareness.

The hidden agenda of unseen elites is a second area that has been
well documented, especially by R. Moore, in the North Sea oil boom
studies. (46)   Much of the analysis is reminiscent, as already
stated, of Walter Lippmann's 'unseen world', out there (in the wider
outscape) where real decisions are made and imposed upon people
which affect the 'seen world' of daily life. (47)   Moore has shown
in his research that there was a lack of understanding in far-away
centres of what was in the best interest of local people.   'Making
it up as we go along' has been cited by Moore as summing up the
attitude of economic planners, which may also be applied to entrepreneurs, who may know what they want in terms of high profits, but
who fail to take into consideration the long-term social consequences of their development and expansionist programmes.

The government, the MPs, technologists, industrialists and contractors, worked discordantly to achieve their various ends often at

cross-purposes during the oil boom.   The inauthentic nature of political action which purports to be in the best interests of the
people has been well discussed by J.J. Rodger, after the Moss Moran
Controversy. (48)   Rodger's analysis has paralleled the distorted
communication and the contradictions behind the public participation
ploy (an inauthentic activity) in which there is a pretence of democratic consultation and open debate about major local issues, but
which in reality are all too often set up to dupe the people.   The
inauthenticity of political and elitist intervention during any boom
is a historic feature, as was the case with the transcape decisions
concerning both the USN Polaris Base at Holy Loch, and McAlpine's
concrete platform building site at Ardyne.   Debate and so-called
democratic lobby are negated by elitist decision-making.

   Many of the industrial and technological developments during the
oil boom reflected the exploited nature of the Scottish economy as a
poor partner to England, not because of any cultural opposition, but
because exploitation is a feature of peripheral areas.   R. Moore,
and I. Carter have shown that historically Scotland has been used
for the extraction of primary resources and that the relative deso-
lation which accompanied it is a product of social and economic
relations. (49)   The incomer-owned transnational corporations
(TNCs) had moved in under the argument that the pressure of the
national interest have required developments, but they adversely
affected traditional local developments.   The 'finite future' (oil
will soon run out) had taken precedence over all in the 1970s.
Tourism and other considerations came second to black gold.   The
North East oil boom studies have shown that the TNCs have needed the
localities more than they needed the TNCs. (50)

   In addition, the Report of the North Sea Oil Panel stated that
where outside developments had taken over, there was a parallel
depreciation of local ownership and control.   J.D. House has shown
there is one ominous uncertainty which hangs over the people with
regard to the future, viz. when oil will dry up.   In fact, day by
day a dynamic underdevelopment will threaten the locality (51) (as
has been the case of so many gold-rush settlements the world over).
Whilst I was in Dunoon it was evident that the initial impact of the
Ardyne venture had much in common regarding these matters with the
findings of the North Sea oil boom studies.   As in these studies
there were signs that economic uncertainty lurked in the East Cowal
settlements, where tourism was affected by the finite schemes of the
industrialists.   In addition, the findings of M. Grieco demonstrated that the TNCs offered guarantees at the start that locals would
be the main employees of the incoming industry but their promises
were seldom realistic. (52)   It was also a characteristic factor
in my Dunoon and district study as will be shown later and was also
substantively reflected in much of the material presented in the
Report of the North Sea Oil Panel (31 May 1979). (53)

   The cultural impact, of large numbers of strangers, moving into
an area, especially from the wider outscape creates a culture clash,
as is brought out in the Scottish oil studies. (54)   However, this
is a topic which is less well discussed.   The seminal Way of Life

Seminars at Edinburgh University (1979) attempted to focus the attention of sociologists and anthropologists on the impact of migrant workers and the oil men upon the local way of life. A.P. Cohen, moreover, has examined the cultural clash and the interesting reaction of what he described as 'cultural accounting'. (55) People become more conscious of their values and traditions when outsiders threaten them and may cling more faithfully to them, as they did in Shetland when the 'oily men' came at the height of the oil boom. The psychological slant taken by Cohen has enabled the researcher to appreciate the personal dynamics involved in an area of study which has tended to be reified. It also corresponds with the concept of social inscape which I have suggested could be usefully utilised. Cohen took into account the impact 'before the first lay-barge and helicopter appeared'. (56) He has referred to 'that moment' and 'that instant' in which the 'sceptre of radical and possibly cataclysmic change was presented', and of 'historical junctures', when people became conscious of impending doom. (57) These ideas correspond with an assessment of the conjuncture of events as suggested in this study of East Cowal under impact.

The impact on a way of life in the wake of the invasion of Mc-Alpine's navvies was not immediately apparent in East Cowal. The effects constitute an invidious process, where lags show themselves within the pattern of life only after some time. However, some people put money first, as G. McFarlane shows in Shetland. The incomers were often preferred as tenants when it came to rentals rather than locals. (58) This was also clear in Dunoon and its locality, as will be demonstrated. It was also demonstrated in the St Kilda story: when it came to the chance 'to turn a penny' many people, even within a small settlement, are prepared to put self-interest before local loyalties. (59)

Lastly, Adrian Varwell, in the Working Papers 4 and 7 of the Way of Life Seminars at Edinburgh University, has suggested that the concept of identity is the key to an understanding of the way of life. (60) Local identity can be challenged by the incomers. 'We are good people in this town', protested a local man when I was in Dunoon, 'and we can't accept these sodden Irish boozers.' Clearly identities were essential to distinguish the sheep from the goats. One must take account of the 'rhetoric of struggle' in Suttles's terms as it exists between groups, and the 'distancing', (61) which are features within settlements under invasion. Suttles has rightly pointed out that identity carries with it outward signs of superiority or inferiority. There are also offensive/defensive muted actions indicating: 'Watch your step'; 'Just so much and no more', etc. Both the established and the outsiders have generally kept their distance and known their place. If it is accepted by the writings of Cohen and Varwell that identity is established with reference to others, then one has to ask: how? And, as overlooked by some settlement studies, invasion is essentially the clash of identities - i.e. of outsiders with the established. This is a matter that is of importance to the study, as will now be briefly explained.

G.D. Suttles speaks of the 'contrived identity', (62) which is the ready-made, manufactured identity which falls in line with images in the media created by the adverts, the cinema or the press. The foisted identity campaign works: it has been noted that people outside the area created local identities, for the purpose of attracting people there (as was the case in St Kilda), or for the purpose of boosting the superiority of the firm, the military, etc. as it moves in. The oil men carried before them the identity manufactured in the press, the TV documentary, etc., as did the US naval men of the FBM submarines. There is the inevitable clash between the 'homegrown identities' and that of the incomers which goes before them in the media and is then propagated by local gossip networks. Flowing from the question of identity and tied up with it, as well discussed by J.R. Gusfield, is the Weberian concept of the 'dual ethic'. (63) Apart from adopting one identity for self, and another for others, beyond the local scape, there is the adoption of an ethic for dealings with people inside the group and for others outside it. Consequently, the impact of outsiders creates dual performances - 'I'd do this to a navvy (an American), but never to a local', etc. In addition, the dual ethic may cut both ways in that the outsiders will also experience the 'consciousness of kind' (64) as workmates/military colleagues, so that there will be one way of acting towards workmates, and another towards locals, and as already noted, some locals often put money before locals when it comes to trade or rentals.

In analysing the clash of identities, one may go further with the analysis by considering the 'master identity' (Suttles), which however is not considered as such in the recent Scottish studies. (65) G.D. Suttles points out that people may identify themselves in sectorial terms, e.g. as West Siders, or Hyde Parkers. Residents in the Dunoon district saw themselves as Cowal folk, and so adopted a 'master identity', but did conserve their other settlement identities.

Thus, the Cowal folk have had subsidiary identities built up by their experience of life in Sandbank, Kirn, etc., along the Cowal shores. Within the area people have divided themselves between those in and out of town. Amongst those who are out-of-towners, there appears to have been a broad local crystallisation of identity amongst the people who state that they live 'by Holy Loch' (beyond the West Bay) or live 'by Toward' (beyond the East Bay), but always within the context of their boast that they are Cowal folk.

As an impact study, this research is concerned with effects of outsiders upon the township of Dunoon, upon the settlements in and around the Holy Loch area beyond the East Bay, and upon the settlements in and around Toward beyond the West Bay. But, the 'master identity of being Cowal folk is always the local cultural account of most of the people with regard to their self-estimation.

What of the mechanisms which have conserved and kept alive the people's local identities? M. Janowitz has shown that the urban press may act as a custodian, fostering sectorial and area loyal-

ties, and integrity. (66)   Once again the importance of the local
newspaper is borne out, which helps, as shall be seen, to cultivate
the identity of the Cowal folk, with Dunoon their local capital and
the boundaries of East Cowal, their ancient parish.   But, I say
'helps' because, as Judith Ennew observes in her contribution to the
Way of Life Seminars (May 1979), citing F. Barth (Ethnic Groups and
Boundaries), the identified are sensitive to the views of the iden-
tifiers, e.g. of tourists, of travel agents, and of national
opinion, (67) to which one may add the popular press and the
channels of television.   The sensitivity of the locality to outside
criticism will be cited in the present study.   Good and bad images
circulated, and often the local loyalties were increased as was the
phenomenon of accentuated identity (see A.P. Cohen, 'Oil and the
Cultural Account', (68)) or an insecurity of identity followed (see
J. Ennew, 'Self Image and Identity in the Hebrides', (69)).   In the
present study, the national press coverage of events concerning the
USN Polaris Base at Holy Loch, and the Ardyne gravity structure
building site played its role.   The national press was accentuating
the importance of fuel and energy to the nation and stressed
national loyalty laying great stress upon the cost of the economic
survival of the UK.

The local Tory groups supported oil expansion, as the nation did
at large, but they were in two minds about Ardyne.   The official
party line had been that Argyll was 'a living county' and that
'sadly many young people must leave Argyll for work.   The opportunity given by oil-related development to keep them here and attract
others in must be taken.' (70)   But most influential Tories were
also aware of the bad effects upon the local holiday image of the
Cowal watering places.   Money came first.   There were faint echoes
of the remark of the Lynds, in their sociological study of life in
Middleton, USA, in the streets of Dunoon.   'People know money but
they don't know you.' (71)   The business people had themselves put
money first when the US Base was set up, and had alienated many
local residents because of it.   They had argued that East Cowal
might be militarised, but if it brought money, it was acceptable.
When East Cowal was on the verge of being industrialised, more money
for some meant less money for others, especially the garage and the
hotel owners.   They blamed the SNP Member of Parliament for promis-
ing that locals would now have employment, that they would not need
to leave Cowal after all, when in fact many were barred from employment.   In addition, they felt cheated by the SNP 'line' which at
the time of the 1974 election promised it would close down the USN
Polaris Base.   And when were the SNP going to give Scotland back
her oil?   Only the bar owners were utterly satisfied - more mouths
meant more beers and whiskies, especially in the case of the thirsty
Ardyners, a matter I shall return to later when considering the cultural effects created by the new labouring class influx.

The local SNP groups, however, continued to protest that they
were not 'prepared to sit back and watch Scotland's oil revenues
being squandered to finance the massive debts which the London government is piling up'. (72)   Most of the local SNP followers
appeared to be against the Irish men in McAlpine's labour force.

Both the strangers from the outside who had jobs at Ardyne, and Mc-
Alpine's collaboration with the French designer of the platforms,
riled many persons.   Some stood by their MP, stating that he had
gone personally to the Ardyne complex to ask if the local labour
force could be cut back because the long-term bad effects upon local
businesses and trades.   Oil-related industry was welcome to the
locality, but the influx of so many 'outsiders' was viewed with increasing misgivings.

Political and economic divisions widened locally when the accentuated wage differentials of Ardyne workers set one man against
another, whilst groups argued for and against the project.   Issues
which had been debated in the outscape by London politicians and USA
oil kings were further discussed within the locality.   The Ardyne
complex brought the Scottish debate over oil and its control, nearer
home.

On the one hand, decline in orders at platform sites throughout
the country caused unease, especially for the workers at Ardyne, and
on the other hand, many residents in the locality felt they had been
cheated because the cost to them socially of having a platform site
in their locality outweighed the need for such platforms.   Indeed,
basins throughout the country were soon to stand empty.   Where was
the justification for so many sites?   What really was the national
interest?

The question of Ardyne did split some local Tory families for the
first time since the burgh began.   The oil question raised the
issue of the English alliance and aggravated the latent nationalism
within older Scottish kinship groups.   In addition, the incoming
labouring classes increased the socialist arguments and gave new
heart to what had always been a weak local minority Labour party.
Further fragmentations took place.

The minority Labour groups generally had supported Ardyne, and
the decision of the Secretary of State to allow McAlpine to build
platforms at Ardyne had their support.   It brought the local males
the opportunity for work.   The Labour grouse locally, however, was
that, after the first months of local employment at Ardyne, McAlpine
had been contacted by the local Tory employers and pressurised into
stopping the employment of local labour to protect their business
concerns.

Local residents in the working-class sectors of the Ardenslate
and Valrose Terrace schemes were annoyed that 'so-and-so' got a job
at Ardyne and was earning £150 a week, when they were being turned
away.   Irish labourers - 'bloody foreigners' - were now getting the
chance to make 'big money'.   An area noted for its tolerance now
regarded the incomers as a threat.   Money had poisoned the minds
and hearts of some local persons.   The Labour following was able
to make capital of the Tory businessmen who had attempted to block
work opportunities at Ardyne to preserve their own interests.   I
shall later look more closely at the economic scape which was under
pressure from McAlpine's Ardyne venture.

The observations of this chapter have delineated the way in which the Ardyne complex was set up, and how industrialisation intruded upon rural Toward.   At the time of the initial shock there were those who welcomed the establishment of the platform-builders because it was in the interests of the nation.   There was also the possibility of employment for the locals.   This at first mattered most, as against the ravage of the ecology.   Others did not welcome the Secretary of State's go-ahead, because the industrialisation en-visaged did not fit in with the 'scape of things' locally, and the social costs were reckoned to be too great, whatever the argument that oil exploration and platform-building had priority over all things.

'Initial surprises' flowed in rapid succession when rumours crea-ted uncertainties, among which was the announcement that the Ardyne platform complex was to be bigger than at first stated.   Many people locally had not had direct dealings with industrialists. They were not familiar with their mode of operation just as they were unfamiliar with the military mind.   In the interplay between government and industrialists in pursuit of their interests, the locals were dismayed and at all times unsure of outcomes for the locality as fears were being expressed that East Cowal would 'go industrial'.

The inauthentic nature of the interplay deserves more comment. D. Taylor, M. Broady, A. Varwell and J.J. Rodger, (73) all show in their Scottish studies how inauthentic were the dealings of the pol-iticians in the Scottish oil drama of the 1970s.   A. Etzioni states that 'the inauthentic provides the appearance of responsiveness while the underlying condition is alienating'. (74)   By alienation, he here means that people are excluded from controlling and deter-mining their quality of life.   J. Habermas, speaking of the 'public sphere', states that it is now 'adulterated and degenerated'. (75) The press, with investments in the North Sea exploration, clouded over the issues adding to the lack of authenticity. (76)

Whatever the protestations of the multinational industrialists, they are intent in the last analysis upon self-interest.   This self-interest was such that industrialists in the name of the national interest secured not only Ardyne, but other shore sites, bringing about a redundancy before some of the platform-builders had secured an order, creating a national disgrace with wastage of mil-lions of pounds in the scramble for local sites.

Once the local terrain is more or less secured by 'the private deal' - although not yet legally secured - the industrialist may accomplish his plans through manipulating the politicians.   It is here the argument is pitched at national need by the government. The outscape has priority over the local scape and the locality must sacrifice its end for the sake of the national ends.   But, the masked government question is - which locality ought to be made to sacrifice its localised ends?

That is why the locals at Dunoon were asking: Why us?   When the argument for a local plant or site is posed, and planning permission asked for, the vertical formal administrative outreach was adopted, but the industrialists had means of masking their case, as was especially so during the national rush for oil in the urgent days of fighting inflation during the late 1960s and early 1970s.   Also communication can so easily become oblique, as will later be explained and demonstrated.   But there is a predictability in the arguments of the industrialists in this situation - the need to create local employment is one predictable;   the need to compete with foreign industry is another;   the good the plant will be for the local economy is another.

The locals often know exactly what arguments will be brought up, so why, in the end, is a project such as at Ardyne secured? Because the politicians, and technocrats succumb to arguments which support the national need, and once that has happened, the invitation to express local objections is low-key and given a narrow time limit.

However, the initial impact and response of the people in the local scape was not quite so dramatic as it was at the time of the USN invasion in the early 1960s.   A second impact has less immediate effect and reaction if it synchronises with percussions coming from overlapping impacts.   Between November 1972 and my departure from Cowal in 1976 there had been only twelve letters in the local press which explicitly mentioned the McAlpine intrusion out of a total of 490 letters written within a period of three years and four months.   This represents approximately only one letter out of every 41.   At the end of the day it was the villagers of Toward and locality who suffered most.   They were immediately involved, but it took them some time to appreciate what was happening.

By the time that the first concrete platform was successfully completed and tugged out to sea in March 1975, secondary surprises were about to take place creating spin-offs and secondary effects, as will shortly be demonstrated.

Chapter 5

THE BUREAUCRATIC TAKE-OVER

The democratic form in the real meaning of the word is necessarily a despotism, because it establishes an executive for the 'all', which is not really the all, and it decides concerning and sometimes against, the one who has not participated in the decision. (Immanuel Kant)(1)

The local authority of Argyll, before 1975, was quite unique. C.M. Macdonald writes: 'Argyll is unique among Scottish County Councils in that it has no recognised headquarters for the accommodation of all the chief officials. This is due partly to geographical and partly to historical considerations, which have prevented any one of the Argyll Burghs from having distinct pre-eminence over the others.' (2) Meetings appear to have been held in different places 'as the council may decide'; indeed, in winter they were often held in Glasgow! (3)

Old suspicions of Cowal in Argyll die hard, as does local ambivalence for the Campbells whose clan chief resides at Inveraray. Dunoonites have never regarded Inveraray as the prime Argyll burgh, and have always insisted that Dunoon District is of immense importance economically. They have always insisted that it has had both the highest rateable value and the highest gross valuation in Argyll for well over a hundred years. In addition, Dunoon, a capital, has had the biggest burgh population in Argyllshire for many decades. Dunoon had a county pre-eminence educationally, and was more accessible to the lowland centres of business and finance than the other Argyllshire burghs. None the less, the administration of the county was not centred in Dunoon. The real administrative anomaly was that the bureaucratic centre was nowhere. Administrative functions were apportioned as follows: the County Clerk, the Chief Constable and the County Engineer were in Lochgilphead. The Medical Officer and the Chief Sanitary Inspector were in Oban. The County Assessor and the County Treasurer were in Campbelltown. The Director of Education, the County Architect and the County Librarian were in Dunoon.

Over the years, Dunoon battled to have the removal of the office

of the Clerk of the County from Lochgilphead as well as the County
Treasurer from Campbelltown to Dunoon.   There was no doubt that
such a diffused administrative structure had to be altered.
Regionalisation in the 1970s attempted to alter the situation in May
1975.   The people of Cowal had hoped that Dunoon would be the District HQ within the new region.   Dunoon's position in Argyllshire
has always been a central political issue.   Locals were proud of
the small burgh which they generally regarded as the more forward-
looking burgh in Argyllshire.

The population figures for the Argyllshire burghs between 1881
and 1951 indicate why Dunoonites demanded more control and the town
status of prime burgh in all Argyllshire.   But Inveraray hosted the
Duke of Argyll or of Lochgilphead in southern Argyllshire shared in
the status enjoyed by the County Council which ruled Cowal and Oban
was the official capital of Argyllshire.   No local could really
identify with any of these and a rift had developed between the
Dunoon Town Council and Lochgilphead's County Council members.

TABLE 5.1 Population of the Argyllshire burghs (1881, 1911, 1931,
1951)

		1881	1911	1931	1951
Inveraray	population	870	533	455	503
Campbelltown	"	7,693	7,625	6,309	7,172
Oban	"	4,046	5,557	5,759	6,226
Lochgilphead	"	1,489	921	974	1,229
Tobermory	"	1,200	988	772	693
Dunoon	"	4,692	6,859	8,780	9,940

Source: Censuses (HMSO)

Before 1975, the Dunoon Town Council baulked at having to render
an account of public spending to the Office at Campbelltown.   Unashamedly Dunoon burghers fought to maintain and control the central
services and amenities of the whole of Argyllshire.   Although the
nebulous County Council administration had immediate responsibility
for the outlying settlements of Kilmunside and of the area beyond
the Bullwood stretching to Toward and beyond, it was the burgh of
Dunoon which mattered locally.   The shore settlements depended upon
the main Post Office, the six banks, the main Cowal Police Station,
the Cowal Fire Station, the Board of Management for the Cowal Hospitals, the chief Cowal businesses and upon almost all the Cowal
shops, the tourist and transport offices, the pier, and in addition
upon the three of five Cowal Hospitals, all of which were located in
the burgh of Dunoon.   The only two ambulances servicing the area
did so from Dunoon, and most of the GPs had their surgeries in the
burgh.   The main services revolved around Dunoon, and as already
demonstrated a great deal else.

Dunoon has been dominated and led by its Town Council, known as the 'Local Parliament'. (4)   For a hundred years, the provosts developed the tourism that had made Dunoon 'the gem of the Costa Clyde'.   The status of the men and women of the Council Chambers at Ewing's Castle House, Dunoon, was ranked highly in Cowal.   The American invasion had only served to enhance the Town Council's position.   Meetings with the top brass of the Washington Naval Department, and the presentation of awards and plaques by the captains to the Council, and handshakes with foremost members of the American Navy Department, who have been accustomed to ambassadorial treatment, raised the small Town Council from humbler liaison and advocacy levels to loftier ones.

Not being industrial, Dunoon District's paths did not cross those of 'the other side'.   Local businesses were largely autonomous, and were not directly dependent upon boardroom decisions in the outscape.   Development in the major development area was centred upon the Town Council and its committees.   As long as the people of the town and area catered for strangers by providing bed, board, and refreshment, there was no serious disjunction between the goals of the people, the Council, and surrounding urban areas.   With the McAlpine industrial intrusion there was strain, because the locally determined tourist goals clashed with the nationally determined industrial goals.   But more about that later;   here one must emphasise the importance of the local controls, vested mainly in the Dunoon Town Council.

It was the power and the status of the burgh of Dunoon which were mainly threatened by the new regionalisation scheme implemented in May 1975.   In 1975 Cowal was incorporated into Strathclyde Region. Glasgow became the centre of the Region and Lochgilphead the centre of the District within Strathclyde.   The dramatic bureaucratic changes and further centralisation, as well as the eventual takeover of local administration by Lochgilphead and by Glasgow resulted from the technocrat's belief in ongoing centralisation.   T. Roszak describes technocracy as:

the social form in which an industrial society reaches the peak of its organisational integration.   It is the ideal men usually have in mind when they speak of modernizing, up-dating, rationalising, planning.   Drawing upon such unquestionable imperatives as the demand for efficiency, for large-scale co-ordination of men and resources, and ever more impressive manifestations of collective human power. (5)

In the face of the unquestionable imperatives, the local councillors and people had little hope of changing the minds or hearts of the faceless ones in the outscape, where decisions were made behind closed doors.   As M. Harloe demonstrates, planners and bureaucrats believe in the enlightened minority taking over, with minimal participation, acting quickly and secretly, with a prior lack of publicity as to actual and precise intent. (6)   At the same time it must be admitted that the local Town Council had often made decisions behind doors with narrow interests at heart in much the same terms,

as described by K. Hudson. (7)   However, there is no doubt that the
Town Council of Dunoon above all had the economic survival of the
area at heart, whereas the technocrats had a grand economic and centralised plan at heart, whatever the cost to localities in the periphery.

The mode of change, as took place during the process of reorganisation, can be traced back to the Report of the Royal Commission of
1969 on regionalism.   Wheatley's Report (as it was popularly called
after its chairman) came as a shock to a local burgh, which had
imagined that the 'status quo' was without end.   When the members
of the Town Council were asked on the 14 October 1969, to discuss
the possibility that the shores of East Cowal would be taken over by
administrative centres on 'the other side', they were asked in a
sense to sign the death warrant of their own Town Council.   The
demise of the smaller councils was part of the scheme of centralisation.   The members of the Town Council faced the horrendous possibility that established modes of decision-making and of dealing with
local problems would soon be radically altered by decisions in
remote industrial centres.   The members were only given until
22 October 1969 to discuss the report.   They were then asked to
pass on their views through a representative.   To crown the situation, only three copies were sent to the council chambers.   Within
four days a special meeting was called of local people who delibera-
ted that 'the people of Argyll and particularly those of Cowal
should be given the opportunity of direct discussion regarding their
own future'. (8)   When it had been a question of discussing the
American invasion or the Ardyne intrusion, the debate was over a
finite arrangement, here there was a question of a permanent settlement which could effect local affairs indefinitely.

The impact had diverse effects locally.   It created from the
start an uneven reaction.   Cowal folk had a dual perspective.
They enjoyed the master identity of being Cowal people, but many had
originated from outside, especially many retired urbanites from 'the
other side'.   There was a marked ambivalence in their social scape
as cultural accounts varied in accordance with the incomers' identification with the locality.   The Dunoon Observer, 11 October 1969,
stated: 'the Cowal shores look across the waters to the rest of the
Clyde estuary rather than to the rest of Argyll'.   Not everyone
would have agreed, but there has been no doubt from a study of
Cowal's historical scape that it has been in effect a colony.
Those who were natives of the old township, and were of real Cowal
stock, were set against the possibility of any merger with industrial areas, as also were the locals who had resided in the area for
over thirty years, or who were at least second generation.   But the
opposition to amalgamation with 'the other side' was not shared by
all of them.   Even the newcomers were divided - some for a merger,
others against it.   The 'cultural account' made under the impact of
invasion, as already touched upon in the case of Shetland, was a far
cry from the situation in Cowal.

Here the 'account' was rather economic and political.   Meetings
from Innellan to Ardentinny discussed the proposal of Dunoon and

area being administered from the industrial mainland.   The local
press described their division.   Ironically, it was ex-provost
Wyatt, a Londoner originally (or must we say once a Londoner always
a Londoner?), who insisted that Cowal should remain with the rest of
Argyll. (9)   The Provost, Judge Harper, stated with feeling at the
Dunoon Ratepayers' Association:

> The proposals of the Wheatley Report are a direct negation of our
> democratic way of life.   These proposals will ultimately place
> absolute power in the hands of a few.   No central or regional
> government can have the knowledge and time to deal with the
> detailed problems of every group of people in the county.

He questioned whether the proposed community councils which had only
an advisory capacity could act as a watchdog.   When asked where a
copy of the report could be had, he was sorry to say that it cost £2
a copy, but that the possibility of a reference copy in the local
library would shortly be taken up by the library committee.   He
added: 'I am just as interested that the public should know all the
facts.   I might well be the last provost of Dunoon.' (10)

Predictably, only two members of the Town Council meeting on the
18 November were in any way favourably disposed towards the report.
Representatives from Troon, Rothesay, Largs, Millport, Campbelltown,
Ardrossan and Dunoon, met at Dunoon on the 15 December 1969 to express their dissatisfaction with the proposals for tourism.   They
protested that urban centres could not and should not manage the
affairs of the seaside town. (11)   Dismay and political uncertainty
hung over the Clyde and the coastal regions, where economic gloom
about tourism had already created despondency.

In the waiting game, the bureaucracy created uncertainty during
long periods of secret deliberations.   An uneasy lull ensued, when
details had become dim in people's minds.   Nothing appeared to be
happening well into 1970.   Strategists know that the impact must
not be dramatised and that the shock must be allowed to subside.
In these ways, the scheming bureaucrat aims to deflate reaction and
protest.   On 10 May 1970 the Presbyterian preacher at the kirking
of the Town Council spoke courageously from his pulpit against the
impending changes: 'Everything today tends towards bigness, and
bigness for its own sake is a threat.... We must the more persever-
ingly strive to find democratic ways of living for little men.' (12)
Little men have little say.

Under impact, immediate reaction within a state of urgency
usually creates a more united front.   However, when people are
threatened with innovation which takes time to develop over a protracted period, lags are created, as people begin to interpret
diversely or indulge in hopeful dreams that change may not occur at
all.   Some read more than others into the proposals.   Accounts are
also largely determined by one's interests - culturally, economically, and politically.   So, it was that intrigue and divisions began
to appear in the Town Council chambers so much so that ex-provost
Wyatt described it as 'Ali Baba's cave'. (13)

No word came from the technocrats beyond the Firth until February 1971.   In the interim period the people became totally distracted by a proposed new housing scheme in the area for the USN personnel and by possible dangers at and from the nuclear base, and by a protest campaign against the parking of American cars in the narrow Sandbank roads.   In other words, the overlap of impacts had confused people's perception and created an overload of stress when clarity and awareness were dulled.

On the 16 February 1971, the government in a White Paper accepted the two-tier system of Regions and Districts to be implemented in 1975.   Shetland and Orkney would be virtually all-purpose authorities.   The people were made aware of events by the shock announcement that Argyll including Cowal would not be within the Highland Region but in the West Region centred on Glasgow. (14)   The people faced the possibility that Dunoon and area would be administered by Greenock which would probably be its District centre, across the water.   The Dunoon Town Council would cease to exist as from May 1975.   Judge Harper commented:

I can foresee many difficulties in this set-up.   Who will, for example organise Dunoon's summer entertainment during the holiday period, and take on snap decision on many matters which crop up during the season?   Local government will be much further away from the people and will I think generate frustration on many local issues. (15)

The initial but protracted phase of impact now began to make itself felt with the officially declared legislative intent of the government.   But, before implementation in May 1975 the initial impact lost much of its momentum as older routines continued and as nothing appeared to happen.   In the four years between February 1971 and May 1975 many uncertainties and fears and divisions were to arise spasmodically.

The first source of division and conflict (bureaucrats do believe in the old adage - divide and conquer) was the statement in the White Paper: 'the boundaries illustrated may be altered slightly after consultation with local authorities and other interested parties'. (16)   The bureaucrats realised full well that authorities are sensitive about boundaries, and what did 'slightly' mean on the map in both geographic and social terms?   Fatalism was inevitable in a situation where the administrative structure and number of Regions and Districts were imposed from above. (17)   The arrangements, however, of the Districts and Regions remained volatile. Sometimes Dunoon was in one suggested District and sometimes another.

When Michael Noble, the Tory MP, came to the Queens Hall, Dunoon, to meet the public and discuss the White Paper, divided views became apparent. (18)   Some people sided with Harper and Wyatt in opposition to any merger with the other side, others sided with a prominent councillor, Mr Thomson (destined to be Dunoon's last provost) in favour.   Ironically, it was the year that Dunoon celebrated its first centenary as a burgh.

The 9,000 free copies of the Centenary Issue of the Dunoon local
newspaper underlined the pathos that year.   In it people read of
the illustrious provosts, of the efforts of Wyatt to secure a worthy
chain of office for the elected leader of the Town Council, and of
the improvements that the Council had brought locally.   Side by
side with the tabloid sheets of the centenary story, they read about
the proposed demise of the same Town Council.   It did not make
sense to many of the locals.

However, there were economic considerations that weighed heavily
for many when 'taking account' of impending changes.   Some argued
that there was more money on 'the other side', pointing out that
with the waning of the summer holiday trade, the economy of the town
depended more and more upon linkage with Renfrewshire and Clydeside.
About 400 locals at that time worked on the other side, and many
tradesmen and firms serviced the local businesses from 'the other
side'.   But the romance of Argyll swayed others.   It was a question of an 'economic account' of the situation in conflict with a
'cultural account'.   Economic scapes clashed.   Some prioritised in
terms of the budget, whilst others took account of Argyll's heritage.   However,utopian nostalgia for Argyll's link with highland
lore asserted itself.   A local poet wrote in support of that
romantic Argyll:

    Argyll, Argyll, a ken ye well
    There's few that ken ye better.
    Free clachan heids frae antlered halls,
    Or biggins' mang the heather,
    Agree, agree tae girt Argyll,
    Avoiding pliskys after,
    As the road and trend in years tae come,
    Is now across Clyde's water. (19)

The area was non-industrial, peninsular, conservative and disproportionately retired, with a largely middle-class population.
Politically and culturally, the people of Cowal had appeared in
recent years to have been relatively united and tolerant.   But,
in 1971, the Town Council was split.   The people were divided over
the proposal that Dunoon and its locality be linked with Greenock
in Inverclyde.   However, they were generally united in their dread
of a Labour-dominated Glasgow Regional Council, but they knew that
they could not back out of the Region.   It was the prospect of an
altered Dunoon District which threw up latent differences.

In the main, the most significant differences were between the
people of the rural settlements (to the NE and SW of Dunoon) and
the people of the burgh.   In the villages, the people were reported
as dominantly opposed to being cut off from the rest of Argyll.
When making my own rounds, I heard people say over and over again
that they did not want libraries, amenities and expensive lighting,
they had left all those things behind them.   They wanted seclusion,
and stressed that they had worked for it over the years before
retirement.   Others, who had not enjoyed the urban delights of 'the
other side' only wanted the sameness they had enjoyed for years.

Village meetings which were reported in the local newspaper confirm the loyalty of the residents to Argyll and their resistance to any administrative merger with 'the other side'.   Councillors Hinge at Sandbank and Wyatt at Innellan denounced the betrayal of Argyll over and over again.   Many repeated Wyatt's description of the White Paper's proposal as a 'mutilation of Cowal'.

It would appear that the latent feelings which divided the burgh and the contrasting attitude of the villages with the burgh's ambivalence revealed a crisis of identity that must surely be the problem facing most migrants.   Many may only react when their assumed and newfound identity is threatened.   Many urbanites had scarcely settled within rural Cowal when they became anti-urbanites.

But why were there only ten letters to the Dunoon Observer about the issue between October 1969 and May 1975?   In contrast, the American invasion had had a diverse modal pattern, as the analysis of the episode of change associated with the USN presence indicates. There were several probable reasons for the different mode of impact in the case of regionalisation:

1 The American impact was dramatic.   It was nationally and internationally sensationalised by the media, accompanied by mass protests and marches.   The regional scheme was news, but designedly undramatic.   The reporting was serialised sporadically rather than sensationalised in the media.

2 The American impact was associated with the growing confrontation in the outscape between East and West, and with the threat of nuclear hazards.   The regional scheme was not associated with the more vital questions of life and death.

3 The American invasion was executed speedily with military precision.   The regional scheme took years of protracted deliberations (and silences) before it was implemented.

4 The American invasion was simpler to comment upon.   The regional scheme was complex and bewilderingly confused.   Knowing what was happening required concentrated reading.   In addition, the White Paper was a lengthy document that presumed one had knowledge of the Wheatley Report, and copies during the critical periods of decision-making in the locality were few and far between.

5 The American invasion was an exogeneous scheme planned and finally implemented by alien militarists in the wider outscape, directly and immediately involving the locality in the American ballistic build-up of missiles, pushing the peaceful locality into the nuclear front-line.   The regional scheme in contrast was endogenous to the process of modernisation, in which technocrats within the nearer outscape devised a plan, which equally affected many peripheral scapes in Scotland, as it had also done in England and Wales.

6 Lastly, the impact of American and McAlpine ventures overlapped

with that of the regional programme, so that overstimulation and an overload of changes had blunted the protests of many people and their awareness of what the implications were, even their knowledge of what was actually happening.

By 1972 the commercial and economic advantages of linkage with the major cities on 'the other side',had begun to win yet more advocates in Dunoon.   John Thomson, a popular baillie, was quoted in the Dunoon Observer as saying: 'Dunoon's future lies across the water where the money is and not in the hinterland of Argyll.'   He added that the Argyll administrators had been 'soaking the Burgh for years', and that it was a spurious argument that there was no community of interest with Greenock, because 'the fact that 400 commuters travel across the water every day gives the lie to that'. (20)

It was becoming more and more apparent that the long-standing political battle between Lochgilphead and local people, particularly in the burgh, was a significant and growing factor in the debate. Already the administrators in Lochgilphead had discussed the possibility of buying Kilmory Castle at Lochgilphead as the District's HQ.   The new provost, J.M. Dickson, was well aware of the increased status the new regional scheme would bring to Lochgilphead, if Dunoon and area did not accept the incorporation into Inverclyde. Meantime, Argyll County Council declared that it would not let Cowal go.   The members declared that its place historically was with Argyll.

By 13 May 1972, the division between members of the Dunoon Town Council had become more marked. (21)   In the chambers, the provost stated that he had been asked to sign a petition to keep Cowal with Argyll, 'which I refused to do', and added: 'For the avoidance of doubt, Dunoon Town Council's position is that they would have preferred to be a District authority on their own with Cowal, Rothesay, and the Island of Bute.'   He then made a statement which repeated the economic link with 'the other side':

There is no community of interest with the rest of Argyll, where the people of Dunoon don't have any business connections, nor can they travel there by public transport.   Experience has also shown that the Argyll authorities are unsympathetic to the people of Dunoon and in recent years development has been frustrated. (22)

Dunoon had been the thorn in the side of the Campbell domain, and history repeated itself, because Cowal was situated between two worlds at the interface, or seam, between the industrial West and the Highlands and Islands.

Meanwhile, the villages collected 3,600 signatures to protest to the Secretary for Scotland against any merger with Inverclyde. (23) An influential local, Judge Harper, who was heartened by the move, stated in the midst of local controversy in Dunoon that a large West of Scotland block could not possibly fulfil the criteria accepted by the Wheatley Report and the White Paper.   He stressed that four points had to be considered seriously:

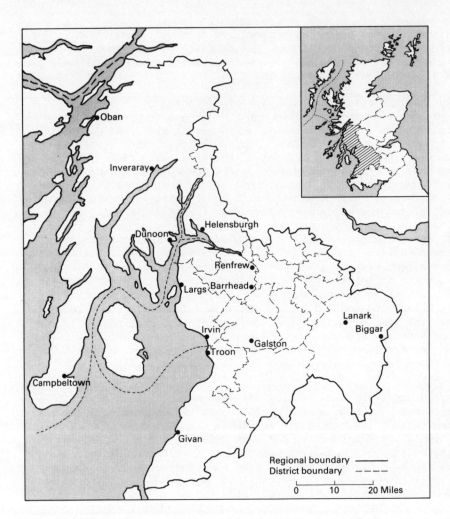

MAP 5.1 Region of Strathclyde and Districts

1 local government services should be provided over areas with
genuine communities with interests and allegiances in common;

2 an authority should be community based; unless its area corresponds with the genuine community, people will not think of it as
their authority;

3 it should be possible for elected members to keep in effective
touch with their constituents on matters for which they are responsible.

4 the government is part of a system of local democracy, not just a
body supplying service over a certain area. (24)

Harper's approach to the question was shared by those who put the
master identity of Cowal first.   Cowal in cultural terms had little
in common with 'the other side'.   At this very time, however, industrialists were offering money to local farmers for sites which
would be suitable for platform-building on Cowal shores.   In addition, the burgh was taken up with local parents' complaints concerning American children.   They were crowding local schools, and were
slowing down the education of local children.   I will consider
these complaints later.   At the same time, May 1975 seemed a long
way off in the summer of 1972.

Little discussion took place until the 1 November 1972, when the
Kilmun Community Association added its protest to that of other
Cowal villagers.   The association was opposed to any transfer of
power to 'industrially dominated areas with all the latent possibilities of political influences and the consequent loss of present
individuality, first-hand knowledge and non-party political administration by local Town and County Councils'. (25)   The political
fears were clearly underlined.   There was rural antagonism for the
metropolitan take-over.   Dunoon, a semi-creation of Glasgow, as
already seen, was not as set against the link with the city as were
the East Cowal villagers.   As people inscaped the situation, many
took account of the benefits coming from interplay between the local
economic scape and that of the more prosperous metropolis and conur-
bation.

On the eve of the discussion of regionalisation in parliament, in
January 1973, there were three groupings, each led by a local influential.   Firstly, there was Judge Harper who supported a merger
between Cowal, Bute and Rothesay.   He had become convinced that
tourism united these localities.   Secondly, Dunoon's provost, Mr
Dickson, was for a merger with 'the other side'.   Thirdly, Mr Wyatt
and Mr Hinge, who were greatly respected in the villages, supported
a continuance within Argyll, which should be administratively cut
off from 'the other side'.   The most salient demarcation of opinion
was between the people of the burgh and those 'furth' (outside) the
burgh, most of whom resided in settlements which hugged the Cowal
shores.   The rural long-standing core of established residents
around Kilmun by Holy Loch were historically and parochially diverse
from the long-standing residents around Toward and Innellan by the

Firth and Loch Striven.   However, most of the residents at either
end of the locality in these areas were retired middle-class people
all of whom were from 'the other side' and whose proud Victorian
homes and life-style were much the same, the only real difference
being that they lived at either end of the locality.   What they
shared most was a retirement dream 'to get away from city life on the
other side', as one objector to the Strathclyde scheme put it to me.

In the confusion, alternative schemes fragmented any possibility
of a block view.   Compromise was inevitable.   The Tory MP, Michael
Noble, secured a compromise approved by parliament that Cowal,
Rothesay, and Bute should merge with Argyll as a District, but would
remain within Strathclyde Region. (26)   The Regional Offices would
therefore be on 'the other side', which would satisfy many burgh
people, who accepted an administrative merger with the industrial
West.   The District Officers would be in Argyll, which would in
part satisfy the more rural residents of Cowal.   But where would
the District HQ be?   This question became the most vital regional
issue and in fact united both the people of the burgh and the people
of the East Cowal shore settlements.   They were opposed to any
Lochgilphead intrusion in the locality.

Firstly, it was a matter of convenience that Dunoon should be the
local HQ because Lochgilphead was over the hills and far away.   The
regular rent inquiries and payments, or educational queries, or complaints, demanded easy access especially for the retired.   In terms
of utilities, the Burgh of Dunoon was to be preferred as the District HQ, quite apart from the historical reasons why Dunoon could
claim pre-eminence over Lochgilphead on the grounds both of its
ancient castle and parish and of its importance as a link-town.

Secondly, and more importantly from the point of view of current
local problems, associated with both the impact of the Polaris Base
and of McAlpine's intrustion, people required a local centre where
prompt decisions could be made.   At that very time by a conjuncture
of events, the people of Toward and of Ardentinny, at both ends of
the girdle of villages along the Cowal shores, called upon the
Dunoonites to support their local preservation societies.   Many
people in their old capital rallied to their aid.   In the halls and
churches of Dunoon the democratic rights of people in Cowal were
voiced and support mustered.   Lawyers from the town and elders from
the churches supported the resistance of the villagers to industrial
take-overs.   The prospect of a local District HQ in Dunoon would
have added considerably to the fight against the major problems of
Argyll which were located in and around Dunoon.   In addition, the
SNP revival had given Cowal a sense of proprietorship.   The shores
were theirs: why should alien people from the outscape exploit
their land?   So why not a local HQ rather than one outside of the
major problem area?

The new District set-up of Argyll and Bute as proposed was contrived.   Its one asset was that it brought together the waning seaside resorts of Rothesay in Bute and Dunoon in Cowal, which shared
the same economic problems.   The ramifications of having these

often rival units within the same economic regional unit did not at that time dawn on many.   People were distracted by the 1973 American riot in Dunoon, to be dealt with later.

When the Argyll Joint Advisory Committee was set up to enable transition to take place from the former County Offices to the District ones, suspicion over the ambitions of Lochgilphead were activated once again.   My neighbours and contacts during my stay in Dunoon put it forcibly: 'Who wants to travel to the ends of the earth to complain about litter on the shores?'   'Why should we come second to the small-fry at Lochgilphead?'   'Can any Lochgilphead office boy know our business?'   'You'd need a sackful of copper to get in touch with Kilmory Castle – it's the back of nowhere.' 'What the hell do the white-collar Lochgilphead blokes know about life under the shadows of the Polaris Base and dry dock and McAlpine's concrete platforms?'

In this protracted period of pre-implementation, cumulative surprises had piled up within short spans of time, with longer in-between periods, when the time-lags created surmise and local divisions.   But none of these mitigated the overall fact that the small semi-rural locality was engulfed within a Region of $1\frac{1}{2}$ million people.

The Lochgilphead debate underlined the need the people had for localised controls.   They had lost the larger issue of centralised controls in the macro administrative management of their affairs; they wanted some say in the microsphere of local administration and welfare.   The local press cited the Town Council's moans that administrators were 'hell bent on getting everything possible for Lochgilphead.   There was real fear that Dunoon and Rothesay would be shut out completely.' (27)   Then in February 1974, Mr Chas Black, a Dunoon ex-provost and popular influential, one of the old incomers who built new Dunoon, died.   He had been a leading businessman in Cowal and elder of the church.   He saw the character and the prestige of the burgh threatened by militarisation, industrialisation and lastly by regionalisation.   Two other local influentails Wyatt (twice provost) and Miss McPhail, the ex-provost who had welcomed the USS Proteus, died during the vital period when Dunoon contested Lochgilphead's claim to HQ status.   The decease of these three formidable Dunoonites weakened the case for Dunoon.

When the SNP electorate twice secured Argyll in the two general elections of 1974, the possibility of altering the regional scheme was revived.   The constituency of Argyllshire had been a Tory seat for years.   The nationalist movement captured the imagination of the Scots with its accent on 'oil for Scotland' and 'hands off our land'.   These and similar statements constituted a clarion call to a growing number of Scots who wanted freedom to decide their own affairs and to shake off the outsiders.   The new MP MacCormick declared at the outset: 'The SNP believes in local government.   We are totally opposed to the concept of putting Argyll into the monster Strathclyde Region.' (28)   His words may have revived hopes, but it was already too late to alter the inevitable on the

issue of Argyll's inclusion in Strathclyde Region.   However, the
issue of the District HQ was more open to alteration.

Whatever the protestations of the SNP and of Argyll's MP, a
massive and expensive campaign to sell the name of Strathclyde and
disseminate information about the Region went into full swing in the
spring of 1974.   The 'contrived identity' of the Strathclyde citizen had to have priority over other identities, however more meaningful were the 'homegrown identities'.   What had been sown and
cultivated within the past had to give way to the new.   Mini-kilted
girls went out from Glasgow City Chambers as Strathclyde publicists
in a planned campaign to spread the work through the distribution
everywhere of brochures and adverts declaring 'we are one' to all
parts of the West of Scotland. (29)

What the regional changes in administrative structure and roles
in May 1975 would mean in concrete terms began to raise unanticipated questions in the minds of the Dunoon business people.   1The
Dunoon Development Association no longer met, and the town and
villages faced a new season without the old advisors and supportive
committees.   Where were the regional offices to be?   What were the
distinctive functions of the Region's HQ and that of the District?

Already in the spring of 1974 when there were reliable rumours
that Kilmory Castle had already been bought, the Advisory Committee
was accused of 'jumping the gun' in the Town Chambers.   Baillie
Thomson, the Town's representative at the Committee who had been
shouted down by the other members, had stated with reference to the
machinations of the Committee: 'they have by reason of secret meetings made sure that there is little likelihood of the new headquarters being located anywhere in Argyll other than Lochgilphead'. (30)   The Dunoon Hospital Board met for the last time a
month before the election of the new Stratyclyde officials.   In the
new Health Board not a single Dunoon person was appointed.   A
letter of complaint had gone in vain to the Secretary of State
stressing that although Dunoon 'had the most important hospital in
the county, they had no say'. (31)

The political scape had also been shaken.   This was initially
made clear when in April 1974 party politics entered into the local
elections of Cowal for the first time.   In the past candidates had
remained independent.   Now, they were seeking to win supporters on
party tickets.   A woman summed up the situation in a letter to the
local press: 'The introduction of party politics seems a retrograde
move, when so many local interests are at present being threatened
by powerful pressure from outside.' (32)   However, the inclusion of
the locality within an urban industrial area did not immediately
alter the fact that the well-known independent faces received the
same support as before. (33)   The merits of global politics would
take time to alter the nature of local elections.

The last provost, Mr Thomson, was instated in a mood of local
despond as leader of the Town Council.   In him were merged local
loyalty and pride in the achievements of Cowal over the years.   But

both he and the people had to accept the fact that their local Town
Council was virtually at an end.   Uncertainty as to many unresolved
questions were added to the lack of information.

Most people faced regional change.   At his 'kirking' (i.e. when
the provost is received by the church and prayed for by the kirk)
the Presbyterian minister said from his pulpit to the assembled last
Town Council:

We have to accept the fact of change.   It is not the first time
in the history of Dunoon that change has had to be faced.
Usually in the past it was accompanied by violence and even
bloodshed.... Arguments in the past of how Scotland ought to be
governed were not settled by the ballot box or Advisory Committees.   The ruins of Dunoon Castle remind us of that.   This time
change has gone through fairly peaceably with nothing more than
an occasional raising of the blood pressure and a certain amount
of resentment and frustration.... A large proportion of the
developments which have made Dunoon what it is were carried out
by the Town Councils.   You and your predecessors have developed
the town in such a way as to make it an attractive place to live
in and for people to retire to.   You have played your part in
fostering tourism so that it is a holiday resort for six months
of the year.   There are two kinds of change: the kind of change
that has happened or must happen;   such change has to be accepted.   Also, the kind of change we make for ourselves.   Remoteness would not make things impossible, only more difficult. (34)

The dramatic references to the ruins of the castle may have reflected in some way how people were feeling, especially the influentials, the councillors and baillies, who saw their Town Council fall
apart and lie in ruins.   But, there was always the possibility that
Dunoon might yet be the District HQ, unfortunately, that hope would
soon be destroyed.

A final decision was passed at Inverarary in August 1974 stating
that Lochgilphead would henceforth be the District HQ.   The manner
in which this took place underlines the pathos of the events and the
bitterness with which the news was received in the town of Dunoon
and its locality.   Firstly, Lochgilphead was recommended in the
preliminary report in preference to Dunoon by 58.4 points to 58.1.
The 0.3 difference was decided upon by the fact that the greater
availability of accommodation for administrative personnel was at
Lochgilphead.

The irony of the situation was that both the American invasion
and McAlpine intrusion had ultimately swerved the decision in Lochgilphead's favour.   The economic scape in the matter of the Council's support of the USN project to acquire more money, and latterly
local hopes of McAlpine employment, had militated against the
claims of Dunoon and area in the bid for political controls in the
political scape.   The actual result of the voting was stunning
because the gathered members had voted 12-12 on the location of the
HQ.   The Chairman, himself from Oban, decided he had to cast in

favour of Lochgilphead.   Few Dunoonites have forgotten the
episode. (35)

Forebodings and fears about a Glasgow regional HQ were common.
The MP, MacCormick, was concerned that rural Argyll and the tourist
settlements would lose out badly, because of the Labour clique in
the city.   He stated: 'They were almost on the point of creating a
virtual dictatorship.   We have only five councillors for Argyll.
The decision will be taken by this Glasgow clique.' (36)   The electorate in Cowal, whether SNP or Tory, were afraid that the Labour
party in Glasgow would impose their priorities and their views upon
Committees in Strathclyde when discussing Cowal affairs, and so
affect decision-making and the running of the town and locality.

The SNP MPs in the last four months before May 1975 added to
existing uncertainty, because they called for the postponement of
regionalisation in view of the proposed creation of the General
Assembly.   The matter was raised in the House of Commons. (37)
Thurso had already written to the Dunoon Town Council to support
their Council's petition for a postponement.   Judge Harper commented in the chambers of the Council at Dunoon: 'We have been forced
into this regionalisation at too great a speed.' (38)   It is the
contention of this present study that it was really dragged out over
time at a slow speed.   But the petition was to no avail.   Undaunted, the SNP, at a December constituency meeting of Argyll people,
met to decide upon an all-purpose authority as in the Western Isles
'composed of those elected to the Regional and District Councils'. (39)   Up to the end of January 1975, the SNP activities only
served to create further uncertainties, and fears escalated.

Shortly before the implementation of Strathclyde region the
people were clearly bombarded by the news of impending changes and
all sorts of possibilities. (40)   Their energies over a longer
period had been diverted in one direction and then in another.   In
the bewilderment and the taxing of their efforts, first of one local
group and then another, realisation lagged for most people.   Divisions of opinion became apparent and these were further complicated
by the split between the burgh and the surrounding settlements over
the inclusion/exclusion issue of linkage with 'the other side'.
The people were still finding it difficult to adapt to the American
invasion so that Ardyne and regional intrusions upon the people
hardly raised much of a response in the local press.   Alvin Toffler
(1970) describes the condition of people under constant change as
one of 'overpowering apathy'. (41)   Reading the details of the conjuncture of happenings, one gets the impression that discussions
between the ex-provosts, the provosts, the Town Council members, the
core of business people in the burgh, and the shore councillors,
went on almost feverishly.   But, most local people were more and
more bewildered whilst misinformation and uninformation piled up,
and contrary rumours spread.

National efficiency, greater co-ordination and a more appropriate
rationalisation of administration had been stressed in support of
the new Regions.   In the case of militarisation and industrialisa-

tion, the local Town Council had supported the national need, but in
the case of regionalisation the cost was to be the extinction of the
Town Council of the Dunoonites' 'local parliament'. So the burgh
leaders could hardly have been in support of centralised administration centres beyond their local boundaries.

In April 1975 the Town Council organised its last event - a
dinner and dance to mark the demise of the Town Council. For 107
years 33 Dunoon provosts and local representatives of the people had
run the town. An air of despondency shrouded the half-hearted
event. The late editor of the Dunoon Observer remarked sadly to me
the day before, 'It is like going to your own funeral'. Certainly,
the drama of the events were pointedly highlighted that August night
when the guests made their exit along the old promenade beneath the
floodlit ruins of the castle walls and the baronial facade of
Ewing's Castle Hill House. Both were local symbols of old Dunoon
on the one hand, and of Ewing's new Dunoon, on the other. Ewing,
the Glaswegian, had attempted to take over Castle Hill when he built
his high wall around it, but the local women had foiled his scheme.
Now in the larger domain of local administrative control, Glasgow
was taking over Dunoon and its locality, building up a veritable
wall of bureaucracy around it. But, the locals could do little
about it this time.

There were some in Dunoon who felt that they were more secure
behind those new walls. They quoted the historian who described
Dunoon as a 'suburb of Glasgow' and the economic linkage between
Dunoon and Glasgow over time. Others recoiled from the association. They preferred the link with the highlands and clans of old
Dunoon. Although they were for the most part retired urbanites
(often from Glasgow), they had left the urban industrial world
behind them when they crossed the waters of the Firth.

The initial impact of regionalisation was to create a local sense
of helplessness. It accentuated the transfer of administration and
bureaucratic controls from the local scape of peripheral zones to
urban centres in the outscape in a spiral of ever-increasing centralisation. The impact reinforced yet more the fatalism engendered locally by the imposition of the Polaris Base at Holy Loch and
of McAlpine's concrete platform building site at Ardyne, by Loch
Striven. One local resident remarked wryly to me in May 1975:
'"Forward" was our town motto. Distrust must now replace it.'

Part Three

THE EFFECTS OF THE IMPACTS

Chapter 6

ENVIRONMENTAL HAZARDS

Bonnie old Dunoon by the hills and sea,
There are lots of bens and fairy glens,
And all of them are free.
There are lots of walks for private talks,
And gorgeous scenery
In bonnie old Dunoon on the C-L-Y-D-E.
(Local seaside song)

The peace of the Holy Loch was shattered once the Polaris Base was established in March 1961. The clang of metal and the continual hum of engines disturbed the tranquillity of the lochside both night and day. Somehow people imagined the noise would abate after the initial period of anchorage. It was not to be. However, people at first had been more concerned with the danger of radiation. The nuclear submarine is an underwater nuclear station. For many it has constituted a greater hazard than any nuclear station because it is a moving object and may collide. People were also concerned that radiation levels could be in excess of safety thresholds because of which nuclear submarines had been banned from thousands of ports across the world. Originally only three submarines were allowed at a time in Holy Loch as a precaution against the danger of massive radiation. Over the years there have been four and other trial submarines on the loch at the same time, as locals in Cowal will testify.

One man described the fears he experienced when the submarines first entered the loch. 'The Loch Ness monster mae or mae no be, but 'a thought when 'a saw the subs coming up the Loch that they wir far worse than a monster. 'A thought they wir turning all the watter intae a killer liquid! 'A ken noo that it's nae as bad as that, but sometimes those fears come back tae me, an' 'a feel perhaps the watter is really dangerous. All o' it.' The water has been regarded by some lochsiders as an altered element, as a few still do today.

Many people in 1961 talked about the radiation dangers that lurked by the banks and commentaries in the national press helped to reinforce their fears.   There were three radiation hazards discussed from the beginning:

1 gamma radiation from the hull of the submarines;

2 the release of cloud containing radioactive iodine;

3 the radioactive liquid in the loch waters. (1)

However imaginary the fears of the local people, such imaginings were real in their consequences.   Fears are real; caution and avoidance are real.   After the initial shocks people near the lochside began to experience spin-off effects brought about by the American invasion such as dread, fear and misgivings.   The very place they had cherished became an evil.   A woman who moved out in the 1960s from the lochside said to me in Glasgow, 'Sure a' loved the place, but it's nae good stayin' whir the pairts ye cherished 'ave a' been contaminated.   Sure 'a ken kids fae Cowal that ave got cancer afore they wir ten.'   But fears pass with time or are displaced by other fears or distractions.

As will shortly be made clear, it was the noise levels and other unexpected effects rather than the radiation levels which were most to disturb the local people after the initial debate over nuclear hazards had run its course.   At the same time, the guaranteed safety precautions at the Base were questioned from time to time, when a rise and fall of radiation fears came and went; but these fears were never totally quietened for some, whereas for others they did not exist, or abated.

I moved into the area in the late summer of 1974 when I did anticipate the people's radiation fears, but was not aware of the local concern over the noise at Holy Loch till I arrived.   In addition, McAlpine's complex had also been set up at Ardyne at the other end of the locality by Loch Striven.   Here too there were environmental effects which also helped to distract attention from the ecological effects of the American presence upon the landscape of East Cowal. It was only when I moved into Dunoon that I realised the people were caught between two environmental hazards.   To be immersed within an environment is essential for any researcher.   It is a form of 'surrender' referred to by Kurt H. Wolff, who stresses that the researcher ought to be aware of the 'pertinence of everything' so as to be in touch with the sum total of life locally. (2)   In terms of the environment, the context of life locally is the ecological scape which needs further explanation.

As stated earlier, the ecological scape is the emergent inhibiting or liberating factors of the environment which create the quality of a setting for living.   The factors of the environment are both the natural features of the landscape and the man-made.   These may constitute hazards or threat, liberation or progress.   The ecological scape refers directly to material dimensions within time and space.   It does not refer to the social and economic factors or to the adjuncts of culture and tradition.   R.G. Baker speaks of

'nesting assemblies' as an ecological arrangement. (3)   The surrounding (or 'circumjacent', as Baker puts it) physical dimensions
not only of hills, sea, and woods, but also of houses, factories and
other man-made elements, constitute the ecological arrangement or
environs within which people in settlements nestle.   The quality of
the setting, firstly in terms of associated features, and secondly
in terms of 'nesting assemblies', needs further explanation.

The quality of a setting refers to the features which affect the
senses and have become familiar features, and to which the senses
have become accustomed.   The ecological scape is affected when any
of these features are altered.   The environment may alter because
of changes caused by new sights, smells, noises, tastes and even by
a new tactile world.   Cosmopolitan inroads bring new levels of experience which are necessarily sensory and are variously inscaped by
residents.

In more recent times the advent of technology and dramatic advan-
ces in science have brought into the landscape not only qualitative
changes which enhance activities, but also new hazards.   On the map
they are registered as topographical features such as 'spaghetti
junctions', chemical factories, nuclear stations or military installations.

In addition, their real presence is mediated by man's perception,
creating a psychological presence.   Thus it is that the ecological
scape may change, firstly through the actual material intrusion, and
secondly through a resultant psychological impression.   The grounds
of the latter may be real or imagined.   It is here that there is
uneven reaction.   Some welcome the change, others fear it.

In terms of hazard, however, there is the element of threat which
lurks in man-made environments, where there is build-up of chemical
forces or of radiation, which are not sensed as noise and smells
are.   These have a real presence, but often do not have a psychological one, because people may not be aware of these hidden
hazards.

Before proceeding with the discussion of the possible changes in
the ecological scape, it will be necessary to establish what terrain
constitutes the ecological scape, hence the need to introduce the
concept of the 'cognitive map'.   When one refers to the impact
brought about by material change, especially as it affects the way
the people see their locality, one is referring to what psycholo-
gists describe as alterations in 'spatial cognition'.   R.M. Downs,
D. Stea, F.N. Shemyakin, R.G. Baker and S. Milgram have discussed
and commented upon spatial cognition, (4) a feature of which is cognitive mapping.   Large-scale environments are perceived by people
as a figurative delineation in their mind with regard to the extent
of an area and its salient features.   It matters to the researcher
that people have variant boundaries in their minds as to the confines of the locality, as will be further demonstrated in this
study.

When I visited 525 interviewees chosen at random at their homes
within the area during the autumn (1975) and winter (1975 to 1976),
I was well aware that my definition of Dunoon and its locality might
not have correlated with that of locals.   It was therefore possible
we could have been talking at cross-purposes.   So at the start, I
made it clear to the respondents that when I referred to 'Dunoon and
its locality' I was talking about the confines as based upon the
Inglis's map (see Map 2.1 on p. 17 of the chapter on new Dunoon).
This delineation of the locality, as it turned out, was acceptable
to 259 of the interviewees (49.3 per cent), all of whom had either
been born within the area, or had been resident there for at least
twenty years.   120 (22.9 per cent) had mixed views regarding the
confines of Dunoon and its locality, 54 of whom had included in
their cognitive map places and areas on the other side of the Firth.
Significantly, none of these was born and bred in Cowal and all of
them had been resident in the locality for a short period, and none
for twenty years or more.   70 others (13.3 per cent) included only
the burgh (Dunoon, Kirn and Hunters Quay) and Innellan.   32 others
(6.1 per cent) included only the burgh and all the settlements to
the south-west (the Ardyne end);   26 (5 per cent) included the burgh
and NE settlements (the Ardentinny end).   Only four (0.8 per cent)
included the burgh only. (5)   14 others (2.7 per cent) were unsure
about the confines and did not respond.   My focus had to be made
clear to each interviewee.

I decided, however, to speak of the burgh, when I referred to the
built-up area of Dunoon, Kirn and Hunters Quay, although in May 1975
the burgh had ceased to exist.   When locals referred to Dunoon they
did not mean to include Kirn or Hunters Quay.   They did so only
when they spoke of the burgh.   Conceptually, local people had been
accustomed to think and speak in this way for over 100 years.   It
had only been a few months since the burgh had ceased to be.   I
respected their conceptual lag, and so I took the people as I found
them.   They referred to the burgh, so did I.   In fact, when I
later had conversations with local people in 1982, many of them
still referred to the burgh when wishing to include all the three
settlements of Dunoon, Kirn and Hunters Quay.   When I was speaking
about 'Dunoon' and its locality' I delineated the local scape I was
referring to in my interviews.   Answers to questions about what was
going on within its limits would have referred to so many variant
cognitive maps in the minds of the interviewees that their responses
could not have been understood contextually.   Just over 50 per cent
had maps in mind which did not 'de facto' tally with mine.   One is
tempted to ask with regard to most sociological community studies to
date, whether their assessments of villagers' or urban respondents'
views have been valid, when the problem of cross-purpose talk had
not been anticipated at the outset by the interviewers or by the
reserachers.

Apart from the way people determine the confines of their local
scape, there are certain ways in which they parcel out the sectors
within it which must also be understood before the effects upon the
ecological scape can be assessed.   People may see the negative or
beneficial effects of an impact within their environment as close to
them or as somewhat distant.

I divided the locality up into three sectors.   Firstly, there
was the built-up area of Dunoon, Kirn and Hunters Quay, which for-
merly constituted the burgh of Dunoon.   Secondly, there was the
south-west sector containing all the terrain beyond the old Dunoon
bathing lido at the south-west end of the Dunoon West Bay and in
which the McAlpine complex was located.   Thirdly, there was the
north-east sector, containing all the terrain to the north of the
East Bay just after the concrete promenade ends at Hunters Quay.
In this was located the Polaris Base.

I had assumed in my approach to the impact study and in my interviews that people sort out the world around them first into the
immediate, secondly, into the less immediate, and thirdly into their
sum.   They inscape their world into a familiar territory which is
their abiding milieu, then into the environs, and lastly into the
total territory.   This parcelling of one's ecological scape into
inner and outer worlds may be referred to as partialisation.
Common and shared experiences which originate from within or from
outside the territories create in time a sedimentation of experience, (6) and so does not remain with the individual: it becomes a
communal one.   Local sets of consciousness may thus emerge from
these plural experiences (these sets of consciousness are described
in this study as social inscapes).

It is therefore important to take account of the partialisation
which takes place when one totals impressions given by interviewees,
or takes into account their inscape of events, which are taking
place within the locality in general, or in the surrounding area
within the locality, or lastly within one's own immediate locale.
The import of these remarks will become clearer later when assessing
the effects of the Polaris Base at Holy Loch and of the McAlpine
complex at Ardyne, which were situated at two ends of the locality
and which were near to some and more distant to others within East
Cowal.

The 525 residents whom I interviewed, not surprisingly, did not
on the whole regard the USN and McAlpine presence as completely
devastating or that they had ruined the environment.   Most of the
respondents pointed out that the familiar contours of East Cowal remained, although Holy Loch and Ardyne had been altered.   There was
an impressive agreement about the attractiveness of the locality in
general, and their own particular settlement of residence and with
regard to their environs.   Certainly, in spite of years of militarisation and of recent industrialisation the liberating features of
the Cowal landscape in terms of scenic beauty had survived for most
people.   To the eyes of the beholders the salient contours remained.   Almost 96 per cent (502) of the interviewees found their
settlement attractive; approximately 92 per cent (485) found the
environs and the locality in general attractive.   There was no evidence that the Polaris Base or the Ardyne complex had altered the
pride and appreciation of the locals in the seascape and landscape
of Cowal.   In the interviews, particular attractions associated
with the ecological scape were identified and noted in my jotter.
Approximately 81 per cent (55 of the 68) of the interviewees from

the south-west; approximately 90 per cent (87 of the 97) of the interviewees from the north-east, and 90 per cent (324 of the 360) of the interviewees in Dunoon (old burgh area), mentioned the beauty of the scenery at least once.   There was no significant difference between the responses of the residents in the three sectors.   Over three hundred mentioned the healthy sea air, and over two hundred the excursions into the hilly country.   Over and over again many of the people stressed that Cowal was a place of beauty. (7)

Was there any evidence that the USN Base, or the McAlpine complex, had made the ecological scape less attractive, or had badly altered some parts of it?   I will examine what evidence there was that came my way, and the reports and account of the local residents, each in turn.

The ancient reputation of the place and the nostalgia that apparently so many had for their Clyde haunts, particularly in Cowal, was always a factor behind conversations and replies to my questions. People painted the past in glowing colours.   There is an old West of Scotland song which refers to the past in nostalgic terms:

Dae ye mind o' lang lang syne
the simmer days' when
the sun shone brighter than
It's ever done since syne.

Apparently in the good old days even the sun shone more brightly. Many live in the utopia of yesterday, presenting the 'inscape of yesterday' as a veritable heaven.   Indeed, in the case of older people, they were living in another Cowal into which they seemed to escape.   In sharp contrast, there were young people locally who recognised the ugly reality of the present and in addition that of the future with its nuclear threat.   They had no past into which to escape.   Someone, who feared the threat of future destruction, had taken the trouble to write on the back of a toilet door at Hunters Quay no less than eleven lines from the 1960s protest song 'Eve of Destruction'.

When people around the Clyde spoke of the locality it was frequently in terms of the weather.   If in the 1970s it was worse than it used to be, it was because something had happened to the sunshine, but the presence of the ballistic submarines seemed, despite realities, to have had very little effect upon the seascape in the view of many folk.   I did take a good long look around me, however, after reading through the graffiti, just in case I was accepting the responses of the interviewees without interpretation and further insights.

In real terms, the landscape and seascape around Holy Loch had both been altered by the military since March 1961.   But, to most of the young people the grey bows of the ships and the black towers of the submarines had been identified with the Holy Loch.   Many of

them had never known the lochside without its USN vessels.   Indeed,
at night, fairy lights dangled from the masts of the ship and dry
dock, as they did from the posts along the old seaside promenades,
and at Christmas Polaris greetings winked good wishes in bright
lights to the people of East Cowal.   During the day, yachts and
speed boats ran alongside, and two fishing boats sailed to and fro
on the waters.   Could the waters of the loch really be radioactive
as some people claimed?

To the older generation there was the memory of the British
Osprey RN Base during the Second World War.   As already mentioned,
the submarine base had been located in exactly the same position on
the loch.   The editor of the Dunoon paper, aware of the association
between the base then and the USN Base, stated in the press at the
time of the celebration of the first decade after Proteus had
anchored: 'The oldsters remember the dark days of the last war when
the same loch gave shelter to the depot ship HMS Forth and units of
the submarine fleets of the allies.   Dunoon and district offered
hospitality to thousands who were based in the area.' (8)   The
'inscape of yesterday' constantly intruded upon the Cowal scene, as
did the old photographs of the town and the environs in the local
press.   It will be seen how the oldsters associated the RN Base
with the USN Base.

Whilst in 1971 the streets of Yokosuka, Japan, were crowded with
thousands protesting against the docking of US nuclear submarines
(also at Saseho, and at Kyoto City), many Scots had become as accustomed to the sight of the grey ships of the ballistic fleets as they
had to the misty days on the Firth of Clyde waterways.   Many locals
had not been fired by the rhetoric of CND politicians, philosophers,
religious leaders and young protesters.   Many locals, in the 1960s,
stood at the pier in groups with placards, 'Go home weirdies', in
their hands.   Many others, however, did not agree.   Later, when
the fish still swam, and the birds still flew over the lochside,
when shell-fish and seaweed were still washed upoon the shores, most
forgot about the hazards of radiation, but some still continued to
be concerned and uneasy.

Not until December 1970 had there been any mention of possible
nuclear hazards since the first protests and debate of the early
1960s.   In December 1970, a fire broke out near the missile-store
aboard the depot ship, it triggered off old Cowal anxieties.   If
one examines the rise and fall of letters concerning the American
presence over the years it is clear that few individuals expressed
their fears in public, nor did the people demonstrate concern collectively.   There had been no deaths of civilians, and no outward
signs of threat.   R.W. Kates points out in his study of environmental hazards that when the sound of a falling tree is not registered
by the sensory system, there is no fear of that falling tree.   He
shows from recent research that even where hazard is established,
few flee from it and few adjust to the effects, especially when the
hazard is not perceived.   He states: 'To experience events does

not imply experiencing consequences.' (9)   People live within
hazard environments as if they did not exist.

Although there was no sensory experience with regard to radiation, there certainly were many people at Holy Loch who were aware
of the noise from the base.   People regularly complained about it
in the Dunoon press.   I therefore had accepted that the local
residents would have brought up the question of the noise at Holy
Loch when I interviewed them at home.   Although I had given them
the opportunity to raise the matter they did not do so during the
actual interviews.   It was, however, of interest that when I was
making my rounds by the lochside one morning, an older lady who had
been one of my interviewees two days before, called me over to her.
She remarked, 'There wis something a' didnae mention to ye the other
day - it's aboot the noise fae those dirty big grey ships oot
there.'   She then complained at length about it and added: 'Do ye
know that at night ma pillow throbs under ma heed wi' the tremors
from that blessed ship.'   Her remarks were in keeping with those of
Margaret Robertson with whom I had talked before the interviews had
begun;   she had cited the stress many of the older people in particular had had to suffer because of the noise.   I wondered why the
problem had not been raised in my interviews.   I did not ask any
direct questions with regard to points of complaint.   Had I done
so, I could have prompted and biased the responses of the locals,
but why had open-ended questions not received a mention of the noise
factor at Holy Loch?

In addition, there had been four letters to the local press about
the noise from the Base between December 1975 and the end of January
1976.   The USS Holland arrived on 7 November to replace the USS
Canopus at Holy Loch.   Two huge depot ships, not one, lay in the
loch, and the noise increased accordingly.   The Sandbank Ratepayers
met to complain about the noise from the Holland engines in December.   I did my interviewing at the lochside in September and
October 1975.

Taking into account the conjuncture of events it became clear
that other matters distracted people.   Local and national concern
in the press about the USN drug abuse was at its height at that particular time and debate over Strathclyde's hold on the locality was
intense.   In addition, the influx of navvies triggered off more and
more local protests, as I will discuss later.   So, I did not interview in the area at the height of the debate on noise.   Instead,
other issues were debated.   When impacts overlap, as they did
during my time in the locality, issues and diverse effects take
their turn and their toll as new circumstances arise.   There had
been an upsurge of local protest over noise in the Dunoon Observer
in the preceding month of August 1975.   The US senior staff had
promised to take special measures.   This, in addition to the over-
lay of other matters, helped to explain why the interviewees of the
north-east were not raising the issue of noise between September to
October 1975.   I did not rely solely upon interviews to assess what

was happening in Cowal.   Press articles and letters to the Dunoon
Observer, and remarks that came my way locally, helped to fill out
the general picture.

There was no doubt that the noise from the depot ships and dry
dock had been a major stressor for people around the lochside.
Over the years, residents brought the matter up time and again at
the Sandbank Ratepayers meetings.   The peace of the local scape had
been shattered, especially at nights.   There is evidence that
people have moved house by the loch to seek other spots, as I discovered when checking addresses and names.

There was some substance to this.   Firstly, with regard to those
who were born outside the locality, those in the south-west who had
moved into the sector since the advent of the USN personnel were
approximately 10 per cent of the residents;   in the burgh they were
approximately 33 per cent;   and in the north-east approximately 49
per cent of the interviewees.   So that as one moved from the south
northwards the turnover of outsiders increased.   Secondly, the
highest proportion of residents born in the locality was within the
old burgh of Dunoon (approximately 41 per cent (149 out of the 360
respondents resident in the old burgh));   the next was in the south-
west (approximately 31 per cent (21 out of a total of 68 respondents
resident in the south-west));   and the smallest in the north-east
(approximately 36 per cent (25 out of 97 respondents resident in the
north-east)).   There had been indications, from informal chats I
had had with locals, that many had moved because of the noise, as
there were in the local press in letters from 'the tired', and 'the
yawners'.

When I showed the 525 residents an article from the Evening Times
headed, 'Holy Loch has a Sinister Air' (24 August 1974), none of the
aged (i.e. 60 years+) agreed that there was anything sinister about
the Holy Loch. (10)

It also became clear that people in the south-west who were
farthest away from the Holy Loch were least aware of the American
presence.   None of the interviewees resident in the south-west
accepted that the Holy Loch had a sinister air.

Taking the above data in conjunction with the previous factors,
there was no indication that most people were unduly concerned at
that time about the dangers of radiation, or that fish were dying
off in the lochside, or that they might be victims of a gigantic
nuclear holocaust.   One local woman, whose home I had not visited,
explained to me almost on my last day in the locality, 'If anything
does happen to the people of Cowal they'll be lucky, because
they'll all go up to the pearly gates together.'   However, 107 of
the interviewees (20.4 per cent) did find the Polaris presence
'worrying'.   All but one of these resided in the old burgh, or in
the north-east sector where they lived nearer to the Holy
Loch. (11)

The military scape loomed up at me when I visited the lochside,
but there was sufficient evidence to show that it was encapsulated
over time within the contours of the local landscape.

The American presence did alter the seascape, but not altogether,
as may be seen from the several holiday postcards depicting the Holy
Loch, which contain the Polaris Base. (12)   In any case, the
Polaris Base was largely afloat and mobile.   Just as the ships of
the Second World War had come and gone, the people felt that their
loch would endure and be as familiar as it had been to clansmen in
the days of the Campbell regime.

The American presence was less obtrusive than it might have been.
No US flags or military emblems dominated the shoreline and hinterland.   The USN senior officers have always maintained a low profile
by insisting that personnel wear civilian clothes ashore.   Seldom
did one see a naval uniform in public.   Only the American cadillacs
and military trucks as they came and went altered the roadscape.

The impact of the Polaris Base was neutralised once the depot
ship had a recognised anchorage.   Familiarisation had established
the USN presence long before any routinisation period had set in on
shore.   Objectively, one may also say that the geography of the
host locality had been altered by the USN Base and that its traditional peaceful scape was overshadowed by the symbolism of militarism and of foreign nationalism.   The vessels and no-entry military
zones altered the morphology locally.   Such changes had been out of
turn; they were not endogenous nor ecologically were they part of
local environmental developments.

Having dealt with what the 525 local residents said regarding the
effects of the USN impact upon the locality, what did these local
residents have to say with regard to the impact of the McAlpine
industrial complex at Ardyne?   I had expected that when I was discussing dislikes, (13) the interviewees would have been loud in
their complaints with regard to the industrialisation at the south-
west end of the locality.   There was none.   I had provided ample
opportunities for residents to raise the matter, but nobody during
the interviews actually decried the churned-up shores, and the
scooped-out basins.   Certainly, changes in the landscape at Ardyne
had been less visible to most residents, the majority of whom lived
north-east of Ardyne.   In addition, although a million cubic feet
of earth had been moved in seven months to form a hill by the shore,
McAlpine landscaped the area in an attempt to compensate for the
altered shores and seascape, so not many of the locals did in fact
have complaints, at any rate not outside of Toward.

In contrast, some people in the south-west area were very critical of an environmental 'eye-sore', not in East Cowal, but on the
other side.   It consisted of the tall concrete Inverkip Tower which
stood incongruously in a rural setting almost opposite Innellan
across the Firth.   When I was in conversation with people, they

sometimes raised their eyes to the concrete mass, which dominated
the rural scape (intruding also upon the seascape) and made some
such remark as: 'That damned monstrosity.   What do you think about
that?'   An Innellan woman said: 'If Harry Lauder had wakened up
one morning to see that ugly pile he'd have changed the words of his
song from "Keep right on tae the end o' the road" to "Take me tae
the end o' the road 'cause a cannie bear it ony maer".'   (Harry
Lauder had once lived in the Bullwood, near Dunoon.)   That concrete
tower was a matter of greater concern than the havoc caused by the
bulldozers at the Ardyne shore, which was for most people in East
Cowal 'out of sight'.   The Toward people, however, were more concerned about McAlpine's concrete platforms rising about their trees
and rooftops, but in terms of numbers they were a local minority.

The Toward Civic Trust made up of local residents did manage to
gain the support of residents elsewhere in Cowal when it came to the
question of noise. (14)

However, in my interviews the noise stressor was not cited.
Most of the homes I visited were situated alongside the busy and
perilous roadway, and yet no one mentioned the noise, or complained
about the dust or the highway dangers.   Was it possible that people
had become conditioned to the noise after 12-16 months?   There was,
however, one factor, which might explain the absence of criticisms
concerning the noisy roadway and other stressors.

McAlpine had commenced the reconstruction of the road from Dunoon
to Ardyne.   There were pavements in the plans, where before there
had been none.   There were new alignments, where before there had
been perilous bends.   Although the bends had added to the scenic
charm of the sea road, none the less, they had proved to be hazardous to local pedestrians, cyclists and motorists in the past.   In
a sense, the new scheme and the work already begun when I came to
visit the local residents in the winter of 1975 to 1976, had neutralised the disfunctions and the hazards caused by the Ardyne
vehicles.   The fact is that locals had for years complained to the
Argyll authorities that their road was dangerous, but Argyll had
other priorities.   McAlpine had also built a car park and assisted
in the building of the yachting club premises at Toward.   These
were to be of lasting benefit to the local people.   In contrast,
the American naval presence had done little to improve the ecological scape of East Cowal.   There was also the rumour that McAlpine
would build a marina for the locality once his men had completed
their task at Ardyne.   It paid McAlpine to buffer the ill effects,
as will be seen later.

So much for the ecological effects of the USN presence and of the
McAlpine intrusion within East Cowal as perceived by the residents.
What did the summer visitors to East Cowal feel about the locality?
To discover what their impressions were I interviewed 148 visitors
at random on the ferry from Dunoon to Gourock in the summer season
of 1975.

There were 148 days inclusively between 3 May and 27 September 1975, these days constituted the official summer seasonal runs on the Clyde ferries, so I randomised the boat departure times, allowing for the weekday, Saturday, and Sunday programmes. (15)   One visitor per trip was interviewed on each of the days during the summer season and were selected at random aboard the ferries.

That summer 625,632 visitors and 83,473 cars crowded the ferries, according to the Traffic Manager of Caledonian Mac Braynes of the Ferry Boat transport group, whom I contacted at the end of the summer season.   It was difficult to accept that these festive crowds were holidaying within Europe's top missile naval strike-zone.   As our brightly coloured funnel blared its carefree way from the pier to the strains of Scottish music, coming from the tannoy, it was almost bizarre to realise that, within a few miles across the loch, stockpiles were being prepared for the destruction of cities and if necessary of nations.

It appeared to me that the visitors saw the grey vessels on the Loch as the ferry crossed the mouth of the Holy Loch, or saw the tower and fins of the Poseidon 'subs', and the naval vans and cadillacs ashore, yet they did not seem to perceive them.   Their inscape of Dunoon district was perhaps that of yesterday, of an his-torical scape with its old ferry Clyde cruises, with bonnie old Dunoon a peaceful refuge from the dust and grime of Glasgow and the industrial settlements 'on the other side'.   The Cowal shores appeared to have been as inviting as of old to many of these people, as the remarks of a letter to the Dunoon Observer, 26 July 1975, bear out.   The writer, living in Paisley, described how he had re-turned to Dunoon fifty years after he had left it as a boy.   Apart from the fact that he did not mention the USN presence, he found Dunoon 'more beautiful than ever, with all the houses freshly pain-ted and tidy streets and gardens.   There must be more paint used on Dunoon houses than anywhere else on earth.... "Lonely I wandered through scenes of my childhood, To call back in memory the happy days of yore."' (16)   The poetry quotation with which the writer ended his letter gives one a clue to his frame of mind, as he walked along the Dunoon promenades.   That frame cut out the ugly parts of the present landscape and imposed upon the scene a scape from the past.   But, to return to the actual interviews ... the people I interviewed were mainly from Scotland and most of these were from the West of Scotland (on 'the other side').   Only forty were from outside Scotland, just four of these were from abroad.   Although the 148 interviewees were not strictly a representative sample, the spread of random interviews over the whole season enabled me to ex-plore some of the impressions visitors had of the locality.   Over and over again the Glaswegian and Renfrewshire trippers explained that they were going 'doon the watter for a breezer'.   The Glas-wegians have referred to Clyde trips as a 'breezer' for over a hun-dred years.   They set off from the grime of the industrial environ-ment to sail in the breeze on the Firth.   Most of my non-commuters were over forty years of age.   Many referred to the days when their

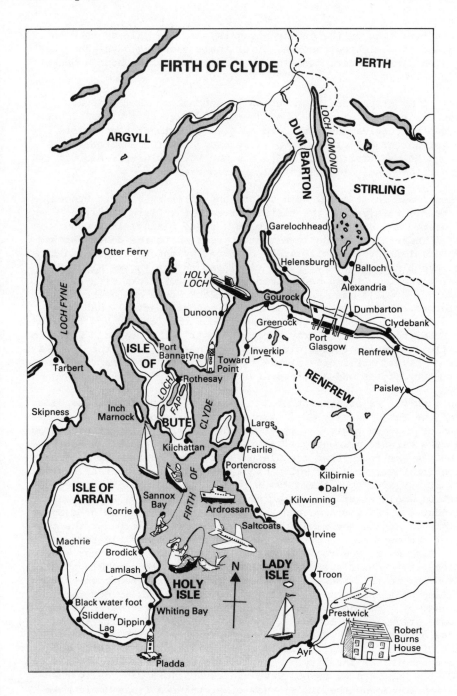

FIGURE 6.1 Places and pastimes of interest to holiday-makers and tourists in the Firth of Clyde (from a picture postcard)

parents took them on the paddle steamers, and they all spoke with nostalgia of childhood memories or of their courting days when they sang with Harry Lauder, 'roamin in the gloamin by the bonnie banks o' Clyde'.

All of my trips were from Dunoon to Gourock so that I could assess their impressions.   The interesting fact is that only four-teen on the ferries had mentioned adverse effects of the Polaris Base but not of McAlpine's complex at Ardyne on the environment, although 58 had visited the Holy Loch and seven visitors had visited Ardyne. (17)   All of these were day-trippers.

When I was in Glasgow, both before and after my stay in Dunoon, some people referred to the dirty shores of the Firth of Clyde. Some blamed the USN presence.   There were complaints in Dunoon also.   There had been letters to the press about the debris around Holy Loch left by the sailors, even dumped by the US ships, and pro-tests about the occasional rusty car lying on the shores with US number plates.   Others had blamed McAlpine's platform site at Ardyne for Cowal's bad image.   Perhaps Jack House had heard the complaints, because in early March 1976, shortly after I had left Dunoon, he wrote in the Evening Times about the love he had for the area under the title: "Dirty: but it's still the dear old Clyde to me'. (18)   Loyalty to the old haunts and nostalgia for the 'bonnie banks o' Clyde' still drew people there, in spite of some complaints about dirty shores and a ruined environment.

So much for an assessment of the impact of both the Polaris Base and of the McAlpine complex on the ecological scape, but what of the impact of the new Region?   It was evident that its impact presented less of a threat 'prima facie' to the ecological scape.   However, the people had fears that the Glasgow planners might think up some scheme for their locality which might make it more urbanised.   In fact, it appeared that there was more fear at that time that region-alisation would alter the character and environment of East Cowal than that the USN invasion and the McAlpine intrusion would.   Under Strathclyde Region the man-made environment was to be under the con-trol of the outscape.   Strathclyde was to be responsible for: roads, transport, sewerage, industry and tourism.   No sooner was the locality under Glasgow than the people began to complain about the rubbish on the roadways, the neglected Dunoon streets in partic-ular, and above all, the time it took for complaints to get through to Glasgow.   Strathclyde councillors could not be expected to have the same pride in the roadways, the townscape, the scenery and the holiday attractions.   What would happen to the shores and the quaint villages of Cowal?   Fears were expressed almost daily when I was staying in the locality.   The local councillors who once sat in the Castle Chambers of Dunoon were the councillors who really cher-ished the lochs and the hills; now other unknown faces would make the big decisions.   There were regional councillors who resided still within the District boundaries, and some of them had been the local councillors under the old regime, but they were now in a dif-ferent political scape, and as will be further explained later in another chapter, they did not have the same control over the local scape.

Strathclyde Region had 7,650 miles of public roads.   But the main ones were not in Cowal.   In fact, when the Dunoonites wanted to make alterations on the A83 signposts so that travellers might take the road to Dunoon, the authorities refused to do so, stating that Dunoon was a 'terminal destination' rather than a 'primary one'. (19)   This only served to emphasise the peripheral status of Dunoon and district, with regard to the central priorities of the urbanised outscape of Clydeside and Dumbartonshire.

By way of reinforcing the fears and uncertainties over the pos- sible neglect of Cowal by far-away officialdom in Glasgow, the local residents in the first winter and spring of 1975-6 had a major com- plaint against the Strathclyde management.   The main street of Dunoon needed to be resurfaced.   No road was more important to the residents than Argyll Street.   For years this road has been lined with the main shops, and carried the main traffic.   On it have always been the main entertainment spots and the most popular town public houses.   For over a century it has been associated with a long line of local businessmen, who brought prosperity to Cowal. Fate had it that the Strathclyde Roads Department bungled its first road job and it had to be in Argyll Street, Dunoon.   No sooner did the new workers cover it in asphalt, than it began to peel off. Over and over again, the Strathclyde roadmen came in, and huddles of locals stood over them sniggering at their inept results.   I used to walk up in the mornings to watch proceedings.   It was fatal for the image of the Region.   Each day people gathered in the doorways of Argyll Street to decry the new regime and to confirm their views, which tended to be negative and hostile towards Strathclyde.   The road marked the old ferry route and at the same time the proud thoroughfare of new Dunoon.   The new workers symbolised 'bungling Strathclyde'.

To sum up, certain general conclusions can be drawn from the assessment of the impacts of the USN Base, of McAlpine's Ardyne com- plex and of the new Region upon the local environment.

Firstly, with regard to the American intrusion, it was clear that whatever the long-term implications of radiation at the Holy Loch, there were no indications of widespread fears locally, but some still remained anxious about possible dangers.   The fact was that there had been no casualties amongst the local population, although there have been mishaps at the base, and no reports of USN concern over radiation leakages.   Noise has been the greatest stressor over the years, which has aggravated local people, as indicated by letters to the Dunoon Observer.   Some local residents have moved out from the vicinity of the Holy Loch because they could not stand the noise.   However, there has been no evidence that a large number of people have been incensed by the sight of the ships and sub- marines on their Scottish loch.   In fact, there are local holiday postcards which present the Polaris Base as a local attraction and trips to the vessels have regularly been organised during the summer

season.   It can be said that the Polaris Base is part of the local
seascape.

With regard to the 'nesting assembly', the landscape around Holy
Loch has remained much the same, American buildings were not too
obtrusive in the mid-1970s, although, as will be seen, the Polaris
Base shore installations were to increase.   Certainly some people
hoped that the USN vessels would go and leave the Holy Loch as it
had been before.   As will be seen, others would miss them.   Communication and access to and on the loch have not been significantly
altered.   Although people have not been permitted to enter certain
shore reserves, these were then few, and many have rowed their small
boats almost daily up to the prows of the vessels.

It must also be said that in Dunoon and in the settlements of the
south-west, the ships have been out of sight for most of the population in East Cowal.   The Cowal people have enjoyed the familiar
contours of the landscape and seascape and of the local villages, in
spite of Polaris.   Dunoon has nestled within bays and hills, as it
has done for centuries.   Whether the people spoke of their own particular settlement, or their environs, or the locality in general,
almost three-quarters of the 525 interviewees said that their
locality, its environs and their settlement were 'attractive'.

Ogburn has explained that the 'superior utility' has pre-
eminence.   Local usage of the land and of the sea do not seem to be
significantly changed.   As has been seen, even the vessels on Holy
Loch have been utilised as part of the holiday attraction.   For
some of the people, the ships have become part of the man-made
tourist environment.

Ogburn spoke of 'selective forgetting'.   Here older perceptions
persisted, and newer experiences have been forgotten, so the 'oldsters' have regarded the area as it has been in 'the old days'.
Around the lochside, many have associated the USN Base with the war-
time base.   'It brings me back to my young days in the war, when
the submarines were here to fight the Germans';   'One often feels
that it's 1940 all over again':   such remarks have underlined the
association between the US naval presence and that of the RN
presence of the Second World War, although they have 'de facto' been
significantly different.   Whether conscious or otherwise, the older
people around the Holy Loch (and they are many) have tended to forget
the threat of nuclear radiation, or of a ballistic confrontation in
which Dunoon and area would be frontline targets, and to remember
instead the entirely different set-up of the last war.   One could
describe them as living in the 'inscape of yesterday'.

With regard to the visitors on the ferries, there did not appear
to have been any great concern about the USN Base.   It was true,
however, that fourteen of the visitors who had visited the Holy Loch
complained about the ships and the submarines in terms of their
ugliness, which contrasted with the apparent lack of concern about
their presence amongst the residents.   In general, visitors still
came to the Cowal shores.   In the summer of 1974-5 they appeared to

come in thousands, whatever the views of some regarding the ugliness
of the vessels at Holy Loch.

Secondly, with regard to the McAlpine intrusion at Ardyne, more
than three-quarters of the local population did not have sight of
the platform complex, tucked away as it was at the other end of the
locality.   Neither the 148 visitors nor the 525 residents interviewed complained about the ugliness of the Ardyne complex.   There
was more concern about the Inverkip Tower standing on 'the other
side' like a hideous reminder of what industrialists might do to the
rural contours of the West of Scotland.

As in the case of the USN presence, there had been complaints in
the press about the noise caused by the intrusion.   These were
voiced especially by the Toward Civic Trust, but not by any of the
residents interviewed at their homes.

The 'nesting arrangement' of the locality with regard to the
hills, lochside, and general landscape, remained much the same, in
spite of McAlpine's excavations, and very much as it had done for
centuries, except for an additional hill, which was created by
McAlpine, and built up by the removed seabed to create the basins.
This hill, however, was near the shore at Ardyne, where it not only
helped to block out the Ardyne platform site, but also was superbly
landscaped by McAlpine, and if anything added to the scenic beauty.
The shores were ruined, however, and access to that end of the
locality was affected; but given the marginal number of people who
used to frequent the area, the effects were minimal.

It was rather the reputational damage to the environment which
was marked and significant in the 1970s.   The press and the media
generally sensationalised local changes.   The press had been negative and often defamatory, but the visitors still kept coming, as
they continue still to do.   To the West of Scotland population,
'the breezer doon the watter' and the 'auld places to take the
wanes', still triggered off images, for the older generations in
particular, of crowded holiday ferries and packed promenades.

Neither the visits of the tourists to the USN Base, nor those to
Ardyne, appeared to have altered the overall perception of the
locality as a scenic attraction.   It appeared that many incomers,
who had taken up residence after the USN Base was established, excluded the Base from their conscious thought as they did Ardyne;
most of them, however, did explain that they would be glad to see
the closure of the Polaris Base and the McAlpine complex, to which
I shall return later.   Was it that they had come into the area in
the hope that soon the Polaris Base and the Ardyne complex would
close down?   They have now seen the McAlpine plant fold up.   The
possibility of the USN submarines moving out draws nearer as the
weaponry becomes more and more obsolete and as Trident takes over.

The local residents have been more conditioned over the years by
the Holy Loch presence.   Many have not known the loch without its
American Base.   The growing numbers of old folk's homes and of

children's homes, and local hostels in Cowal, and the enduring
popularity of the locality as a restful place to retire to, all
point to the continued reputation of the locality as peaceful and
attractive.   Man-made dangers may lurk in the waters, but for the
aged and middle-aged the past has significance in the present.   The
'inscape of yesterday' has prevailed.   For the younger generation,
the relevant factor has been the future promise of vacated American
homes, and perhaps McAlpine might still build them something at deso-
late Ardyne.   These hopes one may describe as the prevalence of the
'inscape of tomorrow'.

It appeared in 1976 the ecological scape would in the long term
be more threatened by the Strathclyde administration.   The local
roads, sewerage, and industrialisation in Cowal have been passed
into the hands of city officials, and the urban control of life
locally has been established as a long-term arrangement, if not
infinite;   whereas the Ardyne and USN intrusion have necessarily
been finite.   In the name of the common good the people have seen
their locality invaded by the military and by the oil men, and they
have coped.   For some time now they have been more uncertain as to
what Strathclyde might demand of their ecological scape in the name
of its 2½ million people.   If they have built the hideous Inverkip
concrete tower in beautiful Ayrshire 'on the other side' in the name
of the common good, what might Strathclyde not have in mind for the
Cowal shores?   In a sense the 'inscape of tomorrow' has held out
great uncertainties for East Cowal within the mammoth bureaucracy of
Strathclyde.   Some roads and amenities had been neglected in East
Cowal in pre-regionalisation days, but how much of the local townscape and landscape would not deteriorate under an executive which
had no idea of rural and seaside needs?   This is what some people
felt in 1976 in East Cowal, especially in the countryside and the
villages.   Others hoped for better times, especially in Dunoon.

Chapter 7

A PLUNDERED ECONOMY

> Social change is not synonymous with development, much less with
> progress.   The latter is merely a sub-class of the former.
> Development is a growth in complexity, progress is development
> plus an improvement.... We may have development without progress.
> (S. Giner) (1)

Conflicting views and attitudes are inevitable in an area under
impact where lags in perception follow upon rapid changes.   Within
a few weeks of my stay in Dunoon I detected swings between optimism
and pessimism, hopes and fears, and between composure and unease in
people's remarks and by observations.   The contrasting moods gave
me the impression at one time of economic boom, at another of economic doom.   Some of these impressions are summed up in the contrasting statements of two local people soon after my arrival in Dunoon
in early autumn, 1974.   The first, a local businessman, said to me
with some bitterness, 'The story of Dunoon and of this side of the
water is one of financial heartbreak.   It's a hard-luck story if
ever there was.   Mark my words this place won't be on the map in
fifty years time.'   The second was a woman whose husband was well
known in the area, 'I hope you've noticed the upturn in Dunoon's
trade and the money that's being made.   The Yanks, and now the
Ardyners, have made up for the days when we needed to depend on
holiday-makers.   And there's Strathclyde, which will lift us out of
a bankrupt County onto the money pile at Glasgow.'

Before sorting out the complex nature of the varying impacts, the
situation in terms of numbers must be presented.   Local economics
are related to the population density, as they are to its categori-
sation of needs across groups.

The totals of naval incomers are volatile because personnel not
only come and go with dependants, but the USN does not divulge accu-
rate statements, especially at a strategic Polaris Base.   At the
same time, the Base denies that its numbers have increased and
understates its true number so as not to create local protest.   To
a lesser degree contractors can also be almost as secretive.

TABLE 7.1 Proportion of USN/Ardyne worker incomers/and dependants
(Autumn 1975)

Population types		Estimates	%
Local residents (including children)	in Burgh of Dunoon	9, 122	71.6
	'furth' (outside) of Burgh	3,615	28.4
1 Total of local residents		12,737	100.0
USN incomers at Base or ashore	Naval personnel aboard Canopus and barge	1,400*	42.6
	Naval personnel ashore (100 of these were on 'the other side')	700*	21.3
	Wives residing in East Cowal	600	18.2
	Children residing in East Cowal	480	14.6
	Civil American technical staff (6 months' stay)	90	2.7
	CBs**	20	0.6
2 Total of USN incomers at Base or ashore		3,290	100.0
Personnel of McAlpine resident locally	Navvies at camp	350	44.8
	Resident in East Cowal	310	39.7
	Wives resident in East Cowal	25	3.2
	Children resident in East Cowal	36	4.6
	American technicians	60	7.7
3 Total of McAlpine personnel resident in locality		781	100.0
4 Sum total residents		16,808	100.0

*   The Guardian (29 September 1981) stated that the number of US
    personnel at Holy Loch was 1,700, but this statistic does not
    include the submariners who come and go; and the submarines
    have double crews as indicated in the text.

** The CBs are a brigade of semi-military American men engaged in
    military construction work.

These 'working approximate totals' were based upon local inquiry
at the Polaris Base, Dunoon Library, the Tourist Information Centre
and at Ardyne camp. Taking the incomers' totals of both resident
and daily migrants (5,121), they constituted a proportion of 28.7
per cent of all persons in East Cowal (17,858). Taking only the
resident incomers of McAlpine and USN personnel at the Polaris Base
and ashore, or at the camp together with their dependants, they represented an approximate proportion of 24.2 per cent of the residents
– which represents almost an 'Outsiders' Proportion Ratio' (OPR) of
one-quarter. Such an OPR was considerable, and in terms of the

local economy could be enormously beneficial, because of more cash
flows locally, or also possibly detrimental, because of more diseconomies.   These negative effects could result from a lack of fit
between local supplies and outside demands upon goods and services,
or because of the economic damages inflicted upon established residents.   The complex nature of the combined demands of the US naval
and McAlpine invasion upon the local economy requires an assessment
of their effects on the economic scape.

The economic scape is the prevailing resource allocation and distribution in the form of goods, services, employment, housing and
the means of production, affecting people's standard of living and
life-style, as well as their perception of them.   How were such
economic utilities affected by the impacts of the Polaris Base, the
McAlpine concrete platform complex at Ardyne, and the newly created
Region of Strathclyde?

At the outset, it must be noted that whereas the impact upon the
ecological scape was first felt immediately after the arrival of the
US ship, the impact upon the economic scape was first felt immediately before the arrival.   In the case of the Ardyne intrusion,
people did not know of McAlpine's scheme, neither the Dunoon councillors nor the local business people, the strategy here was total
surprise, whereas in the case of the USN advent the strategy was to
dangle the economic million-dollar carrot before the local buisness
people after the shock news that Polaris was to be established so as
to buffer it with the promise of economic boom.   In the case of
regionalisation, the strategy of the bureaucrats created uncertainties and regional division, e.g. over specific boundaries and confusing models of local administrative structures.   Moreover, economic implications were primarily in the private sector of the local
economy in the case of the USN and McAlpine impacts, whereas those
of the regional scheme were primarily in the public sector.

In addition, the people of the area had experienced the invasion
of strangers over the years, and in the case of the military, they
had relevant experience in satisfying military needs during two
World Wars.   The economic ramifications of Strathclyde, however,
could not be anticipated to the same extent.   Indeed, for many,
the repercussion in economic terms could not be anticipated at all.
The economic implications of each of the three impacts will now be
assessed.   Before the advent of the USN personnel the attraction of
East Cowal as a holiday area was waning.   The local press cited the
dramatic drop in pier dues in the late 1950s. (2)   There had been
jibes of 'Costa Geriatrica' with regard to the incoming aged, not
only because of its suitability for retirement, but also because of
the 'Old Age Pensioner Holiday Scheme'. (3)   The run-down of the
area as a holiday spot was primarily due to extraneous factors.   In
endogenous terms, modernisation had brought with it increased centralisation of holiday and leisure centres in the nearer and wider
outscapes.   Ironically, just as the new technology of the last century attracted and brought people in the new steam boats by the
thousands to the Cowal shores from the nearer outscape, so too the
new technology of this century attracted and brought people away
from the Cowal shores to the wider outscapes in the new jets.

Whilst the locality was concerned with its economic decline, the American naval anchorage on Holy Loch was announced.   Many people had renewed hopes when they recalled the financial boom during the last war when hundreds of sailors spent their money in the locality. They also remembered that before the Polaris Base was announced a United States naval vessel had unexpectedly anchored off Dunoon and that all the crew had come ashore on a gigantic spending spree. The visit is best described by a local man who recalled the event in the Dunoon Observer as follows:

> An American ship arrived off Dunoon and landed several hundred sailors.   Their coming was undoubtedly a 'feeler' to test the reactions of the locals.   Dunoon went quite mad.   Shops were open until midnight and a roaring trade was done.   Indeed banks reported a huge increase in dollar deposits.   Not long afterwards intimation was received that an American base was to be created on the Clyde. (4)

The memory was still fresh, so too were the gloomy predictions that East Cowal was no longer a prime tourist area.   Some people with vested interests in local business rejoiced;   others were deeply concerned that money outweighed all other considerations and possible social ills which have been proverbially associated with 'sailors hitting the town'.

Seven of the very first letters criticised those who supported the Base, they accused the local influentials of putting money first.   One of these letters made a few pointed observations about the Lady Provost who had welcomed the USS Proteus:

> How surprised I was to hear our Lady Provost and the laymen and all the other councillors referred to who favour this Polaris Base, especially when some of our Christian ministers (real Christians) had us pray for peace.   The same men were against the coming of bishops, and the opening of shops on Sunday the last time an American vessel was here.   Not so the people who had businesses, who did not forget to charge them high prices for what they got, also supplying them with drink to such an extent they were staggering all over the place.   Money comes first with those people.   They don't consider people who come here for a quiet life and who are likely to clear out. (5)

Another letter stated:

> It would appear that quite a number who applaud the decision have nostalgic memories of the war years, when they certainly never had it so good, and in order to recapture a measure of prosperity are prepared to stifle all normal scruples and with true ostrich escapism really believe that tragedy cannot overtake us. (6)

Meanwhile the taxi trade was booming in Dunoon and the surrounding area, as it had never done before.   Indeed, it went so well that an advert later appeared in the press on 15 April 1961, offering Glasgow taxis for sale in Dunoon. (7)   Moreover, several people

who owned cars turned almost overnight into 'pirate taximen'.   For
many in the initial period the star-spangled masthead at Base was a
dollar wand showering gold upon the Burgh of Dunoon and its satellite settlements.

The second series of letters, between 12 August 1961 and 23 February 1963, were written when the local residents witnessed and
experienced the secondary effects of the USN Base upon their locality.   It was a period of secondary surprises and unexpected spin-
offs.   The rumours and the hopes that the national CND protests
would be successful dulled the enthusiasm of the money-makers.
They were not sure whether the bonanza would last.   The protesters,
on the other hand, were concerned that the USN base would remain
after all, but most probably for only three years.   But, above all,
the protesters were pointing out that the locality was getting a bad
name and a nationwide reputation as a radiation zone.   Slowly it
began to dawn upon the supporters of the Polaris Base that the price
they might have to pay was a bad image and that the demise of the
area as a prime holiday attraction would escalate because of it.

During the period of 'secondary surprises' other unexpected negative effects created more misgivings for those who had supported the
establishment of the Polaris Base.   Americans expected credit and
the locals rather naively expected the same honesty to which they
were accustomed in Dunoon and its locality.   Naval personnel and
their dependants were 'short-stay'. Often personnel left the Base,
once their rotation of duty was over, without prior notice.   In the
West of Scotland they use the expression 'doing a moonlight flit'
to refer to people who left home and district without paying outstanding bills.   Dunoon residents had never suspected that they
would be using the same expression to refer to American naval
debtors.

Another unexpected secondary effect upset the very caterers who
were once enthusiastic about the American invasion.   Girls were
walking out of their jobs, often during their working day, to court
American naval seamen.   Girls were refusing to be employed after
5.30pm, even at the height of the summer season, because it blocked
their evenings out.   Sailors were taking girls out on what locals
regarded as bumper spending sprees, and attractive trips to Glasgow
dance halls, cinemas and more lavish city and town centertainment
centres on Clydeside.   There was no doubt, however, that an immediate positive effect with some long-term hopes for the local cycle
of trade was that an area which had a marked summer and winter economic cycle could cater for outsiders all the year round.   Except
for the food shops, and a handful of local tradesmen, most business
people, hoteliers, landladies and landlords who had previously faced
a long winter of ever-increasing costs in preparation for a summer
of ever-decreasing profits, now looked forward to winter profits.
But there were diseconomies which the local residents had not anticipated occasioned by the USN presence.   Nobody had anticipated
that the Americans would be building their own stores and a food
supply centre for dependants.   Imperceptibly USN shore buildings
had been growing in number.

By March 1963, primary and secondary surprises gave place to a
more settled and adaptive period.   At this time an enterprising
local resident set up the Monaco Club in March 1963.   The club was
modelled upon the Las Vegas-type casinos, and was unashamedly
levelled at an officer clientele.   It stood incongruously astride
the old shops of Argyll Street, and in the shadow of the Presbyterian church of St John.   Behind its private doors, huge sums of
money were said to be lost and won.   But there were also stories of
bouncing cheques and extended credit that were never paid by USN
personnel and dependants.   The venture did not last long.

Many businessmen who had enlarged their premises and speculated
upon the needs of the American incomers realised that the Base was
setting up its own stores and amenities at Ardnadam by Holy Loch.
They also became more frustrated with their customers because unapid
bills were on the increase.   The situation became extreme when the
Proteus sailed out of the Holy Loch in March 1963, and the Huntley
took its place.   The President of the Dunoon Traders' Association
complained:

> We are angry and disillusioned at the way the Americans have
> treated us.   We welcomed them to our town, and extended credit
> to them, because we knew that was the way they worked.   The new
> arrivals on the relief ship Huntley are the ones who will suffer.
> It's a case of once bitten, twice shy.

At the same time the Dunoon Observer reported that a spokesman from
the American Naval Building, London, replied to local criticisms as
follows: 'We cannot force a man to pay his debts, but he would be
well advised.' (9)   Business people in the area had been staunch
supporters of the US Base prior to its establishment, they now felt
hurt so that the shopkeepers began to share criticisms of the USN
incomers with their customers for the first time.   The fact was
that they saw new trends taking place within the locality which
would affect their trade with the Americans very badly.

Firstly, the Americans had set up their own stores.   It upset
people that imports at a different cost from the same goods at local
and UK prices were made available excluisvely for the incomers at
discount prices.   On the one hand, customers felt cheated by the
situation and, on the other, many shopkeepers saw their speculations
and dreams vanish into the chill air of the local Cowal economy.   A
letter to the local press made the point in March 1963:

> American goods are available at dirt-cheap prices to our
> country's detriment as they pay no import duty or purchase tax.
> But, now to beat it all we are going to build them bowling alleys
> and recreation rooms.   If we are going to share the dangers (as
> a frontline town), then let us merit the same facilities that
> they enjoy. (10)

The local PX stores were taboo to Cowal people, whilst other local
amenities were available to the incomers.

The Polaris Base was in effect a 'little America', and was becoming more and more self-sufficient in terms of consumables and domestic supplies. Even the service staff at base were usually Americans or married to Americans. For these reasons the American naval
complex had no beneficial impact upon the employment rate locally.
The US Polaris Base has always been run and serviced by its own
ancillary staff. The 'CBs' have done all the tradesmen's jobs;
and US civil engineers come for regular spells of servicing work.
They have been deployed aboard the ships and submarines since 1961.
Only a few Cowal typists and warehousemen have been employed at the
Polaris Base. So, the impact of the American naval presence on
employment in Cowal has always been negligible.

Although the Polaris Base was becoming more self-supporting in
basic domestic supplies, the locality provided the housing, the
schooling, and the hospital treatment. The locals took the
greatest exception to the fact that Americans could outbid them for
local rentals, and at the same time crowd their schools and occupy
their hospital beds. Demands upon public and community services
escalated because the American families had a disproportionate share
of local services.

With regard to housing, the Americans had large subsidies to
assist them in the renting of accommodation. This pushed up the
local rents. The young married couples felt the impact more than
others. The young were an already small minority in a largely
ageing population, their number decreased yet more because they
could not procure rooms at reasonable rents.

The best unoccupied dwellings in the locality were taken up by
senior staff and officers of the Polaris Base. On the eve of the
USN arrival there were 98 empty lodgings in East Cowal of which 88
were available for private rental. The 98 dwellings represented
2.7 per cent (approximate) of the 3,685 non-commercial house dwell-
lings in the locality. (11) When the US Proteus sailed into Holy
Loch 18.3 per cent, 674 of the houses in East Cowal were owned by
outsiders and over half of those were Glaswegians. (12) The ab-
sentee landlords and landladies preferred an all-the-year-round
guaranteed payment to a possible holiday rental for a few weeks in
the year. Houses that had stood empty because of the waning holiday trade were now bringing in money and, whatever the arguments
against Polaris, outside landlords were more likely to cast objections aside about the damaged holiday character of the place. In
any case, landlords and landladies were not prepared to bring politics into economics.

When I came into the locality in 1974, the situation had altered,
because by then there were two specially built American housing
estates, so that demands upon the local housing sector were considerably diminished, but this only existed for a year or so, because
Americans on 'the other side' came over and began to pick up some of
the local houses once they had been reconditioned as will shortly be
discussed. It meant, of course, that some landlords and landladies
now found themselves with empty flats and dwellings on their hands.

Over the years the property rented to the Americans has frequently become neglected. Much of it was over a hundred years old. It had paid the property owners to increase their margin of profitability by cutting maintenance costs. Once the Americans moved to their two new housing schemes the property they vacated was no longer an attractive proposition for holiday flats, still less for the retired. Much of it had to be repaired and reconditioned.

It was claimed in 1976 that every month thousands of dollars aboard the US depot ship were changed into £200,000 and that this money was being pumped into the local economy by the US incomers. (13) However, there is evidence to show most of it went to the outscape. For example, the two US housing estates accommodated most of the Americans living on shore, and these American schemes were owned by outsiders. Given that housing costs constitute a major item of expenditure, one can assume that in fact a great deal of US money passed each month into the accounts of property owners in the outscape. This transfer of money was epitomised in the case of the quite considerable property at Ardnadam where the US Base has most of the shore facilities. These stand where once stood holiday amenities and an hotel. They were bought by the Admiralty as was the once famous pier at Hunters Quay, where well-known international yachtsmen, such as Lord Lipton, had disembarked. The rental for these now went out of the locality and were paid to the Admiralty in London.

This money passed across the Firth like thousands of pounds did for wines and spirits and other luxuries on 'the other side', as also for clothes and electronic equipment. One could count on one's two hands the local businesses which did profit from American custom. There was a 'fish 'n' chip shop', two hairdressers, a cocktail bar, and one club, where American money was spent, together with a clothing shop which specialised in jeans on Argyll Street, and four taxi services. As one Dunoon shopkeeper put it,

If this town has made big money out of them Yankees at the loch, I'd like to know why shops are going bust and why they stand empty on the main street, and why nobody seems to want to buy the old La Scala picture house, barred up now for months in about the best business spot in town.

When the recession came in the late 1970s and early 1980s Dunoon lost some of its most respected businesses like MacPherson's the Bakers (founded in Dunoon in 1876). Had they been so resilient and economically viable because of the so-called local naval economic boom they would surely have survived. It was the outsiders who profited most. Even the US specification export cars were only available from Struthers of Oban.

This part of my research was the most frustrating because local shopkeepers, businesses, and tradesmen, were naturally loath to declare their profits or their losses. The Americans had a local reputation of boasting on all occasions that they were spending hundreds of dollars a week in town. One US Petty Officer said, 'this

joint depends on us, Boy; yea, we've given this coastal strip a
shot in the arm and boy it needs it'.   If this was a typical
remark, did it reflect the true position?   Had I been able to
organise random interviews of the American naval personnel I would
no doubt have had a more comprehensive view, but this study from the
start was limited by the impossibility of having formal and official
access at Base for research purposes.   Moreover, as already explained in the introduction, the research concentrated on establishing what the people felt, and the nature of the effects with which
they had to cope.

With regard to schooling, the impact of the American presence was
considerable.   Local criticism over the years has been noticeably
directed at the education authorities for allowing the Americans to
use Cowal schools.   When in 1967 a dramatic rise in the rates was
announced, the local people laid the blame at the door of the
strained educational resources under pressure from the disproportionate intake of American naval children.   The chairman of the SNP
wrote caustically to the Dunoon newspaper on 28 September of that
year: 'When they can spend thousands of pounds on licensed clubs
and bowling alleys, it is surprising they cannot consider spending
some of it on building their own school and staffing it with their
own teachers.' (14)   The burden on the ratepayer due to the increased number of pupils at local primary schools in particular
became a talking point locally.   This secondary effect had reached
a high point in 1969.   On 15 February ex-provost Wyatt had received
a letter from the Director of Education in Argyll which calmed the
mounting fears.

The letter stated that all USN personnel at Base and all US wives
plus their children were to be added to the normal population of the
county.   What was more significant, US children under fifteen years
of age 'were to be counted twice, as is the case with our own children'.   The letter stated further: 'The effect of this considerable
addition to Argyll's weighted population would in the Secretary of
State's considered calculations make an addition to the County Education Grant that would be more than sufficient to meet the cost of
educating American children in our schools.' (15)   There was, however, a local concern that now the incomers were counted, the local
rates could jump up.   The Director's letter which was published in
the press encouraged a local resident to describe the Dunoon District as 'playing Santa Claus to the Americans all the year
round'. (16)

In the two years between January 1969 and December 1971 the
people often complained at local meetings that classes were fluctua-
ting too much because of the rotation of US personnel at the Polaris
Base.   On 2 February 1971, at a meeting of the Cowal District Education Subcommittee in the County Offices, the complaints of local
parents were aired.   It was reported that the fluctuation of
classes was so bad that one class started with 28 pupils and ended
with 42 and it was stressed that the problem was greatest in the
primary schools of Innellan, Kirn and Dunoon. (17)

The schooling question was to become more acute when, in October 1971, extra houses for the USN personnel were discussed and plans proposed: the influx of extra American children from 'the other side' was necessarily an immediate possibility.   Local critics were quick to react: 'Americans have gone to the trouble', stated a letter to the press on 23 October 1971, 'of organising themselves for housing and have a huge store in Queen Street, and a great complex at Ardnadam.   Why was it that they could not also build their own school?'

It was not until 23 September 1972 that the education authorities put forward any concrete plans to cater for the impact of the incoming school pupil numbers, when a meeting was called at the County Education Chambers.   Here the Director of Education stated that money was forthcoming for additional premises. (18)   It had taken eleven years for any rationalised provision to emerge so that locals could cope with the pressing problem.   The reason for the promise was that Cowal protest was growing louder.

The people were still complaining in the summer of 1974, when the local unrest was reported in the Evening Times of 11 July.   In fact, the matter was raised in the House of Commons. (19)   The cause of the disquiet was the fact that 114 local children, at the start of their final year at the Kirn primary school, had to be moved to the old Dunoon Grammar School buildings at the other end of Dunoon, because of an increase of American children at Kirn.   It appeared to many that preferential treatment for the incomers outweighed any inconvenience caused to the local people.   Some classes were overcrowded for some months, then others took their turn.   The expansion and contraction of pupils confused the staff, now at one school, then another - particularly at the RC school of St Muns in Dunoon, and the primary schools at Kirn and Innellan.   Not until 1974, when I came to the area, was there any realistic building programme for the alleviation of the situation.   Two new schools were to take the extra swell of pupils.   One eventually was built at Sandbank and another also for the RCs at Dunoon.   This local provision explains why there were few people who raised the school question in my street interviews in the autumn of 1974, and later in their homes when I interviewed the residents in the autumn/winter of 1975-6.   As shall be seen in the chapter dealing with the impact upon the cultural scape, local residents had other things on their minds that winter.

In addition to the local schools, the US incomers used the local hospital.   The economic outlay to meet the extra demands made upon the medical services must have been considerable, especially in the maternity unit.   There are examples of additional welfare costs demanded by the USN invasion.   Some residents regarded the naval personnel as the scroungers from overseas.   The situation was not improved by the fact that the Americans had provided for themselves one of the best dental clinics in the West of Scotland.   It was built ashore exclusively for naval personnel and their dependants. Locals could not have access to it.   Once again, the Cowal residents were puzzled.   If the USN could make provision for their

teeth by extra premises, why not for their other medical needs?   If
the residents could not have free dental treatment at the US clinic,
why should the Americans be received into the Dunoon Cottage Hospital?   Many appeared to agree that the locality had played Santa
Claus to the incomers.

The Americans have often protested that they have always paid for
their hospitalisation.   The Dunoonites do not know the details and
where the money goes in NHS terms.   The local residents have pointed out that the inconvenience caused have not been assessed, nor
could ever be costed in monetary terms.   The introduction of private patients elsewhere in the UK to local hospitals of the NHS give
proof of the disturbances caused by special patients.   The Americans in Cowal were in effect private patients.   It is true that
visitors to the UK were welcome to use NHS facilities, but here they
often outnumbered the local NHS clients.   Dunoonites complained to
the press about the crowded maternity unit at Dunoon.   There were
suspicions of priorities given to the patients who were referred to
the Dunoon hospital by the three US medics aboard the ship and that
the dollar spoke louder than human need.   Given the fact that the
Dunoon hospital was not built for the incomers, but for the local
residents, and that the OPR of young US married mothers in particular not only put additional strains at times upon the hospital resources, but sometimes was excessive, proportionately outnumbering
local mothers, one could well appreciate the reason why some Dunoonites had complained.   When I made my own inquiries locally, it was
significant that all six of the nurses I interviewed (four in my
street interviews and two in my household visits) were amongst the
more critical people with regard to the USN incomers.

So, on the one hand, there was a contraction of trade between the
locals and military and, on the other hand, there was an expanding
usage of public services.   The circumstances made a mockery of the
claim in the 1960s that the Americans would bring prosperity to
Cowal.   The locals have rightly complained over the years that they
have not the slightest idea how much the American naval authorities
have paid for the provision of schooling and hospitalisation in the
locality.   If there was a great deal of money, what was there to
show for it?   They have pointed out that, whatever the financial
input, their services for many years had not improved.   If anything, services had remained inferior to those of people on 'the
other side'.   Indeed, when Strathclyde was pressing its case, the
Glasgow technocrats loudly proclaimed that they would improve the
local services of a locality that had been cut off in the periphery
from the larger resources of West Scotland.   How hollow this
promise was will appear later.   What concerned the local residents
was the fact that the money given for the educational and hospital
amenities went to the County chest, and not into the local money
box.   The new schools were late improvements.

After the initial period and the secondary spin-offs, there was a
hollow ring in the claim that Dunoon was a naval boom town.   The
irony was that as the American Navy became more and more entrenched
within the local scape, the personnel at Base became more and more

economically self-sufficient in providing consumables, although at
the same time they continued to enjoy the more expensive commodities
of the UK's welfare state.

There were locals, however, who imagined that the Americans had
brought local prosperity, and openly said so when I conversed with
them.   Some of them thought so, because they had been amongst the
few who had profited as individuals, but most had simply been delu-
ded.   Certainly the image of the American 'big spender' had become
a myth during the US recession of the 1970s.   The profit made by
the relatively few local residents by way of the sale of goods, or
of alcohol, or rented accommodation, must be weighed against other
losses referred to already and against the expensive medical and
educational provisions made available to the incomers.   Whatever
the American payment for these, local services have been seriously
strained over the years, and local clients have been inconvenienced.

What of the impact of the Ardyne complex upon the economic scape?
We must first assess in macro terms what was happening in the outscape during the early months of 1975.

Taking up where I left off in Part Two, Scotland was 'passing
into a new industrial era', with eleven out of the thirteen British
orders for oil platforms going to Scottish sites. (20)   But, by
August, prospects of local boom had changed to gloom.   Orders were
dropping, and by March 1976 it was clear that oil-rig builders in
the UK had no orders at any site.   Map 7.1 presents their plight on
7 March 1976. (21)   The predicament was described as the 'quickest
boom-bust cycle in economic history'. (22)   The prospect for the
workers at Ardyne had suddenly become unsure.   There was little

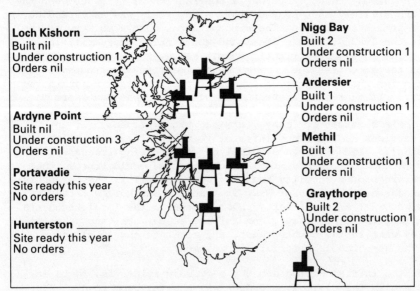

Loch Kishorn
Built nil
Under construction 1
Orders nil

Ardyne Point
Built nil
Under construction 3
Orders nil

Portavadie
Site ready this year
No orders

Hunterston
Site ready this year
No orders

Nigg Bay
Built 2
Under construction 1
Orders nil

Ardersier
Built 1
Under construction 1
Orders nil

Methil
Built 1
Under construction 1
Orders nil

Graythorpe
Built 2
Under construction 1
Orders nil

MAP 7.1   The plight of the UK oil-rig builders (March 1976)
Source: Sunday Times, 7 March 1976.   John Fryer and George Rosie.

possibility of orders coming in after the first avalanche.
McAlpine might continue with other ventures at Ardyne, but would the
work force be maintained at the same level?   Who would go?   The
insecurity was heightened by a statement made by the deputy convenor
for Rig Developments North Sea: 'The oil companies know that they
are eventually going to need platforms.   They are holding off until
the last possible moment when the yards are desperate for work.
It's a big game of chess and we are the pawns.' (23)   Others felt,
however, that the oil platforms would cease to be built.

There were technological uncertainties regarding the older
designs and there was even the possibility that platforms would soon
not be necessary. (24)   Local workers and residents were reading in
their evening paper in January of the shadow cast by the change of
circumstances regarding the offshore service industry, and the
'sudden squall of problems that's blown up down the Clyde'. (25)
Would the 'graving yards' of the concrete complex at Ardyne stand
empty, veritable graveyards of local dreams and bright futures?
The uncertainty, for the moment, only served to spur those employed
at Ardyne to work harder, somehow they felt sure that more work
would come.   'I'm not worried,' said one man at the site to a local
journalist, 'something will turn up, we'll be here for a long time
yet.' (26)

As in the case of the USN impact upon the economic scape, the
effects of the McAlpine workers on local goods, services, and employment will be taken into consideration.

The workers at Ardyne did not shop much in Cowal.   They had
little time for shopping.   As for food, they had their own canteen
at Ardyne camp.   There were those, however, who went into town to
Dunoon's celebrated public houses.   An article appeared in the
Evening Times early in 1975 headed: 'Dunoon Pubs Hit the Jackpot –
Thanks to the Well-heeled, Well-oiled Rig Worker'.   A perceptive
journalist summed up a situation (which was worrying a great many
residents) in the following terms:

The effect of Ardyne on Dunoon and its cluster of villages is
felt in highly contradictory ways.   Money pours in.   Publicans
are prospering.   Landladies have never had it so good.   But the
cottages and flats that once housed holiday-makers have all been
snapped up, first by Americans from the US Navy Base at Holy
Loch, now by men from Newcastle and Leeds, and all parts of
Ireland, lured by the big money of Ardyne. (27)

The manageress of a Dunoon pub was quoted in an article of 2 June
1975, in Glasgow's evening paper, as follows: 'They're great spenders, the McAlpine boys.   In fact, they're fools, and I've often
told them so.   They just drink away all their money.' (28)   The
drinking went on from Thursday pay-night until Saturday closing-
time, and with bottles in hand they drank their 'carry oots' (off-
licence purchase) throughout the Sunday.   Often men with £150-£200
in their pockets would be asking for a 'sub' (payment in advance) at
Ardyne on the Monday after spending it all throughout the weekend.

There were stories about the McAlpine men standing at the bar who placed large bundles of £10 notes on the counter and simply said to the bar-maids, as they ordered drink after drink: 'Tell me when the stack's finished.' The £10 note was locally known as 'the McAlpine pound note'. The facts were that the Ardyne workers had more money to spend than the American incomers. But the locals did not feel happy with a situation where brewers of the outscape, who owned the leading 'pubs', were benefiting and not local business people.

The local residents were also very disturbed because of the loss of tradesmen to the basins at Loch Striven. Residents and shop-keepers had had to phone for plumbers from Renfrewshire and joiners from Paisley when they required repairs. Worse still, there were cut-backs in the bus services due to the exodus of drivers to the McAlpine venture. They were driving Gorman's green buses, or trucks for McAlpine or for subcontractors.

The aged began to feel the effects first. They represented about a third of the outlying population, and depended absolutely upon the buses. How were they to afford the rising taxi fares, which were catering for the affluent McAlpine workers and the 'well-stacked' Americans? The local social workers were considerably disturbed, as were many residents. The shore road to Toward was under reconstruction and was decidedly dangerous at that time.

The impact of the Ardyne venture, therefore, appeared to have affected the people more directly than did that of the USN invasion. It was clear that many people had not yet accepted the Americans after fifteen years, and now on top of everything else they had to suffer from a totally different impact. Certainly, there was the newness of the Ardyne impact, but there was also the diverse nature of the consequences which would remain after the initial impact, and secondary phase. The episode of change affected the round of life more immediately. Employment, domestic services, public transport, and lastly house prices were all altered, when McAlpine's men began to crowd the locality.

The house prices went up due to the increased demand made by the needs of a large contractor. There were also the management and senior technicians, who sought the better houses. The local people, especially the young, were now caught between the greater demand for rentals by military personnel and the greater demand for house purchase by industrial personnel - both consumer groups from the outscape. They were caught between two fires. Worst of all, the strangers were preferred because often money mattered, not local ties, not family status, nor kinship networks.

With regard to the purchase of property, in contrast with the Americans who seldom if ever bought property, the McAlpine manage-ment was buying it. The camp at Ardyne only housed about 350 men at that time, so that the only realistic alternative was to seek accommodation for the incomers locally. Many were transported from the other side, but it paid McAlpine to buy property to cut out the expense involved in transportation. A boat was already chartered

by McAlpine for the men.   Small boarding houses and a few hotels
were bought and used as dormitories.   Many McAlpine men did rent
accommodation.   However, the accommodation between Dunoon and
Toward had always been particularly attractive to the USN personnel
(they wanted to be as far as possible from the noisy lochside), so
they had occupied houses along the shore and also in Innellan, which
was a favourite spot for many officers.   McAlpine had little choice
but to purchase hotels and guest houses along the shore nearer
Toward.   The residents were bewildered yet more, because they saw
their holiday image contract, as holiday rooms and some boarding
houses become dormitories for navvies.   Rumour was rife, when I was
in Dunoon.   Hotels, large and small, were reputed to have changed
hands, often without foundation.

With regard to the schooling needs and hospital care, unlike
those of the Americans, the McAlpine workers' influx had no significant effects.

Before passing on to consider the effects upon local employment,
in particular, it must be said that there were benefits in economic
terms in having McAlpine's men in Cowal.   Firstly, there was a cash
inflow, to some extent for some property owners, for landlords and
landladies, especially for some publicans, and also for the taxi
drivers.   Secondly, there were considerable benefits to the public
such as the newly widened Toward road, and the yachting club
premises, together with the new car park at Loch Striven, all made
possible by the work of the McAlpine workforce.

Whereas the American intrusion had had virtually no impact upon
the employment rate locally, the Ardyne complex, as already noted,
had considerable impact on local employment.   At first, local employers lost many of their best and senior staff who went off for
'flesh-pot' wages at Ardyne.   The drift away had alarmed the shopkeepers and hoteliers of an already ailing holiday and tourist trade
- they were losing their 'old hands' at the start of the project.

One bitter local man interviewed at his home in Dunoon summed it
up: 'I know a lad who gets around £60 a week at McAlpine's for
setting tables in the canteen.   All he does is put out forks and
knives for the men coming in from their shifts.   Here I am labouring like hell for a miserable weekly wage of £28.'   Once again it
was said the 'boom' for some had been a question of 'doom' for
others - such as the dwindling number of bus drivers, so that some
buses could not longer run.   Drivers were lured to McAlpine's continuously, as were mechanics from the local garages.   There was al
also a danger that petrol prices, etc. might have to increase
locally, if the garage owners were to pay bigger wages to keep their
men from going off to Ardyne.   In contrast, the USN Base had not
been as damaging an effect on local transport, nor on the labour
supply.   It was true that Clyde ferries were bringing in the bulk
of McAlpine labour straight from the 'other side', transporting
hundreds of men on daily runs to the jetty at Ardyne.   This outside
source of labour did not affect the main supply of labour in East
Cowal, but, none the less, there had been a sufficient transfer of

local men and women to McAlpine's complex at Ardyne to disconcert
local businessmen and disrupt domestic services.   Moreover, the
drain of tradesmen to the McAlpine Camp affected the local maintenance supply.   There was a working-class emphasis on the blessings
that McAlpine was bringing in the form of work opportunities, yet
here was also the local jealousy of some, and the criticism of
dwindling transport service employees.

As is clear from the presentation of the origin of the work-force
(Map 7.2), no intimation was given that labour would be brought in
from outside the UK.   In addition, the project at Ardyne claimed at
the start that it would provide local employment in a locality where
Cowal youth had had to cross the Firth, and often the English

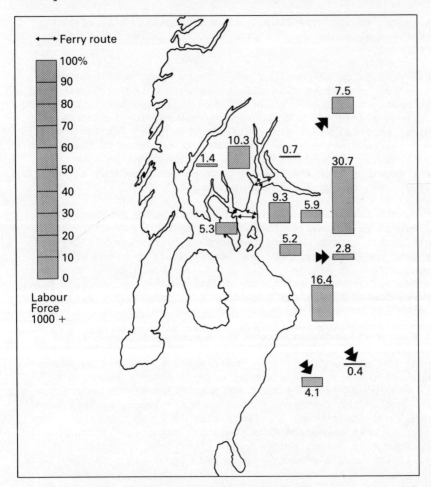

MAP 7.2 Origin of McAlpine labour force
Source: 'Origins of McAlpine's Labour Force', North Sea Oil
           Project, Internal Working Paper 16, G.A. Mackay and others,
           Department of Political Economy, King's College, University
           of Aberdeen, November 1974.

border, to find a job.   Inland and Waterside Planners published the
map on behalf of McAlpine, when in fact the locals were being turned
away from jobs at Ardyne Point.

Uncertainty suddenly descended upon the platform-building industry.   The men at Ardyne who gave up their local jobs had done so by
giving up their Cowal work ties, often in businesses where their
fathers had worked for almost a lifetime.   With the uncertainty of
Ardyne's future, their own future hung in the balance.   They could
hardly return to their former employers who had been put out financially by their exodus.   This meant that for some there was the
prospect of leaving the area after the last orders at McAlpine's,
and this for the most part would affect those who were amongst those
who had had the best prospects in the past of remaining in the area.
Indeed, some were leaving the work before they had a replacement at
their former place of work.   They could not return.

By November 1975 there were signs that some local men were giving
up their work at Ardyne.   Some did so because they could neither
stand the pace of work nor the trying conditions.   Others were involved in industrial unrest at the site.   They had had no previous
experience of striking nor of confrontation with management.   There
were some who became involved and found themselves on the way back
to Dunoon.   They were 'written off' and ashamed.   In the locality
the status of the employed has always been a mark of some importance, where the established have had access to the stable jobs.
Also, some were caught up in a canteen dispute at the camp. (29)
Strikes were events which the locals had read about as taking place
on 'the other side'; now they had become a local event.   In May
1975, 155 men had been laid off, (30) by October there was a strike,
and by 2 November 1975, 200 steel-fixers were laid off. (31)   The
attraction of working at Ardyne for 'big money' became for some a
fiasco.   The local youth could not cope with the situation.

Those who did manage to hold on to their jobs at the basins
earned large wages.   Soon the economic gaps between neighbours
began to divide Cowal residents, especially on the council estates
of Dunoon.   The uneven effects created lags between those who could
afford the new and latest luxuries, and those who were left behind.
In their frustration they saw incomers, on the one hand, enjoying
the benefits of work at Ardyne and, on the other hand, their neighbours also, who perhaps in the previous economic scape had been less
fortunate than themselves.

Having assessed the effects of the USN personnel and of the Mc-
Alpine workforce upon the goods, services and employment locally,
and identified the 'run-down' elements, some residents might object
that the 'local banks were doing well' as one affluent resident told
me in 1975.   Of course, there are no local banks 'per se', only
banks channelling money back to centres in the outscape, just as
there are technically few local 'pubs' in most towns.   One lady
said to me, 'Yea just hiv tae stand waiting for yer ten pound withdrawal fae a mean wee account, like most o' us hiv in this toon, tae
see dollars and £10 notes being thumbed ahead of yea on the counter.

But, it's naebody I know nor naebody anyone knows here.   It's fae big ootfits far awa'.   They dae well tae keep oot of our sight 'a tell yea.'   The impression kept building up that East Cowal had a plundered economy.

But, what about the effect of the American and McAlpine incomers upon local tourism?   This can best be examined in terms of the views of the visitors to the area, and of local residents.

Most of the visitors on the boats I interviewed in the summer of 1975 came from the West of Scotland: 'on the other side'.   The pattern was like the 'old days', with some additional English from south of the border.   The greatest number of the travellers inter- viewed were between 20 and 59 years of age, with only nineteen re- tired. (32)   Significantly, the 'holiday-makers' constituted just over a quarter of the total.   They were touring Scotland and their programme included Argyllshire.

There was an almost daily turnover of guests in many of the premises offering facilities.   Tables 7.2 and 7.3 will give some idea of the effort the locality was still exerting in catering for the visitors.   They show that, whatever the drawbacks in having Polaris at Holy Loch and the platform complex at Ardyne, the local- ity still clung to its tourist industry, undaunted by the bad pub- licity and the competition of the travel agents' attractive packages advertised in the outscape.   Hotels, however, were having shorter- term guests than in the old days pre-1961, but apparently some were still doing a brisk trade, and still boasted that their services were second to none.

As can be seen from the data in Table 7.3, the area to the north-east of the burgh was also plying its tourist trade, although the caravans were adroitly placed out of ear-shot of the USN Base. If one breaks down the number of rooms into types, as made available through the tourist office at the pier in the summer of 1975, one can better appreciate the official number of guests the locality could cater for that summer (Tables 7.4 and 7.5).

Dunoon and its locality could cater for at least 2,559 in its hotels and other 'bed and breakfast' accommodation.   The number is impressive when one considers that this represents approximately a quarter of Dunoon's population.   However, it does compare badly with the situation in 1961.   There were then 137 hotels and board- ing houses advertised in the Burgh of Dunoon.   In 1975 they had dramatically dropped to 49 (see Table 7.2).   Just over 64 per cent of the hotels and boarding houses had closed down since the holiday heyday.   More significantly, Dunoon Burgh had 1,162 rooms (1960) set aside for holiday-makers.   This figure had dropped to a much lower one in 1975, judging from the 94 bed and breakfast rooms ad- vertised in the burgh, and the 21 flats or premises set aside for self-catering (see Tables 7.2 and 7.3).   Rooms available outside the official register are not included, however, but the information I received was that these were almost negligible.

TABLE 7.2   Accommodation available (1975) with Dunoon District

Type of accommodation	To S.W. of burgh		Burgh of Dunoon		To N.E. of burgh		Totals	
	No. of units	No. of rooms	No. of units	No. of rooms	No. of units	No. of rooms	Units	Rooms
Hotel or guest house	3	50	49	1048	8	47	60	1145
Bed and breakfast premises	3	8	33	94	9	26	45	128
Totals	6	58	82	1142	17	73	105	1273

TABLE 7.3   Self-catering premises and caravans for hire (1975) within Dunoon District

Type	To S.W. of burgh	Burgh of Dunoon	To N.E. of burgh	Totals
Self-catering premises	2	21	1	24
Caravans	0	0	48	48

Source: Dunoon Tourist Information Office (1975).

TABLE 7.4 Type of rooms and approximate numbers which could be catered for in hotels and guest houses

Location of hotels and guest houses	Type of rooms available			Sum total of rooms	Approximate number of places for guests
	Single	Double	Twin	Family		
Burgh	182	328	360	178	1048	2092
South-west	11	12	17	10	50	99
North-east	7	18	12	10	47	97
Totals	200	358	389	198	1145	2288

Note: Tables 7.4 and 7.5 allow for three people to a family bedroom.

TABLE 7.5 Type of rooms and approximate numbers which could be catered for in bed and breakfast accommodation

Location of accommodation	Type of rooms available			Sum total of rooms	Approximate number of guests catered for
	Single	Double	Twin	Family		
Burgh	7	43	24	20	94	201
South-west	0	3	2	3	8	17
North-east	3	12	7	4	26	53
Totals	10	58	33	27	128	271

Source: Dunoon Tourist Information Office (1975).

One cannot conclude from the information in the tables that the USN presence in particular, together with the Ardyne worker influx, had been solely responsible for the drop in board and holiday provision. The local economic scape had been progressively affected for some years by the waning UK home resorts as already stated, in the wake of the holiday packages abroad. None the less, it must be admitted that the naval and navvy presence in Dunoon District had not helped.

In my conversations with the travellers on the ferries in the summer of 1975, it was clear that they had more to say about the ill effects of the Ardyne personnel on the area than that of the USN incomers. There were more than twice as many visitors who criticised the Ardyne personnel as there were people who criticised the USN incomers. They all singled out the bad effects of the Ardyners upon the holiday image of Dunoon. It became clear that people from 'the other side' were significantly more critical of the Ardyne workers' ill effects upon Dunoon as a holiday spot than upon the other shore settlements. (33)

Most of the travellers who were from outside the West of Scotland, mentioned the drunken navvies roaming the streets and hanging about the hotel and public house doorways. The people from the West of Scotland were less shocked by the heavy drinking. Given the history of drink aboard the ferries over the years, and the higher incidence of drink in the West of Scotland than in most parts of the UK, this may not have been surprising.

Before passing on to my interviews in the 525 homes of local residents to assess their views regarding the effects of the incomers on the local economy, it is worth noting that the visitors had more positive than negative things to say about the town of Dunoon and its locality. Especial praise was given to the warmth of the locals, and the helpfulness of the shopkeepers and their assistants, and there were enthusiastic English people who had seen little to compare with Cowal's scenic beauty anywhere else in Scotland.

How did the residents whom I visited in the autumn and winter of 1975-6 feel about the effects of the incomers on tourism? I assessed their perceptions and reactions by showing them a cutting from a provocative article in the Evening Times headed 'Anyone who comes here for holidays now is mad' (2 June 1975), which referred to Dunoon.

In contrast with the view of the visitors on the ferries, the residents were more critical of Dunoon's credibility as a holiday resort. 62 (11.8 per cent) agreed with the article, and another 166 (31.6 per cent) also agreed, but with reservations. They constituted approximately 43.4 per cent of the interviewees and were uneasy about what Dunoon had to offer visitors. (34) However, it was the residents from the settlements both to the north-east and the south-west, who were more critical of Dunoon. Dunoonites were proud of their town, so that it was not surprising that 225,

62.5 per cent, of the Dunoon residents interviewed totally disagreed with the sentiments of the article. (35)

Dissatisfaction was chiefly based upon the impact of the navvies. During my eavesdropping in the autumn of 1974, I had overheard people speak on several occasions about the navvies' effect upon the local holiday trade.   People spoke of workers in their dirty togs and heavy muddy boots coming into carpeted halls of once-select guest houses.   There was also deep concern about the purchase of local hotels and boarding houses by McAlpine.   'It'll destory the place: who'll want to come here now,' said someone.   Another added: 'It's no good complaining, the place went over to "bed and breakfast" long ago.'

For the people of the locality, Cowal had a sense of place, which was distinctly summed up as 'the gateway to the Highlands'.   The trucks, the navvies and the rising concrete legs of the platforms were seen by many of those whom I interviewed as the threat of an expanding industrial take-over.   Such fear was ill-founded as it turned out, but when the landscape and the traditions of any local-ity are altered in any way by industrialists local rumour often turns the most exaggerated forebodings into threatening realities. In my interviews with the 525 local residents, 216 people criticised the Ardyne incomers, but more will be said about them later when considering the effects upon the cultural scape.   Out of these there were 50 who expressed fears that the locality would become an industrial extension of 'the other side'.   They represented 23.2 per cent of those who criticised the Ardyne workers. (36)   People locally were uneasy about the inroads of the navvies into their locality because the workers were affecting the holiday image of the area.

Having considered the USN and McAlpine effects on the economic scape, what of the impact of the new regional scheme upon the goods, services, and employment in the area?   The Strathclyde Region con-taining the bulk of the Scottish population within its boundaries, simply engulfed the small domain of Cowal and its handful of coun-cillors.   The area of Dunoon and its surrounding locality thus became a very small sub-unit of the mammoth economic unit of Strath-clyde.   The master identity of the locals had been mainly that of 'the people of Cowal'.   Argyll had been linked with the Highlands and Islands in economic terms, however subsidised it might have been by the monies of the Renfrew and Glasgow visitors.   With regionali-sation, new economies were created in a totally new system.   The familiar economic scape was shattered whilst the sheer magnitude of the regional economic unit of Strathclyde bewildered and confused the East Cowal residents.

The size of the new economic unit cannot be overlooked.   For example, the budget in education had to maintain one of the UK's biggest education units and the largest social work department in Europe.   Suddenly, the small locality of Cowal found itself swal-lowed up by the Region, and people were beginning to wonder if their local needs might ever be on the list of priorities at HQ.   With

only a few hundred school children out of the 530,000 the local protest over either the American impact upon the size and composition
of classes, or the need to build more schools, constituted in the
words of a local resident: 'but a faint squeak in the regional
chambers, where the size of the electorate makes the loudest protest'.   There had been some rumours of change in 1969, well before
the regional axe fell upon East Cowal in 1975.

Sensing the difficulties in 1968 at Dunoon's Centenary Celebration Dinner in November, the guests and their provost found that
their festivities over the history of their Town Council and burgh
had been somewhat eclipsed by the rumours regarding changes.
Provost Harper stood up to make his speech before an imposing cake,
upon which were twenty-seven pictures of the provosts to date.   All
of them had managed Dunoon's economic affairs and tourism from
Castle Chambers.   The provost and a few others, who had been hearing reports, feared that Scotland, like England, would lose its
local controls; when he stood up to speak at the dinner, he
attacked central controls.   After complaining about increasing
bureaucratisation, he stated,

> to add salt to the wound inflicted on local authorities, the
> Royal Commission on the Reorganisation of Local Government has
> been formed.   According to the evidence submitted, reorganisa-
> tion means that small burghs like Dunoon would cease to exist and
> instead large regional authorities would be formed which would
> make the control of central government complete.   There are
> still men and women in this town and county with ideas and
> vision.   It is these men and women who are being frustrated and
> demoralised by a faceless bureaucracy.   Is it not more democra-
> tic and sensible that a community should decide what it wants or
> does not want, instead of waiting for the decision of some
> departmental official, who has probably never heard of the place?
> This ladies and gentlemen is the stage we have reached in
> hundred years of Dunoon's history. (37)

What would happen to their local economy and services, if run and
administered from the outscape?

Willie Inglis, editor of the Dunoon paper, stood up at the same
dinner to pledge his loyalty to Dunoon and all it stood for.   His
family had supported tourism in the local newspaper for over a hundred years.   His words only helped to emphasise the latent sadness
of the occasion, although officially they had come to celebrate,
because his words were those of a man who mourned the passing of the
old.   He ended with tears in his eyes, paying tribute to old
Dunoon, and all that its history represented with the tribute of a
Dunoon poet, Duncan Maclean, taking particular pride in his words:

> Can I forget the place that gave me birth,
> The shrine of sacred memories that I love,
> The fairest, rarest, dearest spot on earth,
> That lifts my soul with thanks to God above,
> Can I forget?   Not till times sun shall set,
> And rise no more for me, can I forget Dunoon. (38)

From the 1969 Report, as some locals told me, till implementation
in May 1975, local people feared for the services of a proud burgh
which were to be run in the future by outsiders who would be financed in the Glasgow City Chambers.   Foreboding bedevilled many
during that period.   The conjuncture of the centenary of the Burgh
of Dunoon and of the Town Council, when loyalties to the town and
its locality were intensified, with the formation of the Royal Commission to discuss the reorganisation of local government sharpened
feelings.

Few people could have anticipated the possible changes after
October 1969, when the Wheatley Report came out.   People wondered
what was happening in private discussion.   But, over the years some
had lost interest in committee meetings till the last twelve months
before implementation in May 1975.   What were the rates to be?
Statements published at the time stated that 'rates should be known
by the end of June 1975'.   The change of authority meant that there
could be dramatic changes in the rates, and there were rumours that
they were to be considerable.

The rumours were soon to be confirmed.   Argyll and Bute had the
fifth highest costs of all the nineteen Districts within Strathclyde
according to HQ calculations.   So huge inroads were made into
people's incomes in the name of rates for expenditure on tourism,
leisure, recreation, libraries, housing, cleansing, planning, and
'other expenses'.   People were shocked by the increased rates under
Strathclyde.

What had now to be taken into account was the fact that costs
covered a vaster area, so that the more populated Cowal area would
have to carry the major load of the costs for improvements in localities on Bute, in the Western Isles, dictated by Glasgow planners;
as was to be the case, for example, in the creation of a large
sports complex at Lochgilphead, costing £200,000 later in
1978. (39)   Although Strathclyde declared its budget sums in round
figures for the District, it departed from the previous practice in
the county statements of entering into detail.   For Argyll, the new
scheme meant that over three years, the older rate would rise by
scale to a 30 per cent increase.   The scale at first would be
between 17 and 18 per cent in Dunoon, for example, and then rise
dramatically till the District was within a far higher rateable
bracket.   Disgruntled people from Dunoon told me over and over
again that they were subsidising Glasgow.

With the growing criticism came local surprise at the enormous
salaries advertised in the press for the new Strathclyde.   A letter
to the Dunoon Observer commented: 'For the majority of the Argyll
ratepayers, the present and future position is alarming.   The
present greatly increased demand is only the very solid end of a
very frightening wedge that will reveal itself in full horror inside
a year or two.' (40)

A local resident observed in the Dunoon newspaper:

Some years ago, I remember a paper given by Captain Hay of Hay-
field at a conference, warning of the danger of the paid official
taking over from the elected representative.   How far sighted
that gentleman has proved to be.   My observations may be parochial, but Dunoon is an area of which I have some knowledge.   I
do not like what I see today as 'so called' reformed local government. (41)

The new set-up had meant that the increased payments from local
residents had gone into budgets for improvements and upkeep elsewhere in one of Scotland's biggest Districts.   'Never have I seen
Dunoon', said Anne Melville, one of the town's most respected residents, 'in such a filthy, neglected state: choked gullies, unswept
streets, unemptied litter bins at the height of the holiday
season.' (42)

In September 1975, on a solitary walk on the promenade, when I
was considering the responses of the local people to my questions,
I was confronted by a resident.   He had chatted with me from time
to time since the day I had approached him in Dunoon streets during
the electioneering days of 1974.   'Hey, there, see those lights
dangling above your head,' he cried, 'those fairy holiday lights
have been strung up along this promenade for years, but under
Strathclyde there's a difference.   They only light up when the
Glasgow "bohyos" tell us, and they are turned off for the winter
when they, not the locals, decide.'   According to my inquiries
later, the maintenance of the lights was by the authority of the
District, but the lighting time was by order of the Region.   It
would appear to be a small matter, but to local people such details
characterise and symbolise the new dependencies and loss of local
autonomy.

A most significant change was that the area was ultimately dependent in economic terms upon the authority invested in the Director
of Leisure and Recreation in the McIver/McKenzie House in Glasgow.
The lack of administrative controls after May 1975, when the new
regional scheme was implemented, will be elaborated in the next
chapter, when the political scape will be dealt with.   One must now
inquire as to whether there were any economic benefits.

Benefits for the people under Strathclyde in local economic terms
were widely publicised.   It was reported that there would be a more
generous loan system for first-time house buyers.   Secondly, it was
stated that the Region would build 44 council houses in the 1980s
within the area.   Thirdly, more money would be put into publicising
the locality as a tourist area.   With regard to the housing, it was
rightly objected by the local residents that the houses would have
been on the planning boards, whether there had been a Strathclyde or
not.   With regard to the loans, already noted, house purchase was
then out of the question for most non-owners.   Available houses
were bought up or rented by the incoming Ardyners.   In any case the
local housing market was prohibitive.   The loans would also have
had to have been considerable to outbid either McAlpine's management
or the outscape landlords who wanted to hold on to the better houses

which more senior USN officers would prefer to rent rather than the
smaller houses on the American estates.

Tourist publicity was promised to the locality by Strathclyde.
It was part and parcel of the glamorised package produced to woo
supporters.   During my visits to the houses of 525 residents, one
man observed: 'The Glasgow powers are not going to put money into
publicising the tourist attractions of a small strip of land like
Cowal.   Like all press statements about what they are going to do
for the public, the big planners promise us a birthday cake, and in
the end they give us a wee sweetie.'

An immediate benefit to the locality, however, when I was coming
to the close of my stay, was the allocation of an additional six
policemen and four wardens.   The people had needed for some time to
augment their small police force which was stretched to almost
breaking point by the influx of so many workers.   In addition, the
traffic congestion and the new huge trucks which often jammed roads
locally had called for much stricter road controls.

By way of concluding this examination of the impacts on the
economic scape by the USN, McAlpine and Strathclyde intrusions, some
points of converging interest might usefully be brought together.

Clearly, the effects of each impact were mediated by the diverse
expectations of the local residents.   In the case of the USN invasion, the people of the locality expected that East Cowal would
become a boom area.   A handful of shopkeepers had gained economically, as had some landlords.   However, these must be weighed
against the diseconomies: unpaid debts, and luxuries at different
costs which were exclusively available at the Base.   There was also
an increasing amount of purchasing on 'the other side', not to mention the inroads into the public services by outsiders and the rise
in rates to cover the additional expenses because of the resultant
strains made upon them.   In addition, there was the bad press,
which contributed to the bad image of the locality which impaired
its tourism.   These had created economic dysfunctions.   The effect
was one of 'let-down' in the economic scape.   And what hurt local
young married couples most was the virtual impossibility of acquiring any decent accommodation at a reasonable rent.

The Ardyne impact also created expectations locally of economic
gain, but here these were associated with more employment and higher
wages for an area that had not gained in employment terms through
the advent of the USN personnel.   The 'let-down' here affected the
local lower socioeconomic groups more dramatically.   Lags were also
created between the minority who managed to hold on to their highly
paid jobs, and the majority, often neighbours, who either could not
get a job, or had lost their job at Ardyne.   In addition, as in the
case of the USN invasion, the housing market during the initial and
secondary periods had been boosted, which profited some, but too
often also brought about diseconomies, which affected many more.
The holiday image of the area in particular had been impaired in the
press by the publicity which journalists were giving to the brawls

and drunkenness of the navvies, as will be discussed further in a
later chapter.

It is not surprising, in the light of these observations, that
the life-style and standard of living amongst the people in Cowal
were inconspicuous and largely unimpressive in terms of domestic
comforts, quality of cars and affluent pursuits.   As will be discussed in a later chapter, there were some young residents working
at Ardyne who did stand out as 'high livers'; who could drink and
'live it up with the best of 'em', as one of them boasted to me in
Dunoon.   But they were a fringe group, and visitors to Cowal did not
come away with any impression of local affluence.

With regard to the Strathclyde story, it was debated at length in
government, in committees, and in the press for years before eventual implementation in May 1975.   The locality had been divided,
largely between town and country over the issues of the Region.
Division was engendered by lengthy discussions over boundaries.
The promise of big monies for economic changes was exploded at the
outset by the dramatic rise in rates.   For the burghers, the demise
of the Town Council which had managed their local economy for over a
hundred years, and the more remote access in the new administration
to a confusing number of offices and officers who were scattered
across the largest authority in Scotland was bewildering.   For the
villagers, it had meant from the start that the urban controls from
which many had escaped, was now an imposition.   Those in the town
who did support the new organisational reforms, were 'let-down' when
they saw the real implications of having to negotiate their affairs
at a distance.   Geographic lags may be lessened by technology, but
communication is not purely a question of technology, but also of
personal access and social interaction.   The access was bureaucra-
tised on a mammoth scale and a psychological barrier created between
Dunoon and the District HQ at Lochgilphead.   Lastly the local
economy, once linked with a budget allocated for under 30,000
people, was now attached to an economic unit catering for 2,578,214
people.

Each of the three intrusions epitomise at macro level the ravages
of 'giantism' plundering peripheral economies in the name of
national and international rationalisation.   Each of the three
impacts are examples at the micro level of 'let-down' and 'run-down'
associated with bureaucratic and technocratic schemes, which purport
to be for the national good or international security.

Just as the oil boom research of the 1970s has revealed the 'run-
down' rather than the 'upturn' of local economies, so too this East
Cowal study indicates that in the long term little people are manip-
ulated and are disposable.

Business people and those few influentials who controlled the
means of local production had grasped the prizes offered and facilitated the intrusions by collusion.   They were often let-down in
turn by eventual unanticipated diseconomies and dysfunctions, and
more often were 'run over' by the relentless pursuit of macro interests at the expense of local interests.

When I questioned the 525 residents at their homes, in the autumn
and winter of 1975-6, about how they felt regarding changes in the
area, the majority complained that there had been little change for
the better over the past twenty years.   They did not necessarily
blame the American or Ardyne incomers, but clearly one could not by
any stretch of the imagination support the claim of a small minority
of residents and of the USN and McAlpine incomers that their
presence had greatly altered the locality for the better or to any
significant extent.   The unease I detected in my interviews with
people in East Cowal was privatised.   There was no evidence in the
locality of any communal effort to change the outcome of events, as
the incomers ran rough-shod over their economy.   Uneven reactions
and lags in perception, together with an overload of outside intrusions, fragmented any possible long-term community reaction of
people in the shore settlements.   Inertia had taken over: an overload of impacts had immobilised them.

Chapter 8

A POLITICAL BABEL

> Politics is about policy first and foremost; and policy is a
> matter of either the desire for change or the desire to protect
> something against change.   But it need not be ... the policy of
> some party or set of ministers or mass movement; it may be the
> policy of a small group in or out of the government.... Politics
> is about disagreement or conflict; and political activity is
> that which is intended to bring about or resist change, in the
> face of possible resistance.   (J.D.B. Miller)(1)

The political scape constitutes the public arena in which power is
exercised and in which controls over people's lives are established,
contended or reversed.   On the basis of what has been described
earlier, it is the institutionalised distribution of power and control in public affairs as exemplified in party politics or the bureaucracy in the affairs of technocracy or of the military, and
within the formal or informal dealings of organisations.   Clearly,
there are political scapes at macro and micro levels.   The important point to make is that the vital political game is played out
beyond the locality in the outscape.   There is little hope of
altering macro decisions.   Indeed, the real centres of power in
relation to peripheral areas are far removed in the wider outscape
so that lags in time and awareness in the local scape are inevitable
with regard to major decisions and significant events in the outscape.   The ambit of life in the local scape is limited, so therefore is that of power.   Beyond in the outscape, power has greater
dimensions and is more far-reaching.   Small may be beautiful, but
small is usually weak.   The import of these remarks will be demonstrated by reviewing the political effects of the Polaris Base, the
McAlpine project, and Strathclyde upon the locality.

The gap between the smaller arena of life and power in East Cowal
and the bigger arena of politics was well exemplified in the case of
the US Polaris Base.   Before the coming of the USN personnel, one
local resident assessed the situation as follows:

> During the past week or two I have been at pains to take a repre-
> sentative cross-section of local opinion and I am struck with the

> steadily increasing apprehension and dismay about this project.
> ... Resentment against the high-handedness of the government in
> saying nothing until they could present a <u>fait accompli</u> is wide-
> spread.   The story of the base is being leaked a little at a
> time. (2)

Others felt let down, not only by the government at Westminster, but
by the Dunoon Town Council.   This is conveyed in the following
observations of a published letter: 'The unctuous and self-decep-
tive attitude of the Dunoon Council in the matter of the Polaris
Base leaves one aghast.' (3)

The town, noted historically for its plebiscites, had been taken
by surprise, and its council members, prone to put the prosperity of
the town first in terms of money welcomed the USN Base.   But there
were others who supported the council members and politically supported Polaris Base on ideological grounds.   As one man put it:
'They helped us during the war against the Huns, we ought to help
them get at those Commie bastards.'   These local reactions were
prompted by political interventions which require some explanation.

In terms of politics certain lines of influence must be identified so as to understand the complexities of intervention or communication between the significant people within the local scape and
the power groups or manipulators within the outscape.   From the
point of view of the locality, communication by outreach into the
larger world can never hope to match the inreach of master powers
within the local scape.   It will be necessary to explain political
dealings further.

Political dealings in general will be either horizontal, vertical
or oblique.   The horizontal and the vertical follow predictable
lines of communication, whereas the oblique does not.   It was R.L.
Warren who identified the 'horizontal' and the 'vertical' community
axes of communication.   The 'horizontal' is the relation of sub-
systems with each other, (4) and the 'vertical' is the relation of
social units with extra-community systems. (5)   So, firstly, there
may be a particular outreach which links ranks at the same levels
with each other ('inter pares').   Secondly, there may be a link
across scapes, which is described as 'vertical' because it is based
upon subordination and superordination along a hierarchical axis
leading to those of higher and greater authority in centres of business, professional enclaves, the military HQs, or government, all of
which are in the outscape.   In this case the individuals contacted
are on different hierarchic levels and do not share the same status
or power.

Horizontal communication although it has formal elements tends
also to be informal and expressive, and is dependent largely upon
face-to-face encounter and charisma.   It is exercised between kinship groups or between people sharing the same membership of a
political party, or religious or ethnic groups.   Conflicts or consensus within these tend to be localistic and 'on the level'.   The
conflicts are dealt with according to commonly accepted procedures

and are therefore predictable.   The communication is a two-way process because it is essentially interactive.

Vertical communication is also in accordance with predictable
procedures, but in contrast it is highly impersonal and bureaucra-
tised.   The exact specifications and rules are formally laid down;
for example, how a Commander at Base communicates with the Admiral
at HQ;   or how the local Town Council or MP communicates within the
Houses of Parliament or with members of the Foreign Office, or vice
versa.   It is also a two-way process.

The oblique communication and interventions which are proposed
within this study are in sharp contrast with the procedures described above.   Oblique intervention is essentially sudden and unpredictable.   It is usually a form of intervention which is always
imposed from outside.   The full strength of such an inreach is
matched by the weakness of the recipients because they are taken
'off guard' or in a state of unpreparedness.   The oblique is of two
kinds: (1) diagonal or (2) zig-zag.

The diagonal breaks free from accepted rules and procedures of
superiors and subalterns, but is usually exercised by discretion
within the chain of command.   Its distinctive feature is the rapid-
ity of implementation because it departs from bureaucratic processes.
However, it is determined and limited by considerations of precedence, and so though its timing is unpredictable, its mode is usually acceptable within the context of the crisis or unusual circumstances.   Institutions and organisations prepare their personnel
and the public for such dramatic eventualities.   However, the
crisis or unusual circumstances are as defined and perceived by the
initiator of the whole process, so the subalterns and the public do
not always understand what is happening.   It breaks free from the
casual formalised superior-subaltern procedures.   Such a way of
acting is justified in the name of the national good.   An example
of diagonal intervention is that of technocrats, whose plans ride
roughshod over the usual regulations and 'modus vivendi' and may be
to the detriment of the common good locally, but for the common good
regionally or nationally.

The 'zig-zag' relation is more devious and unpredictable, moving
in between 'scapes' and across 'scapes'.   Its ploys and shifting
procedures defy prediction in the main as the intervention moves one
way and then another perplexing adversaries or participants.   It
tends to throw off political, economic and cultural controls, often
with disregard for human factors as it seeks to be almost a law unto
itself.   An example could be schemes for the advancement of military prowess and domination.   Juntas and Fascist take-overs are
prime examples of zig-zag machinations.   The military tends to live
by strategy and must be kept in check by the civilian sector, as
also does the technocrat who lives by the authority of the expert
rather than by 'consumer reference'.   The technologists and planners are assumed to know best, so the technocrats tend to run
society by 'fiat' from above and to impose local measures on people,
but under the guise of democratic processes.

It is important to state the military and technocratic agents are professionally prepared for the 'oblique' transaction and adept at coverage, and able to shift ground so as to implement their aims. Their loyalties are to far-away centres of power, and their belief and values removed from the local scene.   Figure 8.1 illustrates the various modes of political communication and/or intervention across various scapes.

This chapter will explore the complex political effects flowing from the oblique intervention, and intrusions within Cowal from centres of power both naval and civilian in the wider outscape.   It will necessarily move backwards and forwards within the political scape at macro and micro levels.   Where there is greater diversity, there is often greater political conflict.   This study will show that with each new impact there was a change in the local political spectrum, and with each, a further weakening of the local people's hold upon events, even within their own local scape.   As will be shown, it was not a question of local people working together to defend their rights, but often a confused and divided people, thrown this way and that as they picked up bewildering cues within the con-juncture of events.   To tap their views, the study will draw upon the responses of the local electorate in Dunoon in 1974, and those of the 525 interviewees in East Cowal in the autumn and winter of 1975-6, and will include some Cowal graffiti as collected in East Cowal toilets between February 1975 and February 1976.   All of these provided some local political soundings.

Beginning with the USN intrusion, one must keep in mind the imposition of Polaris from above and the fact that apart from Harold Macmillan only Franco, the Fascist supremo, had granted the USA a FBM Polaris anchorage in a European host country.   One is also struck by the silence which followed the first nationwide CND pro-tests.   Scanning the research data and the narrative of this study, one realises that the UK's anti-Polaris campaign, which was probably the largest political movement to sweep through Scotland since the depression of the 1930s, had long since lost its political 'tour de force' as macro issues began to recede after the first months of demonstration.   Michael Foot's remarks in Dunoon in the early months of the CND marches of the 1960s sounded hollow when his party was in office during the 1970s.   'Although we have had setbacks, this demonstration and the other demonstrations of the Campaign for Nuclear Disarmament and those who support it are a sign that we are not going to be moved: that this campaign is going to go on.' (6) Michael Foot's voice was heard again at CND rallies in the early 1980s when he was in opposition, but only when CND was revived.   He and the party are to be judged when in office and not out of it.

As events and this study will show, the campaign was betrayed by its once articulate political spokesmen.   Ironically, the arms build-up since then has grown enormously in the locality.   Polaris is now Poseidon, deterrence is no longer respectable, because 'second-strike' weaponry is regarded as a virtual admission of defeat.   The 'military ways' of Washington through oblique dealings established not a Polaris Base as such, but a Poseidon Base, whose

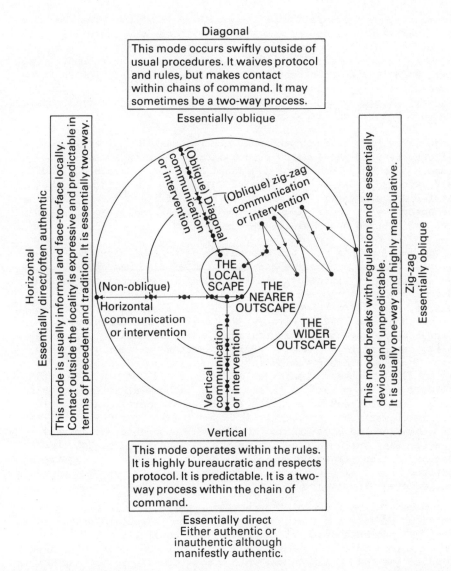

Diagonal

This mode occurs swiftly outside of usual procedures. It waives protocol and rules, but makes contact within chains of command. It may sometimes be a two-way process.

Essentially oblique

Horizontal

Essentially direct/often authentic

This mode is usually informal and face-to-face locally. Contact outside the locality is expressive and predictable in terms of precedent and tradition. It is essentially two-way.

(Oblique) Diagonal communication or intervention

(Oblique) zig-zag communication or intervention

(Non-oblique) Horizontal communication or intervention

THE LOCAL SCAPE

THE NEARER OUTSCAPE

THE WIDER OUTSCAPE

Vertical communication or intervention

Zig-zag

Essentially oblique

This mode breaks with regulation and is essentially devious and unpredictable. It is usually one-way and highly manipulative.

Vertical

This mode operates within the rules. It is highly bureaucratic and respects protocol. It is predictable. It is a two-way process within the chain of command.

Essentially direct
Either authentic or inauthentic although manifestly authentic.

FIGURE 8.1   The macro/micro context of communication or intervention between agents across scapes

destructive capacity far outweighed that of Polaris.   The Poseidon
multi-warheads were devised to shatter with maximum annihilation,
and did not merely constitute the 'quid pro quo' of a nation prepared to return a 'first-strike' blow with a sobering second.   The
term 'Polaris' had been conserved almost as a cover-up for Poseidon
years after Polaris was supplanted by the more effective weapon
system.   The Canopus, one of the best US depot ships, still carries
the word Polaris on its ship shield!

The 1964 Labour government scarcely raised the nuclear issue,
although many of the leading personalities had been active in de-
nouncing the Holy Loch Base.   Michael Foot, Tony Greenwood, Judith
Hart, Richard Crossman, and Barbara Castle had all joined in the
earlier CND protests.   Later, however, in office they were less
courageous, when their party extended the American presence at Holy
Loch and secured a UK Polaris system.

The local people have had grounds to be cynical about the Labour
party's stance over Polaris and the issue of disarmament.   Reading
the Labour party statements, it is evident that out of office and
government, party members were loud in their condemnation of
Polaris, but once in government the matter was dropped.   This was
so once again in 1973.   Firstly, Ron Hayward, the Labour party's
General Secretary, at the launching of the Labour party's foreign
policy document in the summer of 1973, stated explicitly that the
next Labour government would issue the Americans an invitation to
leave. (7)   Secondly, Denis Healey, former Defence Minister, said:
'We will open negotiations to secure the withdrawal of the Polaris
Base.   We will seek to persuade the USA that there is no case for
Polaris submarines to have British bases.' (8)   The ULMS/1 ballistic submarine had been created in the USA, and there was no real
need for the continued presence of the US submarines on Holy Loch
because the long-range potential of the new type did not require an
overseas base.   In J. Habermas's terms, the Labour party had
proved to be 'inauthentic'. (9)

A Dunoon Grammar School teacher, a Mr Smith, continually raised
the issue of Poseidon in the early 1970s, and strove to create a
local CND pressure group at that time, but to little avail.   One
man explained to me, 'Mr Smith, and Mrs Robertson before him, have
tried to get the locals to see what a monster Polaris is, and how
we must all get the country talking again about it, but the Labour
party's a big useless lot.   They let CND down in the end, so what's
the use.   We're only a few Labour folk here, and our loyalty is
sorely tried.'   As has been seen, the locality was largely Tory
over the years;   the few Labour followers required a strong lead
from outside, and moreover, spokesmen whom they could trust politically.

In my interviews, during the electioneering campaign in the
autumn of 1974 on Dunoon Streets, it was clear that the Polaris
issue was not dead locally, although it was no longer a vital macro
political issue.   Instead, the voters were more preoccupied with
UK economic issues such as inflation and price controls, or with

national issues such as Scottish oil and wage differentials.   Local
people had lost faith in the pronouncements of the Labour spokesmen.
Many more Cowal residents were committed over the years to taking an
anti-socialist middle-class stance, so when they were disillusioned
by the Tories they turned to the SNP.   The SNP Manifesto had called
for the removal of the USN presence in Scotland, but the issue was
swept under the carpet within Cowal during the electioneering days
of 1974.

The SNP Manifesto explicitly stated:

The SNP does not want Scotland to have nuclear weapons or bases
in Scottish territorial waters.   Existing nuclear bases were
sited in Scotland without the consent of the Scottish people, and
these are clear examples of how London makes use of Scotland for
installations thought to be dangerous. (10)

And the SNP were powerful locally, having in February captured the
Tory seat for the first time in an area that had been a Conservative
stronghold for years.

On Friday, 4 October 1974, a national upsurge of the SNP was
cited by the Nat-Opinion Research Council.   It was supported by the
fact that there was an increased support for the SNP from 21 per
cent in February to a historic 28 per cent in October. (11)   Would
the swing and the Manifesto's declaration reveal the latent feelings
of the people around Holy Loch about the American presence and the
ballistic missiles stacked in the hills of the region?   When I
checked the local SNP handouts there was certainly no mention of
nuclear bases, nor did the American presence find even a passing
reference in any political SNP speeches.

The fact was that the majority of local people, represented by
their pro-Polaris councillors, had been led from the start to support Polaris, and, as already seen, to help Dunoon and its locality
to survive financially.   The minority who had protested at the
start had been isolated.   The SNP wanted the majority vote, so in
spite of the SNP Manifesto, the local SNP workers and their candi-
date did not make an issue of the Base throughout the campaign.
Propaganda does work, and the coals were there to fan, but votes,
not principles mattered above all else.

As S. Lukes indicates, much of what goes on in politics is empty
ritual: 'systematically distorted communication' emphasises the
inauthentic nature of much that passes for open dialogue. (12)   The
CND efforts locally, during the disclosure of the Poseidon missile
installation aboard US ballistic submarines, proved to be futile CND
protests.

The national parties debated numerous other issues.   But, gross
deceit had taken place in American politico-military circles.   The
new 'first-strike' weaponry had been installed on Holy Loch in 1971,
without the knowledge of the members of the House of Commons. (13)
The Pentagon had stated that the deployment of the Poseidon weaponry

would be indefinitely postponed, yet locals knew that the James
Madison was being loaded with Poseidon missiles by the depot ship
Canopus, as reported in the Dunoon Observer of 22 May 1971.

The macro/micro interactions between Washington and Holy Loch not
only cut across the local scape, but apparently cut out British politicians.   On one of the toilet doors at the Dunoon pier someone
had scrawled the words in large letters: 'Dunoon - the 54th State
of America.   Yankee Rule!'   David Fairhall commented in the Guardian (29 September 1981) on 'the cosy American connection' in which
never has the use of emergency of US missiles on FBM submarines in
terms of operational rules 'been disclosed even in outline for
public scrutiny and debate'. (14)

In addition, the local people never had an anti-Polaris lead from
their local leaders in the Town Council.   The Americans, in terms
of the local political scape, enjoyed the protection of provosts and
councillors, whose pro-American stand had been an enduring factor,
except in the case of one or two atypicals within the Town Council.
The Polaris Base had been financially profitable for some, certainly
at the start.   USN authorities had maintained a high-level contact
with the members of the council over the years.   This was cultivated formally through higher echelon communication and shared symbolic ceremonials in both American and British national commemora-
tions, special suppers and banquets within the locality.   Informally, the officers' wives, often wearing their Annapolis gold rings
(their husbands enjoyed high status as Annapolis graduates), organised select social evenings for the families of Town Council members
and other local influentials.   There were also musical evenings at
the Commander's mansion by Holy Loch, to which the local leaders
were invited.

Obviously, the American presence strove to consolidate the
'status quo' and build upon it because it paid it to do so.
Leadership locally had to remain intact because it happened to support the US presence.   It was strengthened from the point of view
of added status, because officials of the highest order, from the
Secretary of the US Navy down, called to meet the Town Council on
special visits, and there was contact with Congressmen from time to
time.   The Cowal people were divided, however; some applauded the
visits, many more simply stayed at home.

In outscape terms, the governments, whether Labour or Tory, did
not appear to want to see an end to the American presence, whatever
the protestations of the Labour party before regaining office.   CND
was suffering in the 1970s from a national apathy over the old
issues of nuclear disarmament, and repeated let-downs by Labour
spokesmen over the years.   In terms of national policies, there
appeared to have been a laissez-faire attitude towards what went on
at the Base, especially after the British established their own
Polaris Base at nearby Faslane.   Was it because Britain's submarines were installed with the Polaris system by the USA, which
was, in fact, a totally American installation?   Was the US Base at
Holy Loch guaranteed, in other words, as long as the UK required
the US ballistic system on its submarines at Faslane?

Judging from my Dunoon electoral soundings in the autumn of 1974, there were indications that there was considerable aggravation over the American presence on the grounds of being a local nuisance and such-like social factors which will be dealt with in the next chapter.   More people wanted the personnel to go and even the influentials were beginning to have mixed feelings about the USN incomers. A growing number, because of the blacks, were uneasy about their presence, which had political undertones.   There were many, as will be seen, who wanted the Polaris Base to close.   In spite of local SNP spokesman's statement that Polaris was a dead issue, I felt that one had only to scratch the surface locally to find latent anti-USN feelings in East Cowal.   Over the years local protests have had to be ignored or 'mystified' by the Commander at Base. fact, his role has been crucial throughout, in macro and micro terms.   He has had to play to so many galleries - both military and civilian.

Commanders, at the Polaris Base have been caught between 'the demands' of the civil-military upper echelons of the US Navy Department and the local influentials and Cowal citizens.   The full story of the stresses and pressures upon the Commander and his senior staff will never be known.   When I approached the USN authorities back in 1973 through an influential friend in the USA for information regarding the constitution of the Polaris Base, its lines of command and its civil-military relations, I was told the information was classified.   When I asked to see the Commander at Base I was passed on to the Community Relations Adviser at Sandbank Naval Centre, who as it transpired knew very little about the organisation and was truly a lay person outside of the inner sanctum of the organisation.

Given the need to assess the civil and political pressures at Base, and keeping in mind the distinctions between 'militarism', 'military ways' and 'civilianism', I had to turn to the ideas of D.R. Segal and M.W. Segal. (15)   The Segals suggested three models of organisation: the 'pre-bureaucratic', the 'bureaucratic' and the 'post-bureaucratic'.   These could be applied to the USN Base. In the monolithic organisation bureaucratic procedures are mainly charismatic leadership vestiges of an older military ethos now surviving in the 'militarism' of the Flag Officers and combat personnel and operational staff.   Whereas the bureaucratic procedures embody 'military ways', as implemented by institutional managers such as civil naval department administrators, e.g. in Washington.   Post-bureaucratic procedures are in evidence within the 'civilianism' which stress dialogue and collegiality as propagated by the newer technical managers and experts in the Navy Department.   The relevance of these often conflicting strands of activity will now be shown.

Figure 8.2 presents the conflicting salient influences which have impinged upon the personnel at the Polaris Base from the beginning and, as shall be explained further, upon the Commander in particular.   The lines of influence have become 'stressors' creating a problem for the Commanders, standing as they do between the mili-

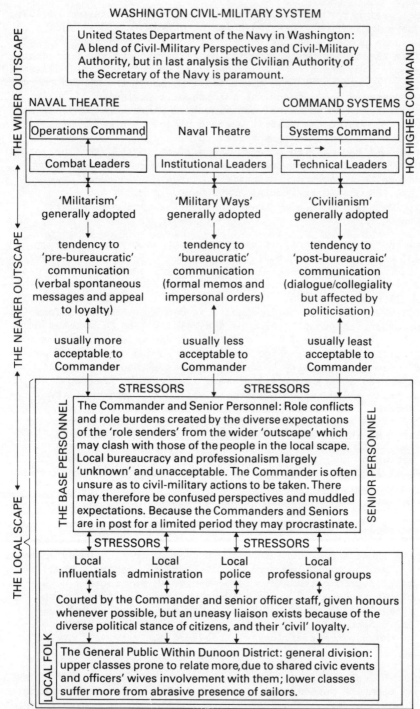

FIGURE 8.2 The salient military influences impinging upon the Commander and senior staff at the Polaris Base

tary outscape and the civilian local scape.   Most of the Commanders
have favoured pre-bureaucratic controls by reasons of their Academy
background and combat training.   Because of the conflict of principles and values between the civil and military scapes and because
of the unease with which 'militarism', 'military ways', and 'civilianism' coexist within the 'military scape' itself, the Commanders
could not possibly have been 'direct' in their dealings with locals,
especially when they have had to satisfy elites of the Washington
outscape in the last resort, whatever the costs to others.   Their
dealings have always had to be devious and secretive.

D. Sutton presents three key factors accounting for the field
behaviour inconsistencies of Commanders. (16)   These are: that
officials will conclude that there have been 'none'.   Naval men
have stated locally that informal reprimand is common at Holy Loch.
Also, the studies of P.Y. Hammond describe how the naval personnel
resent the intervention of the civilian Naval and Defense personnel
in military affairs. (17)   The best alternative is to handle the
problems within the overseas base itself, no matter how burdened the
Commanders may be.

With regard to the racial problems which are 'political dyna-
mite', the overseas Commander is largely thrown back upon his own
resources.   The racial problems at Base will be further described
in the next chapter.   In the USA the Base Commander can utilise the
'Command-Community Relations Committee' which includes representatives of both the base and the local community.   Such committees
provide him with an organisation framework for the discussion of
racial problems as they arise and to make it possible for him to
work in harmony with those who have influence locally and sympathy
for his problems.   The overseas Commander at Holy Loch lacks these
supports.   Navy Instructions No. 5350.6 also provides the Base
Commander with guidelines, but these apply more to the situation in
the States than they do to an overseas base.   A document, 'Military
Personnel Stationed Overseas and Participation in the National
Guard' (1964), caters for the situation outside the USA, but in
practice the Commander has to face the overseas problem of racial
antagonism locally and abide by his own judgment and insights.   On
the other hand, the men know their rights according to the United
States Commission on Civil Rights: 'The Negro in the Armed Forces'
(1963), and are quick to claim that they are being discriminated
against and that the Commander has not played his proper role on
their behalf. (18)   Every junior seaman can approach his Congressman, but the process is rather formidable and in an overseas base
the Commander may hide behind the local attitudes as a veil for his
own indifference or 'laissez-faire' policy.

From an examination of the Annual Opportunity Reports from 1963
to 1967, there have been only a few reported attempts by Commanders
to reduce discrimination off-Base.   If this has been so in the USA,
where there are more controls over the community-base approach to
the racial issues that can arise off-base, then one may wonder how
many Commanders at Holy Loch have taken action to lessen the problems that negroes have had to face within the naval quarters and
ashore.

The Commander at Holy Loch has to secure the good-will of the host country.   However, everything comes second to the military mission itself, so that at all costs he must secure the strategic post so important to the Department of Defense.   Pragmatism matters to the military man, and ultimately the military objective is paramount, whatever people's rights.   C.W. Mills writes: 'The military mind indicates the sharing of a common outlook, the basis of which is the metaphysical definition of reality as essentially military reality.   Even within the military realm, this mind distrusts "theorists", if only because they tend to be different.' (19)   And J.M. Swomley jnr points to the military preference for swiftness of action and impatience with democratic discussion and compromise. (20)   Diagonal intervention is favoured from above.

The second consideration is the possibility that the USN Commander's activities may be skewed by the fact that he is 'captive' within the local upper socioeconomic groups.   Pressures are brought to bear on Commanders by local power-elite groups.   There is an endless round of suppers and banquets, not to mention the local civil events, which the Commander is expected to attend.   These may have the effect of neutralising his mind and outlook, taking the elitist point of view and not considering that of the people at large, especially the lower socioeconomic groups.   When I was in Dunoon he lived in a mansion, 'Ardbeg House', like one of the old Glasgow tobacco grandees.   Sutton says that the Base Commander has to struggle to free himself from undue influence from the top sector. (21)   In this situation the Commander may act against the better interests of the majority of the locals, siding with elitist groups.   He is in charge at the Polaris Base for a relatively short period;   the local power-elite are there all the time.   They can make things difficult for him in the eyes of the host country's ruling bodies and government, which may jeopardise his position at the Polaris Base, and be reported 'back home'.

Commanders also depend on local dignitaries for references, as they face the proximity of retirement from the military.   So, they may simply adopt the view of the important hard-core of families locally, however unjust or distorted their views might be.

It may happen that the Commander becomes so involved in the milieu at 'boomtown' that he neglects some organisation issues at base.   One will never know the dilemmas which civil-military liaison have posed for the Holy Loch Commander.   Sutton writes: 'Often the harmonious base-community relationship can be taken as a symbol of successful management.' (22)

Sutton quotes a retired base Commander: 'I do not believe you get the backing of superiors if trouble develops.   They want you to push the programme but not to create any ill-will.   If trouble does develop ... you change the base commander.'   It is the Senate Armed Services Committee which decides ultimately on his removal or promotion, not merely the CNO (Commander Naval Operations), so that the civil contacts are often 'the' important ties, and at all costs the Commander will strive to preserve political harmony. (23)   When the

interests of a base do not match those of the local power-scape, the
Commander may be seen to adopt the 'civilianism' of the local power
elite, rather than the 'military ways' and 'militarism' of his naval
colleagues.   Indeed, living ashore, he could become estranged from
the combat captains, and in their eyes become identified with the
institutional bureaucrats, losing 'connective tissue' as leader at
base.   The situation is confusing, but thankfully for him the position is short lived at the Polaris Base.

Thirdly, the Commander may have internal communication problems.
The Department of Defense does sometimes issue conflicting inept
directives to bases.   There are well documented cases of this. (24)

There have been instances where friendly relations are given priority locally, where the Commander has informally supported racial
discrimination to conserve these links.   Weak cues from HQ put res-
ponsibilities and decisions squarely upon his shoulders.   The Judge
Advocate is sometimes called in to interpret the naval directives,
and his interpretation may be adopted, but if it is enforced it is
the Commander's responsibility.   The advocate in any case always
adds 'in my opinion' to his interpretations.   Legal confusions have
multiplied in the past.

The organisation of the Polaris Base changes continually as submarines come and go, bringing several repercussions for the American
families ashore and Polaris personnel at the ship and dock.   The
span of the Commander's cognition contracts and expands, or may even
snap at a time of too great a change.   Predictable precisions in
organising the interdependent parts is made possible by the messages
the Commander receives regarding the incoming vessels, but he cannot
be sure of the timing of supplies to meet the ever-changing needs of
Polaris, both in material terms and in personnel.   G. Homans, P.L.
Berkman, L.A. Zurcher jnr and R.W. Little have demonstrated in their
studies, much of them participant observational, that the coming and
going of ships, or personnel, bring about structural changes which
demand adaptation and a modification to leadership style to suit the
different needs of the personnel. (25)   'Consideration' is one
dimension which will need to be evidenced in the attitude of his
command towards the incoming SSBN crews, but at the same time, the
Commander may be attempting to establish a tightening of shore discipline to placate the local authorities or the host country's government.   Add to this the fact that the joy and jubilation on returning from a submerged stint rubs off on to other crews and personnel.   There is need not only to balance the needs of general
order with the needs of returning crews, but an 'initiating structure' must be carefully planned so as to weld the incoming personnel
with the shore and ship personnel.

It is this constant change which obstructs the easy management of
affairs for the Polaris Commander.   US supply ships to Holy Loch
carry crews whose loyalties are not those of the more permanent FBM
personnel, nor are they so socialised that their behaviour ashore
would measure up to the discipline of Polaris personnel.   To the
Commander these men are largely an unknown quantity, as also the
locals.

But what of the Community Relations Adviser at Holy Loch; is
this position not the answer to the problem of civil-military relations, and to the issue of fusion between FBM personnel and the
local residents?

To assist the Commander in his management of the local civil-
military relations is the Community Relations Adviser, a British
Ministry of Defence appointment, who apparently has to be female.
An advertisement for the post was published in the <u>Dunoon Observer</u>
<u>and Argyllshire Standard</u>, 20 October 1973.

Situations Vacant

COMMUNITY RELATIONS ADVISER
The Ministry of Defence has a vacancy for a Community Relations
Adviser, female (age 25-45), with the United States Naval Forces
at Dunoon, Argyllshire. The duties are to give guidance and
advice to American Forces personnel and their families stationed
in the area and to establish Scottish-American contacts with
local organisations and private individuals, and provide information on local and national activities of interest to the American
personnel.

Due to the nature of the work there can be no set hours and
some evening and week-end duties are not unusual. It is essential, therefore, that applicants should be of single status without domestic commitments.

Good education and appearance, outgoing personality, initiative and ability to type are necessary. A car is essential, for
which mileage allowance on duty is paid. Salary scale, £1850 to
£2136, four weeks' holiday a year. Application forms to be re-
turned within two weeks of the date of this advertisement, en-
closing a recent photograph.

Interviews will be held in London.

The employed Community Relations Adviser has to be immediately
answerable to the Commander, but her employer is the British
Ministry of Defence, which appointed her after interview in London.
It might appear at first that the appointment of such a person might
indicate that the USN Base would be able effectively to liaise with
the civil authorities and influential organisations in the locality,
and that the Commander had in her a specialist and local adviser.
(However, the woman appointed when I was in Dunoon was an outsider.
The locals respected her, but saw her as a temporary worker.) She
is also appointed in the outscape by a Ministry selection panel
wholly divorced from the Scottish scene. She is not a military
person, and so cannot be wholly identified with the military.
Being immediately answerable to the Commander, there is also a
danger that unpopular Staff decisions could be traced back to her.
On the other hand, being neither identified by USN personnel with
the military, nor the local people, she could become a gossip
centre, where USN personnel could speak of problems either on duty,
or on leave. Either way, she is in a vulnerable position. In

this situation the Community Relations Officer tends to 'escape' and become involved in organising travel packages and personnel excursions to Scottish beauty spots, or historic places.   When I eventually called to see the Community Relations Officer in 1973 I found her walls covered with many travel posters, and her desk strewn with tourist brochures.

Certainly there emerges from the available facts a great deal of stress within the monolithic military scape at Holy Loch, wherein 'militarism' and 'military ways' impose structures not only within the organisation but also upon those who are not in uniform.   The Commander must be devious to survive at the margins whilst dealing with the elusive machinations of the militarists in upper command and the bureaucratic HQ demands made upon him.   There is the 'civilianism' which politically involves him in 'oblique' programmes to extend naval installations ashore in the peaceful settlements, by creating the impression that the influentials have everything to gain by having a naval boom town in Argyll.   The US Naval Department demands that the personnel have a low military profile so that they usually wear civilian clothes in town with no flags in sight, few military cars, and fairy lights on the grey bows and stern of naval vessels.   'Assimilation' is the battle-cry of the civil echelons at Washington;   so in Dunoon the errands of the naval wives at homes for the elderly and for deprived children attempt to humanise the whole exercise of military imperialism.   The activity may manifestly be charitable, but latently it is largely political, however personally sincere some individuals may be.

Having dealt with the Polaris Base in terms of its political scape, what can be said about the McAlpine project at Ardyne?

Under the impact of the rush for oil, the rig and concrete gravity builders strove to secure sites in an irrational fashion.   The SNP MP for the area, Iain MacCormick, was busy protecting the interests of his small electorate against these giant inroads, especially during 1974-5.   He saw the US's quest for a solution to inflation through oil development as another example of England's intrusion in Scottish local affairs.   He accused the Scottish Office of being the 'English Office' and the government of interfering with local planning applications instead of leaving decisions to local authorities. (26)

The SNP MP and his electorate were blocked by a conspiracy of secrecy at both Ardyne and the Scottish Office.   McBarnett has elaborated upon this elsewhere, where he shows that onshore development plants and rig-building sites kept people out, and any information jealously to themselves.   I myself found it easier to have access to the decks of the USS Canopus and the Base installations than I did the Ardyne complex.   Information was not available either.   McBarnett points out that the oil development chief 'made it a point of principle never to allow access except under very special supervision, or for official press facility trips which gave very little idea'. (27)   As seen already, the mode of impact associated with Ardyne had elements of secrecy and oblique dealings.

The locals had heard of the McAlpine venture in the <u>Dunoon</u>
<u>Observer</u> of 4 November 1972, which was shock enough, but in the
issue of 9 December 1972 they learned, as seen already, that a forum
met to review the options for Ardyne at the Excelsior Hotel, Airport
in the first week of December.   Planning and debate seemed to be
denied the locals from the start.   Discussions of importance were
stated on 'the other side' close to the airport to suit national and
international influentials.   The effect was to increase a sense of
local helplessness.

The McAlpine venture had accentuated the macro events of the UK's
national drive for oil, and the Scottish debate as to 'whose oil' it
was.   The SNP followers watched helplessly.   In spite of Scottish
national protests decisions were made across the border to explore
Scottish waters and to set up sites for platform- and rig-building
on Scottish shores, while Tory followers quoted the national need,
and saw the whole North Sea programme as an Anglo-Scottish effort.
The McAlpine venture took everyone by surprise when announced in the
tabloid columns of the <u>Dunoon Observer</u> of 4 November 1972.   The
area was a tourist centre, committed to attracting holiday-makers,
which was already strained by the USN presence.   A local hearing
was called for.   However, in the first week of December, McAlpine
staged the main forum for discussion and declaration of intent, not
in the locality, but on 'the other side'.

Contacts were made in the outscape, where the power lay.   An
immediate effect was that the Town Council felt left out of the
whole affair, negotiations having been made almost exclusively with
the Argyll County Council.   This had not happened with the USN
invasion.   Then the town councillors were brought in from the
start; not so in the case of McAlpine's venture.

The oblique and zig-zag tactics to secure the shore at Ardyne,
already outlined in an earlier chapter, were clearly successful.
The local farmers and the stretch of shore terrain were already won
over by McAlpine whilst the locals were pursuing other matters.
Minimal information had been leaked out as McAlpine senior management took advantage of the situation in which London officials gave
maximum leeway to industrialists prepared to procure oil rig or
concrete platform building sites throughout Scotland.   Planning
permissions had never been easier to procure.   Local people felt
angry.

The political mood that pervaded the area at that time was highlighted for me during the autumn election of 1974, when the SNP
staged a huge local motorcade on the last Saturday afternoon before
the electorate went to the polls.

Forty-seven cars moved through the locality, beginning in Argyll
Street.   They were led by a breakdown van, carrying aloft a
battered and rusty blue Tory car with its party stickers.   It hung
from a small crane, like a man on the gallows.   The streets echoed
with the strains of 'A Scottish Soldier', and as the cars followed,
bedecked with SNP streamers, the whole spectacle resembled a victory

parade. In the middle of the long line of cars was a large float
with three large dummies of the Labour, Tory and Liberal leaders,
sitting upon three drums of 'Scottish Oil'. Underneath was a large
banner: 'Look - they're stealing our oil'. Meantime, a long line
of Tory cars came up a side-street to Argyll Street, hooting their
horns and shouting out abuse. I was handed a small leaflet: 'Work
for Scots at Ardyne', which went on to state: 'It's our country,
our oil, and our industry.' It was not an SNP handout, but it reflected the agitation and concern of many Scottish people.

In the midst of local controversy the timely publication of a
booklet, 'Ardyne Tomorrow', appeared which was to have a dramatic
effect upon local opinions on both sides. It was free and politically significant for the public at large, and well timed. What
did it have to say? Why was it politically significant?

The booklet, published by request of McAlpine and Sons, was in
print when the first concrete gravity structure platform was successfully floated out into the Clyde in March 1975. It appeared to
offer a pledge that the area around Ardyne would be restored after
the completion of the required rigs. It also set out alternative
plans for local discussion. Its content and format reflected the
concern of the construction engineers for the ecology and social
quality of life locally, utilising the expertise of staff from the
universities of Aberdeen, Edinburgh and Birmingham, the Clyde
Estuary Amenity Committee, the Clyde Port Authority, Clyde Yacht
Clubs Association, Scottish Countryside Commission, Scottish Development Department, Scottish Marine Biological Association, Scottish
National Trust, Shellfish Association and Toward Civic Trust, and
others.

A million cubic feet of earth had been moved. Justification was
required. Fishermen were also afraid that the herring fishing in
Loch Fyne might be damaged irretrievably and many local people, as
has been shown, were concerned about socioeconomic repercussions in
Cowal, so the booklet came as a welcome discussion document. The
document declared itself to be independent, and set out to present
an outline for a working party, to be distributed to administrators,
local influentials and put in public places such as the library in
Castle Gardens, Dunoon.

The 'Foreword' opened as follows: 'Sir Robert McAlpine and Sons
are pledged to the restoration of their oil platform construction
site at Ardyne at the conclusion of their leases and planning permissions. This would probably conclude their active involvement in
this beautiful corner of Argyll.' (28) With regard to the uncertainty expressed (notice the word 'probably') on the question of the
time scale, it stated: 'Other assumptions may prove equally wrong.
It is assumed that Ardyne's place in the North Sea oil story is to
last perhaps ten years.' (29) Those who were 'for' the scheme saw
employment prospects in it; those who were against it saw an end to
it in the near future. In addition, the impression taken from the
publication at meetings and in local groupings was that there would
be other projects at Ardyne once the platforms were completed,

perhaps a marina, so that the drastic impact at Ardyne would have
been justified.   However, today the site is a derelict and aban-
doned spot.   By 1977, the place had quickly wound down, and well
within a decade.   In fact, the 'futuribles' made the whole document
for those who cared to study it rather nebulous.   One effect of the
Ardyne venture was to expose the public to sophisticated overtures,
and dubious public relations exercises.

   What the document ignored was the USN presence.   The area was
still under the USN impact and would McAlpine's venture not add to
it?   In fact, a flight over the area is described in the brochure
without any reference to the vessels at Holy Loch.   The conjuncture of events, emphasised in this book, demonstrates that the impact
of one intrusion cannot be isolated from the overlap of others.
The fact was that McAlpine's venture may never have been allowed, if
the increase in socioeconomic pressures locally had been fully taken
into account.   McAlpine was well served by the publication of
'Ardyne Tomorrow', because it was in reality a political document
which allayed local concern about both present and future matters.
Firstly, with regard to the current employment situation, it gave
the impression that the incoming work-force would not be too large,
whereas the number was far in excess of a thousand.   It was impossible for locals, or myself, to get a precise statement from management.   Secrecy usually shrouds the work-details of firms, especially so at that time, when they vied with each other for orders,
sites and manpower in the rush for stakes in the shore development
associated with the North Sea explorations for oil.

   Local residents had been concerned that the contractors might
leave behind them a wasted shoreline.   But after the publication
people were stating locally that McAlpine would build a marina on
the Ardyne site.   (This sailing centre scheme was the second
'option' of six in the document.)   Certainly, the McAlpine sponsorship of the study and published document had succeeded in pushing
aside the old mistrusts created by the planning schemes, when Ardyne
had been secured amidst oblique dealings.   These were all above the
law, but were commercial ploys, so that yet another giant from the
outscape had succeeded in plundering local resources to the benefit
of the outside concern, whatever the costs locally.   The rumours
about a marina and the golden future for Ardyne, once the platform
programme closed down, were then locally in circulation and a bright
'future scape' was then predicted.

   The document referred to its dealings with Argyll County Council
and its commitments to the Council, but the County Council was
shortly to pass away with the new regionalisation that came into
force exactly four weeks after the publication of the document.
There is enough legal ambiguity here alone to make one wonder
exactly what rulings or commitments were valid after May 1975.
Enough ambiguity had existed before - when the County Council was in
control.

   The macro political patronage of a government anxious to catch
up with foreign rig-builders aided outscape control of the work-

force.   It brought into the locality a giant enterprise which
prioritised in terms of international interests, and whose future
plans had, of necessity, to be dictated by events and power scapes
outside the locality.   The nationwide crisis over inflation, and
the widespread belief that 'oil was the answer', made it impossible
for the handful of people around Ardyne and the rural population
within the vicinity to devise a strategy which would attract widespread support for their protests over the intrusion.

Throughout the early months of planning and bartering at Ardyne,
the Town Council had no profile, and it was to remain so throughout
the years of production at Ardyne up to the demise of the Council in
1975.   The SNP MP stepped into the situation and took upon himself
the central local role.   It might be argued that the Town Council
was not to be involved because Ardyne was outside the burgh.   However, so was Holy Loch, but the USN personnel and government at that
time had respected the political standing of the Town Council (that
local parliament) with the knowledge that the ruling committee members of the old capital of Cowal saw the American presence as good
for business and local commerce.   When McAlpine moved into the area
the contractor knew well that local tourism, services and commerce
would be threatened so McAlpine avoided the local centre of business
and tourism and stressed the national need in overtures to the
County Council, although it would be Dunoon which would be most involved and most affected in socioeconomic terms locally.   The significant centres to which the firm paid its respects lay in the outscape, not at Castle Chambers, Dunoon.   The Town Council was to
fold up in May 1975; the McAlpine intrusion added to its weakening
role as a Cowal institution.   The involvement of the MP within the
area in all matters related to McAlpine's venture stressed more and
more the irrelevance of the Town Council in its last months in
office.

In local scape terms, the Ardyne venture also had a divisive
effect politically.   Secondary unintended consequences consisted
mainly of splitting the SNP followers.   Firstly, there were those
who managed to work at Ardyne, and secondly those who were turned
away.   The irony was that at first they were encouraged to apply,
and then were refused employment.   There were locals who told me
that the change of tactic was to satisfy the 'Tory' shopkeepers and
businessmen.   The oblique tactics were dictated by expediency.
There was a sense of 'let-down', which for some turned into political disillusionment.   The Ardyne venture had helped bring into the
locality anti-Irish feelings which had political undertones.   In
this instance the conflict of interests both political and religious
in Ulster were dragged into the local political arena of Cowal, and
antagonisms created between lower socioeconomic groups.

For approximately five years before McAlpine's local venture
there appeared to have been strong anti-Irish feelings, which
appeared to have been fostered locally by the Orange Lodge.
Although the Lodge did not itself become associated with gun-
running, a local Cowal man with Orange Lodge connections was convicted in Glasgow High Court of conspiring to rob the Ardyne wage

van at gun-point.   The money he was to have taken was to have been
for the anti-IRA cause in Ulster.   The trial at Glasgow was particularly embarrassing for the local population, because the man was
from one of the most respectable business families of Dunoon.
There was national coverage in the press, whilst the local press
reported the main story and the family left the locality.

There is no doubt that change over the years in endogenous terms
had moved in the direction of greater tolerance and openness, as has
been shown in the assessment of the historical scape in an earlier
chapter, but the McAlpine navvy invasion in conjunction with the
events in Ulster and the intrustion from outside of a group of
Orange Lodge campaigners created exogenous change in the opposite
direction.

I decided to explore the feelings of the locals by noting political slogans or snide remarks which appeared as graffiti in the local
toilets between February 1975 and February 1976.   There was an
underworld which could be explored and where inhibitions were thrown
aside.   As they were to show, the graffiti indicated that there
were political battles being waged between the youths of the area
and the incomers which had in fact been alien to the locality.   As
it turned out, the findings threw some light upon local political
animosity.   I checked Dunoon male toilets early each Monday morning
throughout twelve months from the last day in February 1975 to the
first day of February 1976 inclusively.   I was assessing the impact
of a male work-force, hence the exploration in male toilets.   The
toilets of the old burgh were well distributed: three in the town
centre, three to the south-west of the pier, four to the north-west
(one closed down after my research began), and one at the pier.
Outside Dunoon, I regularly checked toilet graffiti in the main male
toilets at Toward, Ardentinny, and Sandbank.

Obviously, the graffiti were largely concerned with the usual
vulgarities, etc.   Toilets in East Cowal were much the same as anywhere else.   However, within Dunoon, statements concerned with the
Ardyne workers and related matters were scrawled on walls approximately six times a month on average, whereas those concerning the
USN personnel and related matters were written about three times
monthly inside the ten toilets visited.   The three toilets visited
'furth' of Dunoon, in sharp contrast, seldom had graffiti which referred to the incomers.   Dunoon graffiti proved to be of significance in a political context.

Whereas only one reference to the USN presence locally had a
political flavour, all but three of 77 graffiti within Dunoon did
have political connotations.   The term 'IRA' figured in statements
in 38 out of the remaining 74 graffiti.   'King Billy Rules'
featured in 14; 'Republican' in 9; and the other 13 statements
represented a combination of terms mentioning either 'papes' or 'the
Boyne' in contexts such as: 'Ulster is British - keep the papes
out.'   More than half of the statements with a political flavour
were written on the walls of the toilet by Kirk Brae in the centre
of the town nearest the bus-stand for Ardyne buses.

But, there were gibes against both the Irish and against the
locals, side by side.   In fact, 30 out of the 41 statements regarding the locals and associated matters were scrawled upon the walls
of the Kirk Brae toilet.   It would therefore appear that given the
position of the toilet near the Ardyne bus stop, the anti-local
remarks came probably from the Irish Ardyne workers, whose remarks
were countered by some local men who were also working at Ardyne.
One heard horrific stories of the fights between the 'Irish papes'
and the 'orange lads' or the 'Wasps'*.   But, in the other toilets
the anti-Irish remarks with political allusions, etc. were not
usually countered by anti-local remarks to the same extent.   It
could be that sixteen graffiti at the Hunters Quay toilet to the
north-east of Dunoon which were anti-Irish were the work of local
men who were not working at Ardyne, as also just a few graffiti in
the other toilets apart from the pier at Dunoon.   This would fit in
with the growing frustration locally amongst Cowal men, in particular, over their inability to secure employment at Ardyne.   Given
the number of Ulster and UK bombings associated with the IRA, and
the influx of Irish navvies and the upsurge of an Orange Lodge group
locally (who incidentally had won favour with one of the local
councillors), the anti-Irish male grievance expressed itself politically in strong terms.   There was no doubt that events in the outscape had aggravated the situation.

What of the possible confrontation between the Irish and the
Americans?   As shall be demonstrated in the next chapter, the
Americans and the navvies hardly ever met, because generally they
frequented different haunts.   So political confrontation was only
occasional.

Having dealt with the manner in which the McAlpine intrusion had
affected the political scape, what of the Strathclyde take-over in
Cowal?

By way of summing up the way in which the local residents
inscaped the impact of Strathclyde, and the associated changes that
accompanied the change involved, it must be noted that from 1968
people were politically divided over the whole question of reorganisation.   The bureaucracy involved set up the regional scheme in an
oblique fashion.   The decisions were made over a long period in an
almost stop-go fashion so that people became confused, and when eventually decisions were made they appeared almost unreal, and divided
the people.

As already indicated in Part Two, the people were split over the
reform of local government, and even those who were in favour were
divided over details.   The split was mainly in the burgh; outside
it the villagers were opposed to the regional changes.   This division of town and country, of villager and burgher, and of burgher
with burgher, meant that regionalisation had opened up rifts across
an area once noted for its cohesiveness.   The people around Holy
Loch appeared to have lost their trust in the townspeople of Dunoon

* This stood for 'White Anglo-Saxon Protestant'.

because they had seen how town leaders and influentials had put the prospect of making money out of the American invasion before the inconvenience caused to the villagers around the Polaris Base. At the other end, the people living by Ardyne and Toward had also seen how the Dunoon people had welcomed the prospect of more employment for the young, chiefly in the burgh, at the expense of the inconveniences caused to the villagers. Money had divided; once again the old axiom of the Middleton studies applied here: 'People know money, but they don't know you', or to quote the old Latin tag: 'Pecunia non olet' (money does not smell). At the secondary surprise level the Strathclyde impact had further divided the locals. It has been noted that the Town Council was divided over the issue of Strathclyde. Obviously, none of the council had wanted the demise of the Town Council, but given the decision of government, nothing could be done. It was, however, the old issue of whether Cowal should be linked with 'the other side', or with the Highlands, which really was the next big concern of the council members and their followers.

For many, especially the SNP and Tory electorate, being in Strathclyde had the effect of altering the political profile of the locality. The Labour party was strong in Glasgow, and given that ultimate authority in regional terms lay with Glasgow, fears grew that the Labour elite there might interfere with Cowal.

McCormick voiced his concern soon after the general election; and complained, on 9 November 1974, in the Daily Express: 'Half the people of Scotland are in danger of coming under the dictatorship of the Labour leaders of Glasgow Corporation.' Locally, the people of the villages were openly talking about 'the mutilation of Cowal' and the Labour party's hand in 'the carve-up'. Many people in the burgh, especially the elder and senior citizens, also mourned the demise of the Town Council and the ending of the long line of provosts. The regalia and the chain of office were now museum pieces, which added injury to injury by their eventual removal to Lochgilphead. No one had ever expected that such a thing would happen. It was the unkindest cut of all for proud Dunoon.

The struggle between Dunoon Burgh over the years to secure all County Council offices at Dunoon has already been referred to, and also the political struggle between the officials at Lochgilphead and the Dunoon Town Council. Earlier, when the new reorganisation scheme was first discussed, Lochgilphead appeared not to feature, but as already noted, the town lost out to Lochgilphead by the narrowest of margins. The effect was one that left the burghers both annoyed and humiliated. The removal of the regalia of the provost's office to Lochgilphead, referred to above, rounded off the last sad episode for Dunoon's old parliament. Worse things, however, had happened.

When the change-over to Strathclyde was not only in debate, but being prepared for by the authorities, it was suggested that in the future Argyll be known as West Strathclyde. That was in the winter of 1975. The Dunoon Observer printed a letter from an angered

reader which epitomised the mood and the protest that the change
created.   The issue of 15 February cited his objection: 'Are we in
Argyll now to become West Strathclyders?... Will his Grace the Duke
now have to change his address to West Strathclyde instead of
Inveraray, Argyll?'   The decision met with the full onslaught of
the entire county, which may be demonstrated by the fact that over
6,000 signatures were collected in Cowal, many more than had ever
been collected in protest against the Polaris Base!   By April the
suggestion had had to be dropped and 'Argyll' remained as the postal
address of the County.

It would appear that for many the Region was considered on the
whole to have been harmful.   Many took it as adding yet again to
the waning image of the old burgh, whose motto, 'Forward', looked
rather ludicrous in the circumstances.   For many, the Council
Chambers at the old castle house had been the political arena where
local grouses and indeed ideas could be tabled and immediately reported in the local press.   Strathclyde ruined all of this.   But,
there were some who saw the passing of the Town Council as a bles-
sing, because for them it epitomised the ending of local privilege,
which will shortly be discussed when I review the responses of the
local residents to my questions during my stay in the locality.
Before I do so, the question of creating local Community Councils
will have to be considered, because it is linked with the fragmentation caused by the creation of Strathclyde.

The authorities had hoped that the new Community Councils, which
would complement the Regions, would attract the electorate.   The
Councils were designed to be the mouthpiece of the local electorate.
Strathclyde adverts described them under the banner headline: 'Community Councils: The Part You Can Play'.   The setting up of these
proved to be problematic.   Firstly, they were to be established
within Districts by a scheme to be drawn up by the District Council
to be submitted to the Secretary of State for Scotland, not later
than 16 May 1976. (30)   Without entering into the exact nature of
these councils, suffice it to say that when I left the area in February 1976 the fragmentation over inclusion or exclusion from
Strathclyde had blocked communal discussion.   Secondly, the suggestion that under a hundred people of a small village could form a
Community Council, or take the form of a larger one on a 'locality'
basis fired some Dunoonites to create a council to serve the locality, but villagers wanted their own council.

Division, already created by the regional debate, was further
exacerbated by villages competing with villages in the race to have
a Community Council, whereas Dunoon argued for a larger locality
council.   All this debate took place before the 'Draft Scheme For
The Establishment of Community Councils' was sent to the area by the
Argyll and Bute District Council in which areas were identified with
the polling districts.   So some suggested that there could be as
many as 45 Community Councils in the new District, which people considered a huge joke.   Some went it alone, because, after all, the
councils would only be advisory;   for example, a Community Association was set up in Hunters Quay on 9 July 1975, on totally different

lines from the Draft Scheme.   The result was that political confusion followed.

Taking the points made earlier in this study concerning concepts
of change, impact and community, it is clear that the Community
Councils opened up problems of identity for the people of the locality.   Overall, there was the 'master identity' of Cowal people, but
within it a more and more specific set of identities, either of
settlement or locational (e.g. 'By Holy Loch', 'By Toward').   What
the draft scheme (as set out by the new officials) did was to give
the public notice that it was proposing to establish areas within
electoral boundaries as community units from which people could be
elected.   Notoriously, electoral boundaries do not coincide with
those of meaningful communities.

Having commented upon the conjuncture of events and the divisions
caused by Strathclyde, it will be worthwhile assessing my street
interviews with the local people which may elucidate some of the
political effects, and the import of Strathclyde in the eyes of a
cross-section of the electorate at that time.

Before reorganisation in the autumn of 1974, when I interviewed
people in the streets of the burgh, only nineteen out of the 130
chosen at random had explicitly stated in answer to an open-ended
question that they wanted removal of the locality from Strathclyde. (31)   There seemed to have been less concern in 1974, but
in 1975-6, when it came to my interviews after reorganisation in 525
Cowal households, I found that all but seven of the 525 interviewed
had read the supplement on reorganisation attached to the Dunoon
Observer just before the implementation so that interest was great
and, in contrast with the street interviews, opposition was impressive with 336, 64 per cent of the people selected randomly for
interview actually stating that they were opposed to reorganisation.
There were 109, 20.8 per cent, however, who agreed with it, and
also 80, 15.2 per cent who did not indicate what they felt. (32)
One may be able to deepen an understanding of what was happening by
taking a closer look at the people who were opposed to Strathclyde.

A greater proportion of the rural residents whom I interviewed
(61.8 per cent) were opposed to Strathclyde, most of whom had supported the SNP MP.   With regard to those who supported Strathclyde,
all were Tories by political preference.   78 of them had only been
in the locality under ten years, with only three who had resided
there for more than twenty years.   As Tories, they were less inclined to listen to McCormick's repeated attacks on the scheme.
Where linkage with 'the other side' was strongest, agreement with
regionalisation was greatest.

What was of interest was the fact that sixty-one locals referred
in conversation to the ending of local privilege, in one form or
another.   About half, 30, of these spoke in terms of 'the face that
did not fit' when it came to having a hearing in the old days of the
Town Council.   R. Taylor, a community worker in Cowal, wrote of the
'Ach Him - A' Kent His Father' (Oh him - I knew his father'). (33)

With it, went the stigmatisation of certain families and the glori-
fication of others.   It was evident that more than half of those
who were opposed to the continuance of the older set-up had felt
that a good effect of the regional reorganisation was the thwarting
of parochial privilege.

There was another political sounding which I took during my 525
interviews in the autumn/winter of 1975-6.   Political opinion is
often expressed in story-telling and often with the aim of exposing
the stupidity of government or of those in authority, or simply to
conserve group prejudice or group hostilities.   This may be the
best weapon to use, outside of formal polemical confrontations.
The newspaper cartoon serves as an example of a similar political
tool.   Often the repeated story says more about the political situation than learned commentaries.   Sometimes the stories are mere
fabrication, and at other times symbolic, and sometimes true
accounts, but whatever their source or veracity, they may be a
political cement, drawing people together when under threat or
coping with alien inroads.   Three stories which were passed around
locally struck me as worth quoting to the 525 interviewees to serve
as an indicator of local reaction and as a measure of local cynicism.   The first story (which I will shortly repeat) was used particularly to check out cynicism with regard to Strathclyde.   It had
political undertones, and I knew from informal conversation it was
making the rounds within the gossip network locally.

The Strathclyde story in vogue in East Cowal during 1975 was
about a Kilmun roadsweeper, to whom a letter was sent from the
Glasgow bureaucrats just after reorganisation.   The story described
how the letter specified that he was to go personally at the start
of each working day to his local District HQ where he was to be informed of his daily duties.   The District HQ happened to be Lochgilphead.   For those not familiar with the public services and the
distances in Argyll, such a journey would have meant a whole day's
journey.   He had no car, so he had to go into Dunoon, take a ferry
to Gourock, catch a train to Glasgow, and then go by bus to Lochgilphead (which buses were very infrequent).

The second story which I repeated with a view to testing local
reaction was concerned with a bizarre American wedding in Dunoon
where the bride, a local girl, left her reception to throw herself
off the Dunoon coal jetty into the Firth of Clyde, because she had
discovered that the night before 'the best maid' had slept with her
American naval groom.   It ended with the best maid preventing her
at the coal jetty from taking the plunge (as it happened, it was at
low tide!)

The third story dealt with an incident concerning a semi-nude
McAlpine navvy, who at two in the morning was saved by a taxi driver
from the hands of an irate husband in Dunoon because he had been
caught in bed with the local man's wife.   Chased right up to the
taxi cabs, with the husband still in hot pursuit, he failed at first
to hire a driver, because, as he admitted, he had no money.   The
taxi driver, who eventually took him, did so on trust that he would

pay upon arrival at Ardyne camp.   They left in the nick of time
with the irate husband shouting abuse on the pavement.

163 (31.1 per cent) of my interviewees had heard the first story,
or a similar version, which had political innuendos and was slanted
against the Strathclyde Bureaucracy.   Only 78 (14.9 per cent) had
heard the second, and only 66 (12.6 per cent) had heard the third
story. (34)   Figure 8.3 presents the origin of the stories and the
residence of those who heard them.   The political story slanted
against Strathclyde had been mainly passed on in Dunoon centre as
also were the other two stories.   Dunoon was clearly the gossip
centre, especially of snide political talk.

What relevance had the story-telling to the political impact of
Strathclyde as presently discussed?   The political sphere at micro
level is played out within informal settings.   Often debate and
political influence are most effective in neighbourhood haunts,
where political expression finds a way of saying things in the idiom
of a particular group, or class, or settlement, etc.   Just as in
the case of the toilet graffiti, so too here I took the opportunity
to sample the local cynicism and the political undertones by using
unconventional methods.

Evidently, Dunoon was operating not so much as a centre for
scandalous stories but rather as an informal information centre,
quick to pick up politically loaded observations (as the locals
would say, 'the latest').   Such a sharing in shop doorways confirmed shared convictions about Strathclyde.   The anti-Strathclyde
story served to cement town and rural people.   Town contacts were
talking with the people 'furth'of Dunoon about their shared anti-
pathy.   They did so on Argyll Street, which road, as already seen,
was an embarrassment to Strathclyde.

Unlike the USN and Ardyne impacts, Strathclyde was affecting
every single household, because of the increased rates.   Common
plight and adversity have a way of uniting people.   The issue of
Strathclyde had been divisive before and during the first months
after implementation, but in the spin-off period, people appeared
to be more united against Strathclyde.

Summing up the impact of Strathclyde upon the political scape, it
is immediately evident that neither the effects of the USN presence,
nor that of the McAlpine intrusion had shaken the political scape,
as did the new regional scheme of Strathclyde.   First of all the
USN presence had actually strengthened the Dunoon Town Council's
position by giving it added status.   Whilst the Ardyne venture
weakened it, the Strathclyde scheme destroyed it altogether.   There
is no doubt from the reading of the history of Dunoon and of Cowal,
that the Town Council was 'the' central local institution, with the
greatest political influence at micro level.   Ex-provosts and ex-
councillors and baillies, because of their attachment to the council and offices within it, had also enjoyed local political prestige
because of it.   Three of the greatest influentials, Mr Black, Mr
Wyatt, and Miss McPhail were ex-provosts whom the USN senior staff

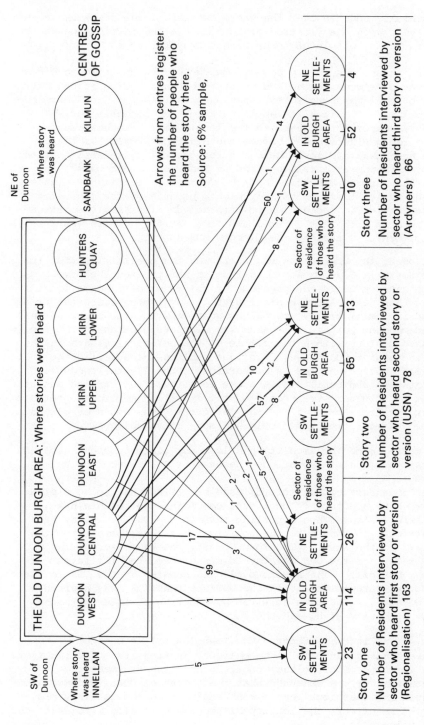

FIGURE 8.3 The centres of gossip with regard to the three stories and where transmitted

had carefully courted over the years because of their status in the locality.   With the creation of Strathclyde the institution which had been their vehicle of power passed away for ever.

In addition, the County Council was gone.   With it ended old feuds waged between Dunoon and county; but now the political battle at micro level was simply realigned and hostility in fact increased politically.   The locality would have to face Lochgilphead, whilst the shore councillors presented the local view.   Lochgilphead through reorganisation had become the District centre, so that Dunoon and Cowal had lost their bid for greater self-determination. The locality was at first weakened by inner divisions caused in part by the Strathclyde debate.   And the Community Councils at that time created, rather than healed, divisions, because of the confusion over boundaries.   Opposition to Strathclyde after implementation was uppermost both in the rural and town areas.   There was evidence of cynicism against the Glasgow bureaucrats.

Moreover, in outscape terms, there was the possibility that the Labour party in Glasgow would intrude in and through the powers at HQ upon an area where the presence of the major parties in local politics had been almost non-existent.   Any independence the area enjoyed in administrative terms had gone, now it also appeared that any independence within the wards was also evaporating as the locality was caught up within the battle of the political giants in the wider and nearer outscapes.   Oblique tactics characterise the political machinations of the major parties.   Locally there had been confrontation and conflicts, but the locality often carried out its debates and counter strategies 'on the level' in horizontal terms and usually face-to-face; now the political games would be played in macro terms, often indirectly and more often obliquely.

In macro terms the locality had lost any claim it might have had to local political independence, because of all three impacts.

The Commanders of the Polaris Base since 1961 had to be diplomatic with regard to the locality's complaints yet maintain a 'militarist' stance when reporting them to the US HQ.   They had also strictly to adhere to the political messages coming from the Secretary of the Navy.   The Town Council was respected by the CNO and Secretary of the USN, as the Commanders courted the favour of the Town Council.   The numerous plaques donated by the USN to the Town Council are memorials of the USN's successful sway over the local council.   The Base survived by adopting oblique approaches towards authority at HQ and the local Town Council.

The Ardyne incomers ignored the Town Council at Dunoon. McAlpine's moves had also to be oblique, putting first the interests of the firm and offering the County Council the argument that the national fuel crisis demanded that the shores of Cowal become industrialised and that local employment would bring the locality prosperity.   In effect, the local parliament was totally irrelevant and highly vulnerable.

Strathclyde had the greatest micro effect upon the political scape because with regionalisation the Dunoon Town Council ceased to exist, and Lochgilphead, the old rival, had become the District HQ. When the rates rose dramatically, people realised that they could no longer walk up to their administrators and argue face-to-face about their predicaments.   Dunoon and the locality were now within the grips of one of the largest regional administrative units in Europe.

Chapter 9

CULTURE CLASHES

It is expectations about one's life evaluations of present and
future, which guarantee or bedevil any social system. Where the
mentalities of a people diverge from the social predicament surrounding them, tensions and frustrations erupt. (H. Brody)(1)

The cultural scape has earlier been described as routine patterns of
living, consisting of customary behaviour, and rituals within a
social calendar. The routines are mediated by conventions, traditions, and customs, giving rise to expectations. The cultural
scape is essentially observable 'ad extra', but is also associated
with the mentalities of people, hence the expectations.

In everyday living people will become accustomed to each other's
mode of behaviour, and however unacceptable it may be to some of
them, it will be part of the 'social construction' of life in which
they find themselves. (2) The cultural scape is socially construc-
ted over time within established local patterns of behaviour, and
the smaller the locality or settlement, the more aware people will
usually be of alternation to the routines. Some social scientists
with David Schneider restrict 'culture' to the mentality of people;
however, Richard Feinberg objects to this, (3) and lays stress upon
the established order of behaviour (in Ogburn's terms, the well
tried 'utilities'). The cultural scape as described in this study
lies somewhere in between, being part the established order and part
the dominant mentality. The latter gives rise to expectations regarding norms and also any familiar deviance from the norms. The
overall quality of life is the outcome of habit and expectation.
H. Brody observes in his Inishkillane study that maintenance of culture under pressures is crucially dependent upon 'consciousness', (4) which is in keeping with A.P. Cohen's ideas referred to
earlier. These contributions complement those of W.F. Ogburn who
stated:

Culture once in existence persists because it has utility.
Forces that produce changes are the discovery of new cultural
elements that have superior utility, in which case the old utilities tend to be replaced by the new. The slowness of culture

184

to change lies in the difficulties of creating and adopting new
ideas. (5)

When lags occur, as already pointed out, there will be a clash of
expectations.   Some stay with the old, some accept the new.   Such
preferences when shared within the groups or collections of people,
are transferred from being individual cognitive acts to take on a
social and collective importance.   Consciousness is established
within customary and familiar shared activities wherein shared perceptions and values are crucial, but which also have proved over
time to have utility.   People will be slow to alter the old utilities.   The families, groups, institutions, and milieus, to which
they belong will act as a brake.

H. Brody shows that self-criticism and comparisons that are
mainly social, financial and sexual, play a part in determining
whether people change their behaviour under the impact of contact
with people who have another way of life to theirs. (6)   The dominant ethic may be determined by socialisation within homes, schools
and churches, but also by other societal views and taboos created by
the media.   The media provide outscape pressures which modify the
locality's older social, financial and sexual utilities.   In other
words, the cultural scape is the outcome of traditional and customary practices which endure and survive as utilities.   When people
arrive from the outscape, they bring with them, their own habits and
orientations, which may increase the influence of the outscape
locally.

Some introductory remarks about the reaction of people in an area
under impact will help to identify some of the possible diverse
effects at psycho-social levels.

Older people may often live in the past, judge, and act by the
past, not always because they wish to be difficult, but because they
may be simply out of touch, or slow to keep up with events.   As
already observed, the new often does not affect all the people in
the same way, so that there are uneven effects throughout areas
under impact - socially, financially, sexually, etc. depending upon
the type and mode of impact.   The younger people live more in the
present and are attracted by the outscape as reflected in the
media.

The older Cowal people were less conscious about what was happening.   Others, although fully conscious of events and changes, did
experience the confusion that follows cultural shock due to the
changes which accompanied the passing from the state of initial
impact to that of spin-offs, and the period of gradual adaptation,
broken by unexpected events and experiences.   The younger people
were less confused and often welcomed the cosmopolitan inroads.

In this chapter the cultural effects of both the USN Base and the
McAlpine complex at Ardyne will be assessed each in turn.   Clearly,
the Strathclyde impact could hardly be compared with these in terms
of a cultural impact in 1976.   When I left Dunoon the locality was

chiefly adjusting to new bureaucratic effects rather than any cultural one in the case of Strathclyde.

Firstly, with regard to the USN invasion it was not only foreign but was also, in terms of the US culture, a culture within a culture.   This has already been referred to when discussing the 'military ways' and the 'militarism' that characterise the US navy.

The USN Base confronts the peaceful shores and its tourist industry with the symbolism of war and of foreign nationalism, both of which tend to throw up sceptres of the unknown, the mysterious and uncertain.   Such a situation inhibits interaction between the USN personnel and many of the local people.   In addition, there is the question of clashes in interest, or wants.   Sometimes there is a convergence of interests, sometimes a divergence of views, but usually a confrontation of values and interests.

Secondly, the military culture is itself two cultures, as Moskos points out, (7) there is the officer culture, and there is the enlisted culture.   Each will be considered during this narrative.

The cultural effects of the USN personnel will now be assessed chronologically from 1961.   The initial impact gave way to secondary surprises and social jolts.   The initial shocks were reviewed in Part Two.   The secondary effects, or spin-offs have now to be discussed.

In the autumn of 1961 disturbances caused by USN men ashore had forced the Captain of Proteus to introduce a curfew.   The local press of 9 September 1961 reported: 'Sailors on the American ship Proteus are now under an 11 o'clock curfew, imposed by their Commander Laning.   The curfew follows several incidents in town in recent weeks.' (8)

That autumn, when the Costa Clyde reeled under the impact of hurricane Debbie, the district was to reel under the impact of new shocks as the incomers began to make more inroads into the social texture of life in the locality.   In addition, the letters to the local press were complaining about the 'mores' of the USN crews - they were 'misbehaving' in public with local girls and causing considerable scandal in Presbyterian Dunoon.   A Dunoon man criticised the sailors in the Glasgow Evening Times in January 1962:

Since the arrival of the American sailors at Dunoon it is only out of politeness that the community has suffered in silence the embarrassment caused by Some American sailors keeping their secret passion anything but secret.   Any Scottish girl and boy behaving as these sailors do would be thrown out of railway stations and other public places by the scruff of their necks.

Another Dunoonite, referring to 'heavy petting' in public, observed: 'We in Dunoon don't like it, the summer visitors don't like it, and Dunoon with no major industry of any kind depends entirely upon the summer visitors for their livelihood.' (9)   In February a local

American dependant hit back at the criticism of the USN personnel:
'It is a bit disgusting that these "nice" girls don't have more respect for themselves, their parents and their country.' (10)

But the biggest impact was created later when it was reported
that the illegitimacy rate for Dunoon Burgh had jumped from 6.3 per
cent of births in 1961 to 15.3 per cent in 1962.   The number of
illegitimates in Dunoon had increased from six in 1961 to twenty-
four in 1962.   It was the second highest rate in Scotland of all
counties, cities, large and small burghs, and landward areas.

Presbyterian residents complained that USN personnel were dating
girls who were under sixteen years of age.   The Sunday Mail of
1 April 1962 discussed the matter under the banner headlines:
'Don't Date our Girls Call to Proteus'. (11)   The article reported
that a deputation would approach the captain, composed of local
magistrates.   The deputation were to tell him: 'Stop your men from
dating schoolgirls under the age of 16.'   The ship's spokesman, a
typical militarist, replied to the local protest: 'Our men are expected to behave like gentlemen, but whom they date is a matter of
personal preference.' (12)   An irate father had complained about
the typical American sailor who would court a schoolgirl under sixteen as someone beyond control, stating: 'anything the Captain
would say to this type of man would be as ineffective as singing
hymns to a tiger'. (13)

By May, the USN personnel were fairly bewildered by the reaction
they apparently had caused.   Especially when they read the following letter of a local in the Dunoon Observer:

Disgruntled Americans would do well to remember that Scottish
upbringing and education differs substantially from their own and
that such a document as the Kinsey Report is unlikely to make us
feel that their methods produce results we would like to see in
this country. (14)

But something more serious than the dating habits of the USN personnel had been raised.   A young girl had written in the issue of 16
June 1962 stating that 'there are brothels in Dunoon'. (15)   The
letter, however, was largely ignored.   Perhaps it was regarded as
incredible - certainly no one took up the allegation - but it was to
be the harbinger of a local scandal a year later.

At this stage the Cuban crisis had blown up, and the American
image had received a Western face-lift.   In addition, the USN personnel had become more and more involved in local charities and were
involved as sponsors of projects for the aged and particularly for
the children's home at Dunclutha.   Their local image had been
improving, and photographs in the press of their welfare activities
improved their local standing and image.   Public relations exercises were succeeding in reducing tensions.

In addition, by 12 December 1962 all hope of those local residents who were shocked by the USN cultural inroads was destroyed.

By 177 votes to 34 the House of Commons had blocked a proposed bill to terminate the agreement with the US government for the siting of the Polaris Submarine Base.   The USN would be in Cowal for a long time.

The local press of 15 December sadly reported the deal that had made the Polaris a fixture on the Loch: 'It had become known this week that there were secret understandings in the agreement by which the Americans had been given Holy Loch as a Base ... Britain was going to be offered a submarine equipped with Polaris missiles.' Some locals were concerned about the broader CND and military issues, but at that time most were more concerned about narrower issues in terms of culture clashes in Cowal.

Certainly by the spring of 1963 an uneasy routine (almost fatalistic) had settled upon the locality as the locals attempted to adapt.   Inevitably, there were petty confrontations between incomers and locals.   Regular letters which were critical of the USN personnel appeared in the local press.   In June 1963, the following poem in the _Dunoon Observer_ summed up much of the argumentation between local residents and the USN incomers.

THE AMERICAN-BRITISH VIEW
Sir to the editor.
What fun it must be to write letters
which later appear in the press,
And in them give vent to your feelings,
Finding faults upon which to lay stress.

What fun when the weather is ghastly,
And it keeps all the tourists away,
To forget that it is due to the weather
And instead blame the old USA.

What fun when you can't get a taxi,
Because there are none in the ranks
To say, 'Well we all know who's guilty,
Of course it's the fault of the Yanks.'

What fun to invite new arrivals
To drink just one final Scotch more,
Knowing well that its strength will affect them
Then their antics to naively deplore.

What fun to maintain that we're cousins,
And our customs are therefore the same,
And then when you find out that they're different
To say, 'Well of course they're to blame.'

What fun to be sent here on duty,
And not shut your mouth like a clam,
But rather inform all and sundry
On the merits of Auld Uncle Sam.

What fun to give way to your feelings,
And belittle the things that you see,
And although you may only drink coffee,
Say frankly you cannot stand tea.

What fun to maintain that the nation
To which you so proudly belong
Is bound to be right in all matters
While all others are bound to be wrong.

Yes, it's fun my friends to be naughty,
And express your own personal views
By writing an unsigned epistle,
And disrupt good relations anew.

But remember that those in the squadron
Were sent here by higher command,
And merit the kind of a welcome
That kindness of heart should demand.

Although they aren't here by your asking,
And you on Polaris aren't sold,
Remember they're here for one reason
A sailor must go where he's told.

And neither must it be forgotten
By those who are guest on our shore,
That we live this way 'cos we like it,
And criticisms rightly deplore.

And so let us bury the hatchet,
But let us by all means have fun,
So why don't you pick on the English
As many for ages have done.

PS.   What fun just once more to be beastly,
Like those others who've all done the same,
By asking the editor not to give you
Any clue to this Sassenach's name. (16)

The letter, however, did not deal with local unrest over what many
people regarded as sexual exploitation (17) of Cowal girls by US
sailors.   Women locally had had a lesser place in cultural terms
within a male-dominated society, (18)   none the less the sailors'
'dollie' image of girls, and their US brand of male chauvinism (pro-
jected in their 'hello baby' attitude towards girls) troubled many
local parents, especially the Presbyterians.

Willie Inglis, the late editor of the Dunoon Observer, told me
that when the US seamen first came he was approached by a seaman at
Dunoon pier.

'Hey, Buddy, can you tell me where the cat house is?'

Willie explained that there was no cat or dog home in Dunoon.

'Buddy, don't you get what I mean, I wanna get laid somewhere.'
Willie replied, 'Listen son, this is a respectable town, we want to
keep it that way.'

Male military overt sexual permissiveness is a universal phenomenon. US military sexuality and its more accentuated virility cult
are well described by N. Mailer in Why Are We in Vietnam?, and in
naval terms, e.g. in the novel of D. Ponicsan in Cinderella
Liberty. (19) In these novels is summed up the irresponsible young
military man's attitude towards foreign women, in particular. Some
young seamen had little respect for the Christian status of woman as
conserved by Presbyterianism.

Navy social contacts were mainly with women. Boomtown studies,
upon which one may draw some comparative material to flesh out a
theoretical discussion of the civil-military relations in a FBM
boomtown, cite the casual and steady relationships the servicemen
have with local girls, such as that of W. Caudhill, who observed
that the local authorities recognise the buffer function of prostitutes and 'vice' areas so as to protect the good citizens from the
frustrated servicemen. (20) Roger Little presents interesting
figures with regard to the army which can throw some light on the
probable behaviour of the seamen in the locality, and 'on the other
side': 62 per cent of the sample both in Korea and in Japan had
episodic sex with prostitutes. These figures in Little's study
concur with other research showing that about a fifth of the
servicemen do not engage in any sexual activity with local women,
about another fifth have regular mistresses, and the remaining
three-fifths have casual relationships with prostitutes. (21) In
fact, according to the citations in Dixon Wecter's When Johnny Comes
Marching Home, sexual behaviour has not changed much over the generations. According to the officer in charge of the venereal dis-
ease section of the American Expeditionary Force from 1918-22, about
71 per cent of all US soldiers in France had sexual relations during
their stay abroad. (22) Figures of between 65 and 70 per cent do
tally over the years and in different places. These figures have
serious implications for local people such as those of the West of
Scotland and the events detailed in this study reflect them.

The diverse heterosexual habits of the incomers, especially the
'dating' of younger girls, greatly affected the behaviour of some
local girls, causing friction between families and the USN
personnel.

Some local girls did welcome the easier attitudes of the incomers
towards sex. However, there was perhaps greater enthusiasm on the
part of the many girls who came over on the ferries from 'the other
side' to date USN sailors. (23) An irate American woman living in
Dunoon angered Dunoon parents when she observed in the local press
at the height of the local criticism of American permissiveness, on
28 April 1962: 'Your lassies look quite capable, mature, and
willing to me.' There was evidence, however unwelcome to local

parents, that some girls were delighted with the easier attitude towards earlier courtships, and with the less inhibited behaviour of the men from the Polaris Base. (24)

It would be wrong to suppose that the American personnel had no standing morally in the locality. There were locals who were 'for' them as well as those who were against them and biases often misrepresented the true state of affairs. And at all events many were impressed with the married officers' moral behaviour. The married officers were generally praised by the local families, whereas the behaviour and attitudes of some USN ratings shocked them. But, as shall be shown, the more liberal attitude of some officers with regard to the permissiveness of the sailors ashore puzzled many. One local put it to me, 'Because they speak like us, and because we drink their Coke, and eat their burgers, we take it that they are like us, but they are a whole Atlantic apart.'

Dunoonites were disgusted with the petting sessions on the 'prom' and even in the main street. Even in 1976 people still complained about them. Some regarded Dunoon as Cowal's 'sin city'. In the early 1960s US vans with high-powered lights scanned the shores to detect sexual escapades in the night. The impact of USN permissiveness was marked. Also, to the local people's consternation, it had been announced in the summer of 1963 that a VD clinic was to open soon, at the Dunoon Cottage Hospital. Moreover, after a police raid in August 1963, a Dunoon 'call-girl' facility, consisting of at least twenty-two girls, had been exposed. (25) What grieved local people was the fact that the USN senior officers did not appear to be concerned with the effects caused by the escapades of their men ashore. Vans searching for 'immoral shore practices' was about the best they could do, whereas people were more concerned about explicit sexuality in broad daylight.

The Minister of the High Kirk in Dunoon commented on the apparent lack of concern at the Polaris Base. The Minister's words were cited in the local press on 26 October 1963:

It also seems to be that the American authorities have been extremely lax. I cannot imagine that they would tolerate the kind of behaviour this town has suffered in an American town of the same size.... And if we may judge from the press, their spokesmen have been evasive and even impudent when the matter has been drawn to their attention. (26)

All the USN Commander could say about the situation was as follows: 'There are in Dunoon no indoor bowling alleys, no swimming pool, and no gym available, where the men can work off their youthful energies; so where do they go?' (27)

One can appreciate the stress endured by submariners under water for months at a time. Add to the limitations of enclosure, the total cut-off from society and the emergency drill the men have to go through so that they may be able to fire their 'throw-weight' of atomic destruction sixteen times, at the rate of one missile per

minute at different alien targets.   One seaman said that they never
know till the final second of 'blast-off' if the drill is 'for real'
or just 'make-believe'.   Another described his relief on breaking
into the daylight of normal living after a tour like this: 'Imagine
what it's like to come from that tin box in the dark deep where your
eyes see nothing for weeks but nuts and bolts, to see a real sexy
"broad" in the daylight!'

On the other hand, at the opposite extreme is the tedious life
aboard the service vessels of the Holy Loch, especially during the
misty and cold winters.   One is able to understand how drudgery on
the one hand and tension on the other may create 'breakouts' ashore
where life contrasts with the tedium aboard, or in a submerged state
on an alert mission.

In March 1964, in the House of Commons, the South Ayrshire MP
asked the prime minister:

When the Prime Minister was discussing the question of Polaris
submarines with President Johnson, did he raise the question
whether the American government should make some financial contribution to the mothers of illegitimate children left behind by
these Polaris submarine sailors?   Is he aware that the illegitimate birthrate and VD figures in this area show a considerable
increase, and if he doubts that will he get disguised as an
American sailor and go to Dunoon on a Saturday night and find out
for himself?

The prime minister replied: 'I did not discuss any of these by-
products of the Nassau agreement.' (28)   The local concern of East
Cowal parents, particularly, in the end succeeded in convincing
senior USN staff that the men ought to be encouraged to seek their
'flesh pots' on the other side of the Firth.

According to my burgh and local investigations, there were only
two spots in town in the mid-1970s where a sailor could contact a
prostitute.   Most brothels were on 'the other side'.   After the
'call-girl' scandal, almost all the prostitutes left the town.
Many locals had made life difficult for them.   In a small place
like Dunoon it is impossible to be an effective anonymous 'call-
girl'.

However, most USN personnel had in fact steered clear of prostitutes.   The USN personnel who wanted a more glamorous 'date' of an
impersonal nature could always phone up a Glasgow or West of Scotland agency, where the usual escorts were provided, but at exorbi-
tant rates even for overpaid American naval personnel.   To the USN
personnel the price attached to 'a date' (as they described it) was
like the price attached to a commodity.   However, many of the men
managed to associate with girls in Glasgow without much trouble,
'and buck free' as one sailor crudely put it to me.

My principal source of information regarding Glasgow came from
taxi drivers.   After explaining that I was carrying out a study of

the USN personnel in Scotland at Glasgow 'Unie' (university) I was
passed on from one Glasgow taxi-driver to another who knew what was
happening.   The picture that emerged was what one might expect of
overseas servicemen.   There were flats for 'sexy parties' known to
the sailors, to which they were introduced by their naval sponsors.
Most of the flats used were rented by USN personnel.   There was one
problem, however: the winter weather on the Firth could make the
journey to the other side 'impossible'.

When the winter weather makes crossing difficult the men were re-
duced to 'playing "kissy-bear" and "huggy-face" to funky music in a
pub basement in Dunoon', explained one of my American contacts.   It
was in the winter that trouble often broke out between local lads
and the USN personnel over the relatively few local girls available.

There were not many young girls locally.   From the 1971 Census
it can be seen that there were 445 burgh girls between 15 and 29
years of age, and in the burgh as many as 865 single males of the
same age group.   There were at least as many USN single personnel
as the local males, so it could be said that in the mid-1970s there
were approximately four times as many single males to single girls
of this age group.   The more marriageable girls, who were under 24,
amounted to 410 according to the Census. (29)   With the influx of
hundreds of young seamen the competition for these girls increased
significantly.

Although there was exploitation of local girls and literally 'a
traffic' in girls on 'the other side', many Americans did marry
local Scottish girls.   This effect is more easily documented and
more convincingly demonstrated because of available statistics.
Table 9.1 shows that each year on average in the thirteen years
between 1961 and 1973, approximately forty girls married USN personnel in Dunoon in comparison with the overall average of approximately 88 girls.

In 1965, 47 out of 93 non-US brides were maried to USN personnel
in Dunoon, i.e. more than half.   Generally girls married locally
are presumed to be local, given the regulations regarding local
residence, but sometimes outsiders can arrange matters so as to
marry outside their own place of residence.   But I am not going
simply on the figures, because the retiring registrar told me that
most of the girls marrying USN sailors in Dunoon were, in fact,
local girls.

The numbers were impressive because the USN personnel are in the
area from eighteen months to two years.

Although this is not a situation like that in Inishkillane, in
which Brody found that most girls wanted to marry the stranger to
move out from the more remote backwoods to the brighter life, (30)
there were some who sought to move out to the States, as eventually
at least 415 local girls did.   One local cynic had his opinion:
'It's all them Tony Curtis and Frank Sinatra sailor films that give
the lassies their urge to find a sailor.'   It was rather unfair,

both on the Americans and upon the local girls, but there may well
have been the wish to get away from the semi-rural world of Cowal to
the brighter lights of what to many were the dream cities, apartments and luxuries of a world produced by Hollywood.

TABLE 9.1 Male USN personnel marriages with non-USN females and US
women in Dunoon compared with other marriages in Dunoon (1961-73)

Year	Marriages of USN personnel to non-US women	Marriage of USN personnel to US women*	Other local marriages	Total number of registered marriages
1961	9	0	52	61
1962	36	0	50	86
1963	31	6	39	76
1964	34	2	41	77
1965	47	3	46	96
1966	44	1	53	98
1967	35	5	49	89
1968	22	5	53	80
1969	23	4	60	87
1970	36	2	73	111
1971	42	10	50	102
1972	33	4	61	98
1973	23	6	53	82
Total	415	48	680	1143

Source: Statistics as from General Branch (RG Office Scotland),
          Ladywell House, Edinburgh.

* The number of USN personnel marrying US women over the period was
  minimal every year except 1971.   Most of them were the outcome of
  long-term courtships begun before arrival, or with the daughters
  of USN married personnel.

The situation was further complicated by the racial stresses
within the USN organisation.   There was an increase in black naval
personnel at Holy Loch in the 1970s.   They attracted attention and
certainly were popular with some local girls.   White and black
seamen began to clash.   Some local white males joined in the fighting in a situation which led to a major USN riot.

On Saturday night, 13 October 1973, the main streets of Dunoon
echoed with the sound of crashing glass as twenty-two shop windows
were shattered by black Polaris sailors.   Fighting broke out and a
local youth was stabbed.   The residents of Argyll Street were ter-
rified.   Six ratings, three of them black, appeared in private at
Dunoon Sheriff Court on the following Monday - according to the

Daily Telegraph of Tuesday 16 October. By 7 November, the number
of sailors connected with the rioting had risen to ten; seven of
whom were black. (31)   There had been an uneasy atmosphere building
up amongst the local youth and the black American sailors.   The
irony was that the shopkeepers who had been the main supporters of
the USN Base from the beginning were the victims of the confrontation.   The shattered premises of almost every single main shop in
town shocked the public.   The incident was reported, amongst other
international newspapers, in a Florida daily newspaper, in the
Daily Cincinnati, and in the Buenos Aires Herald. (32)   Concern
within the Navy Department was great because of the international
news, and the poor image of the Base which had been created abroad.

The Commander sent his apology to the provost, which appeared on
20 October in the local press.   It ran as follows:

COMMANDING OFFICER'S APOLOGY
Provost John Dickson has received the following letter from
Captain Albert L. Kelln, Commander of Submarine Squadron Fifteen,
Holy Loch:

Dear Provost Dickson,
On behalf of the American Government, and especially the Navy men
and the 1300 American wives and children here in the Holy Loch
area, I sincerely apologise for the disgusting conduct of a few
American men last Saturday evening.   For whatever reason the
incident occurred, there is no justification nor excuse for this
type of behaviour.   We Americans look upon this with shock,
shame, and regret.   As you know, the vast majority of us try
very hard at being good neighbours and residents of the area.
We are extremely proud that as Americans, we have the opportunity
to live in Scotland, a land which was home to so many of our
grandparents, and which has contributed so much to the American
culture.

We are also extremely aware that by the efforts of our small
group of men and their many daily personal sacrifices we are able
to make a significant contribution to both of our countries.

With deep regret for the past, I ask that you convey my feelings to the community.

                                                    A.L. Kelln

Four days later, the Secretary of the Navy, Washington, arrived to
see the Base Commander and to apologise to the Town Council.   The
Commander apologised to the public, which had been the only USN
apology given to the people of East Cowal.

At the same time as the above events, the Base advertised for a
Community Relations Adviser, and one had the distinct impression
that the Navy Department wished to show how unhappy it had been with
the local outrage.   The Captain was more than embarrassed by the
whole episode.   But what had led up to events that weekend?

There were local male convictions also, and there were white as
well as black naval personnel involved. For some time the locals
noticed that blacks were on the increase, as noted already. Black
USN personnel were attracting the local girls. They were regarded
as the best dancers and their clothes and life-style were more
colourful. They gained a local reputation for being more generous
in their relationships with the girls and treated them with more
respect. Some of the FBM white sailors were put out and peeved.

On the dance-floor at the Seamen's Club, Ardnadam, especially at
'discos', or boy-girl events, Polaris black seamen were soon in
confrontation with the white personnel over girl partners. They
decided in the circumstances to avoid Ardnadam Seamen's Club and
went instead to a local tavern in Dunoon for a quieter scene. Here
the local white males reacted badly to them. They taunted them.
A Cowal spokesman reported to the Daily Telegraph, that,

there had been a gradual build-up of tension between local youths
and unattached men, and the more affluent, often bizarrely
dressed, American Navy men. In the summer when there are
holiday-makers and day-trippers from Glasgow there seems enough
company to go round, but when the town is thrown on its own resources there is more competition for what female companionship
is around. The locals don't like to be beaten by a Yank and
they seem to take it more badly if he happens to be
coloured. (33)

The girls drifted from the Ardnadam premises to follow the blacks
for drinks and a more relaxed dance session.

As seen already, racial integration in the US Navy has a sad
history, and the Base, according to locals, was caught up in racial
conflict where 'Black Power' was quoted, and unease expressed by
the personnel. However, the racial issues were more or less contained within the naval organisation, but outside the Base there
were less controls. C.C. Moskos writes: 'The most overt source
of racial unrest takes place in community centres in dancing situations.' (34) A well-known commentary on American 'mores' of servicemen, 'Project Clear', indicates that almost three-quarters of
the large sample strongly objected to negro servicemen dancing with
white girls. (35) These statements are highly relevant to racial
issues in the naval boomtown of Dunoon.

The white personnel at the Base realised what had happened and
followed the local girls into Dunoon on Friday 12 October. There
were white locals ready to join forces with the white US personnel.
At the tavern there was more than one explosive situation that evening between the white and black American seamen. According to one
version, white USN personnel, abetted by local lads, at the end of a
disco session, blocked the bar from the black sailors. Another
version which was quoted in the court and press, stated that an in-
sulting remark made by a local lad to a black rating in a toilet had
sparked off a fight. (36) Seven Cowal lads were later convicted of
brawling. The black sailors were outnumbered, and apparently got
the worst of it that Friday evening.

The next night, a group of Polaris black seamen, shouting Black Power slogans and giving the black salute, took their revenge, as they saw it, upon the white town of which the main street shops were eminently symbolic.   Intent on revenge, they marched into town from the top end of Argyll Street, systematically breaking every shop window on both sides of the street, except one.   What followed has already been described.

Eight letters were written following the incident, and old complaints and unresolved grievances were revitalised.   But the locals were not that critical of the outrage because they realised that seven Cowal males, at least, had had a hand in the situation.   What was not so well appreciated was the racial unrest at Base which had been smouldering for some time.   The black salute was given later in the court when the seamen were tried.   It bewildered local people.   Amongst the white personnel involved the salute meant more than the isolated shore incident.   After the unfortunate incident, the US authorities stepped in and people noticed that the number of black sailors at the USN Base dropped.

The next big shock for the people came with the news that (soft) drug addiction in the locality was the worst in Britain.   The statement was made in 1974 by the police drug squad in the various church guilds, in a series of lectures to alert the parents in the locality to the drug threat for their youngsters.

In the USA the smoking of cannabis is tolerated in certain States, and is socially approved in certain regions.   US seamen were receiving the cannabis from home, but strangers from 'the other side' of the Firth were also involved.   Local people were uneasy and named the Canopus the 'USS Cannabis'.   Whilst I was living within the locality it was claimed that at least 200 men were found to be in possession of drugs within a year, (37) but not all of these, by any means, were brought to the Sheriff Court.   The fact was the US mail, which was a possible mode of importing drugs, did not go through the British postal system.   At that time, when a drug squad search discovered a group of Americans in possession of cannabis, or LSD, they were handed over to the USN authorities, so that many cases were not reported locally.   The extent of the traffic and the involvement of the locals caused great concern, especially when it later became clear that submariners at sea were also given to drug abuse, with twelve men guilty of smoking marijuana aboard.   They were crew members of the Casimir Dulaski, a ballistic missile submarine. (38)   The press stated that the drug traffic was an internal affair.   However, the Sheriff Court convictions prove that civilians were also involved.   Just after I moved out of the town, a USN fireman aboard the USS Holland stated that 'hash' was locally available: 'It's easy to get.   The guys pick it up when ashore in Dunoon.' (39)   The situation was grave because seamen on active service were implicated and locals were also involved ashore.   Cowal parents had their youth to worry about, but all citizens were concerned about the possible danger of a nuclear accident whilst men were drugged.   Drugs were said to be 'pushed' at the small gardens on Argyll Street where the toilets are.   They

TABLE 9.2 Convictions in Dunoon Sheriff Court excluding CND demonstrators

| Impact periods when convictions occurred | Type of conviction | USN personnel and dependants | | | |
		Depot ship personnel	Sub-mariners	US depen-dants	Totals
1 During initial impact (after anchorage of USS Proteus March-July 1961	Motoring	2	0	0	2
	Drug offences	0	0	0	0
	Other	7	3	0	10
Period one totals		9	3	0	12
2 Secondary phase of 'spin-offs' Aug. 1961-Feb. 1963	Motoring	51	0	0	51
	Drug offences	0	0	0	0
	Other	24	3	0	27
Period two totals		75	3	0	78
3 Tertiary phase - uneasy routinisation March 1963-Feb. 1976	Motoring	669	3	0	672
	Drug offences	19	0	0	19
	Other	193	17	3	213
Period three totals		881	20	3	904
Sum totals		965	26	3	994

Source: The data was collected from the Dunoon Observer, which reported all Sheriff Court proceedings.

* American dependants had only 3 convictions in the period.

Local	West Scot- land	Non-American Other Scots	Rest UK	No fixed abode	Abroad	Totals	Sum total	USN % personnel and depen- dants	Locals %	Others %
12	8	11	4	0	0	35	37	5.4	32.4	62.2
0	0	0	0	0	0	0	0	0.0	0.0	0.0
10	1	3	2	0	1	17	27	37.0	37.0	26.0
22	9	14	6	0	1	52	64	18.8	34.4	46.8
67	64	71	7	0	0	209	260	19.6	25.8	54.6
0	0	0	0	0	0	0	0	0.0	0.0	0.0
41	29	15	1	0	0	86	113	23.9	36.3	39.8
108	93	86	8	0	0	295	373	20.9	28.9	50.2
1262	449	434	144	42	0	2331	3003	22.4	42.0	35.6
11	3	6	1	0	0	21	40	47.5	27.5	25.0
538	141	139	24	0	3	845	1058	20.1	50.9	29.0
1811	593	579	169	42	3	3197	4101	22.0	44.2	33.8
1941	695	679	183	42	4	3544	4538	21.9	42.8	35.3

called them 'the perfumed gardens'.   One local cynic pointed to a
veritable heap of 'goofy' sailors after a local disco session and
observed, 'They're defending us.   God help NATO.'

In addition, there was a growing concern about the increase of
crime and breaches of the peace.   Table 9.2 presents their occurrence.   The data indicates that 21.5 per cent of the 1,238 reported
non-motoring offences in the local press between the first USN crime
of May 1961 and those of February 1976, were crimes of USN personnel
(not including the minor convictions in other courts, for example at
the Police Court at Dunoon). (40)   The motoring offences of the USN
personnel were 21.9 per cent of the 3,300 local motoring offences
(up to February 1976).   Moreover, USN statistics do not represent
all the drug offences; already referred to, they were often handled
in secret by the US authorities 'in camera' aboard the depot ship.

In the period there were only three officer USN non-motoring
offences.   US Officer behaviour was usually exemplary.   The offences were mainly those of the seamen.   The local people's proportion
of non-motoring convictions was 48.5 per cent of the 1,238 total for
the period May 1961-end of February 1976, as may be calculated from
Table 9.2.   The proportion of the local residents' share of the
3,300 motoring offences was 40.6 per cent; as noted that of the USN
personnel was 21.9 per cent.   In other words, the population of USN
non-motoring offences was almost exactly the same as that of USN
motoring offences.

So, the figures show that the claim at Base that most USN crimes
are motoring offences is entirely wrong, and supports the opinion
and research of Moskos that the military may boast of discipline,
but that on shore that discipline is clearly doubtful.   The militarists live in an enclave where discipline is coercively maintained
within a caste officer/seamen system.   Once that caste system is
non-operable in a civilian milieu, the whole disciplinary system
weakens.   Judging from their behaviour, the officers at the USN
Base have demonstrated throughout the years a sense of discipline
founded upon military values – the most senior officers and captains
were usually Annapolis graduates, whose normative compliance and
militarist views have already been stressed.   This state of affairs
contrasted with that of the seamen whose compliance appeared to be
coercive.   It was mainly the POs who enforced the commands of
seniors in forceful military style.   They were backed by a tough,
heavy-handed Shore Patrol (SP).   However, they could not be omni-
present and were often singularly missing not only in trouble spots
in Glasgow and on 'the other side', but also when the riots of the
autumn of 1973 broke out in Dunoon.   When no PO or SP came in
sight, discipline broke down.

In addition to the above distinctions with regard to the discipline of the men and their orientation, there was a difference
between the orientation and values of the submariners and the ship
personnel.   (The former were named by the latter – 'the bubbleheads', and the latter by the former – 'the seaskimmers'.)   The
training, the military experience and cycle of duty, as already seen

in an earlier chapter, differed significantly. The submariners had
been convicted in Dunoon of some of the first shore assaults. Significantly, the mid-1970s saw them spending only a short period at
the Polaris Base, after a mission at sea, before returning to the
US.

At the Base there are also rotation problems which may affect
discipline. Firstly, there is the continual renewal of the personnel because of their termination of posting overseas, so that every
two years the Base is manned by new strangers. Getting to know
them takes time, so that relationships tend to be shortlived.
Secondly, there is the coming and going of submarines and supply
ships with the consequent straining of organisational controls at
the Base, where stress is worked out in town by fights between
supply ship personnel and depot ship sailors, and also between
'bubbleheads' and 'seaskimmers'. As an American sociologist, herself a wife to an American serviceman in an overseas base, stated in
the context of rotation: 'Within this short period of duty goes the
short-term perspective - "why get interested. I'm leaving
soon."' (41)

In addition to the problems cited above, there are gross dispari-
ties in terms of privileges which accentuate the split between officers and men. The married seaman has to manage abroad without his
dependants, whilst the commissioned are able to do so because of
privilege. Even the married Petty Officer (3rd class) cannot share
the privileges of officers in having their household goods transported free of charge from the USA. (42) In addition, they have a
'Temporary Lodging Allowance', which is not granted to the enlisted
from Petty Officer (3rd class) downwards. Wives are transferred at
the expense of the naval authorities under sponsorship, in the case
of the commissioned, but not in the case of the enlisted (from the
same cut-off point at PO level). These factors are also cited by
Moskos, who states that, because privileges are concentrated at the
top end of the ranks, 15-20 per cent of enlisted men do not have
their wives with them abroad. (43) As a result frustration is
inevitable for many seamen.

Taking into consideration the above problems, how did personnel's
conceptions of life locally play its role in the impact of the military upon life in the local scape? Although enlisted crews and
senior staff have rotated many times with complete change of staff
over the years since the Proteus sailed up the Firth, a sedimentation of collective views has been built up amongst the Americans,
and so a particular 'social inscape' of life was set by 'outscape'
people, as their experience gelled, and was passed on to mates.

Each American serviceman had a sponsor before he arrived at Holy
Loch. The sponsor was chosed for him at Holy Loch. In advance of
the replacement's arrival, the sponsor wrote to him and gave him
introductory information suited to his rank (they shared the same
position within the military structure). He met the newcomer at
the airport and accompanied him to the locality, acting as his
mentor in the first crucial months till he himself left. Thus it

was that, although there was a high turnover of staff at Base, old
stereotypes and perceptions tended to endure.   This created a particular 'social inscape' of life locally, which was conserved at
Base, and which contrasted with the way people saw themselves
locally.

Each replacement was also given a booklet about life locally on
arrival; its contents and views tended to reinforce the naval
stereotype of life locally.   I was fortunate in being able to
acquire one from a naval contact.   It was strictly for USN personnel.   It is worth describing.

The booklet as such had no title, but on its cover there was a
statement of welcome from the Commander of the US Naval Activities
Personnel at Holy Loch.   Four pages of the booklet were about the
people of Scotland, the other 37 were about the Polaris Base itself.
With regard to the Scottish people presented in the four pages, the
clans were described, the kilt, the Gaelic, and the Church of Scotland.   However the clans had a marginal role; the kilt was mainly
for special occasions; Gaelic was almost non-existent except in the
Isles, and, as will be demonstrated, the Church of Scotland and
American worshippers seldom if ever came to pray and commune
together.   After the above inclusions, the booklet dealt mainly
with consumables and military privilege.   It was these which held
the key to understanding the invading military culture of a highly
materialistic consumer society.

Stresses were created by the overseas American chauvinism.
Moskos refers to it, as have so many commentators over the
years. (44)   The US personnel carried with them the values of the
American outscape which naturally, for them represented the superior
life.   Material standards were in contrast, and the latent ideology
often carried with it the bombastic claim of a well-nourished incomer whose 'bravado' and arrogance have sometimes merited the old
tag: 'over-paid, over-sexed, over here'.   'Social inscapes' back
home were carried into the new situation where outlook clashed, and
so trouble was bound to occur.   One local told me that he was
'driven over the top, when a seaman boasted: "Even our cauliflowers
are bigger than your trees."'

Invidious comparisons were made by US personnel between the
higher standard of living and material cultural benefits of America
and those of the host country.   C.C. Moskos observes that servicemen from the States boast of the 'land of the big PX' and cites that
even in the front line in Vietnam soldiers of the USA had an abun-
dance of radios, cameras, and photographic accessories. (45)   The
latent ideology of the USN incomers was 'Americanism'.   It constituted a pervasive pride which was not only talked out, but 'acted
out' ashore.

American military commentators detect the widespread serviceman's
belief that America is the best country in the world and that its
products and creature comforts are unrivalled.   The seaman abroad
will be inclined to romanticise, but the stress on materialism

parallels ethnographic studies of working-class and middle-class
Americans in civilian contexts. A.J. Vidich, E. Chinoy and H.J.
Gans, to mention only three, give evidence of this. (46)

Another factor was the boast that American military policy was
best.   The political loyalties of the sailors and officers was
maintained and fostered by force of regulations and sanctions both
formal and informal.   R. Nauta cites Janowitz's statement that a
characteristic of the military is an ideology which emerges from the
explicated political views that are fostered and indoctrinated at
base. (47)   There is an identification between military honour and
politically defined Averican ends, especially when the US military
confronts Russian dominance and its communist ideology.   'We're
here to protect you' has often been heard with chagrin by Dunoonites
over the years.   What was the culture clash created by these
salient USN social factors?   Culture is held and usually passed on
within the family unit.   What effect did the USN invasion have upon
it and its life-style?

The salient American culture evoked particular family reactions.
As cited in the Shetland studies in a previous chapter, so in the
wake of cultural invasion, families held on to their cultural heritage and local identity.   Families became more Cowal-minded.
Moreover, the very expectations of the incomers with regard to the
locals and their stereotypes of Scottish Highland life, created in
their turn a local renewed stress upon the Scottish culture, its
folklore, and the identity of the local men of Cowal, so that one
detected in the Dunoon Observer more and more articles about Scottish culture.   Families, already SNP-minded, became more aware of
their heritage.

When the Americans arrived, family life in Cowal remained much as
it had been in some important ways.   The grown sons still had to
leave home.   Father was still very much the breadwinner.   With the
growing holiday downtrend, a wife would have been fortunate indeed
to procure a seasonal job.   However, for those with children, life
was far more dramatic.   There were parental fears because of the
threat of drugs, greater sexual permissiveness and a significant
modification of parental authority.   The incoming Americans did not
appreciate that parents in East Cowal did demand that their young
daughters conformed to a life of obedience and respect and were home
for 11p.m. at the latest.   On the other hand, there were parents
whose children had American classmates, and whose daughters had US
boyfriends.   Other fathers and mothers had an American sailor for a
son-in-law, together with the exciting invitations to the United
States for a christening and summer holiday.   Some local ambivalences were therefore apparent.

Married life and home life remained much the same, however, for
most.   Many parents became more protective and family life for a
minority did become more enclosed.   Others noticed the greater participation of American naval husbands in family tasks.   American
husbands did share the chores of the home; they did wheel their
babies in prams, or toddlers in push-chairs down main streets in

Dunoon or along the promenades - something rarely seen before 1960,
either in Cowal or on 'the other side , from accounts I was given by
older parents.   Local parental styles did alter to some extent, and
although there is no knowing whether this came about by the example
of the incomers or not, the new American styles of parenthood did
not go unnoticed.

In addition to the family, the religious institutions of the incomers presented certain interesting aspects.   The role of the
Presbyterian ministers was not only as religious notables, but as
guardians of family values.   They also ran major social events and
organised charities, using their parish centres as community
centres.   Around the ministers were the 113 elders, who were all
local notables or influential laymen. (48)   Their part in establishing the tenor of life, and the ideals to be maintained, cannot
be underestimated.

I visited each of the ministers of the Church of Scotland and all
the vicars and priests of the locality in turn, and from my conversation with them was able to piece together certain facts and certain impressions relevant to the effect(s) of the USN invasion upon
the church and parish life of religious groups in the locality.

What surprised me was the minimal contact the Americans had with
the Church of Scotland.   There were relatively few Presbyterian USN
marriages and baptisms.   For example, three of the eight ministers
had been in post for six to seven years, and yet had only baptised
between four and five US babies in their churches.   There appeared
to have been more USN marriages at the Dunoon kirk, where the
minister told me he married on average two a year.   Most agreed
that there was not much church contact with the American naval personnel over the years at parish events.

Most of the USN personnel, according to the ministers, had been
Baptists.   The local Baptist church was almost entirely Americani-
sed, with its accent upon participation at the services and in the
running of parish events.   The parish magazine, In Touch, could
have been an Ohio publication.   About 50 per cent of the parish
creche children were USN infants.   Almost a third of the congregation was American.   The Social Concern group and the mini-fellow-
ship group had the closest links with the USN dependants.   The
Baptist pastor had much to do with the black seamen and was greatly
respected by the USN officers.

The RC parish was also much affected the USN incomers.   The
priest had been in Dunoon five years.   He and his curate said they
were most involved with the Polaris Base, and went to say Mass regularly aboard the Canopus.   The parish priest commented, 'The
Americans have done us a power of good.'   There were seventy
American pupils at the Catholic primary school in Dunoon.   About
one in seven USN personnel at that time were Catholics, often the
Americans represented about a third of the parishioners (there were
1,200 local RCs).

The involvement of the Americans in the life of the parish was considerable, said the priests.   To demonstrate this, I was shown the parish registers.   Between 1970 and 1975 there were no less than 118 US baptisms out of a total of 321.   In the same period there were approximately thirty American weddings.   The priests said that the Americans took part in socials as well as in church services.   The parish priest summed up the beneficial effects of the Catholic naval injection of new life in the parish by saying, 'As far as I'm concerned, the Americans are a breath of fresh air', adding, 'Often about half the children in our school are American, and the teachers find the kids an example.'

There remained the Scottish Episcopalian Church, the Apostolic Church, the Jehovah Witnesses, the Church of Christ, the Mormons, and the Salvationists.   The significant religious group amongst these were the Mormons, whose members sometimes increased fourfold when a new depot ship came in.   In the Episcopalian Church there had only been three USN marriages in fifteen years, and twelve baptisms.   These were more than there had been in some of the minor Presbyterian churches, but it was dramatically less than what there had been in the RC parish of St Muns.   Contact with the Jehovah Witnesses, like that of the Mormons, was often considerable. Clearly, the minority religions were more affected by the Americans.

The observations of the clergy and the facts show that there was minimal contact with the majority religion of the Presbyterian Church, as also came across in my interviews with the residents in their homes.

However, the USN senior officers fostered formal links with all of the clergy.

Contact and religious involvement cannot be judged purely by marriages and baptisms, but they serve as a general indicator, and my talk with the clergy did show that an inverse state of affairs had been created by the American presence.   The bigger cars and the more affluent used to be outside the kirks on Sundays, now they were outside the Baptist or RC churches or outside the smaller halls, citadels, and places of worship of the minority churches and fellow- ships.   Sunday was different now, because a Scottish Sunday for the people of Cowal was quiet, without servile work, and 'holy', even in 1976.   But, for the Americans, Sunday was 'odd-jobs' day, and the day for baseball or American football.   The Presbyterian Sunday was much more strictly observed in Cowal than it was on 'the other side', so the American Sunday did create a veritable culture shock for many 'Sunday observers'.

The Americans were also outgoing and more talkative about their belief.   Their T-shirts told the world they had a mission.   One middle-aged local man complained to me, 'I don't mind religion, but these American religious fanatics overdo it.   They're Jesus Christers in jeans, with the holy message written, not in a book, but on the seat of their pants.'   The more reserved kirk-goer could not take to the new disciples, with their guitar sessions, clapping

hands and extrovert witness.   For many Presbyterians, the Americans
were an enigma, whom they tended to see as people of extremes in
sacred, or secular terms: 'Saints or sinners', said another puzzled
informant.

The American impacts upon the world of leisure, in the form of
entertainment and also sporting pastimes, call next for some
comment.

One main impact made by the USN presence to the local cultural
scape was felt upon the stage, particularly in 'show business'.   I
contacted the principal entertainment agency in the West of Scotland, and professional artists through contacts, who had 'played
Dunoon' since the anchorage of Proteus in 1961.

The Clyde was known for its Scottish summer shows with the usual
comedian in kilt and 'tammie', with the repertoire of old Scottish
songs which Lauder had made famous, himself once a local resident of
Dunoon.   The points made by the various stage contacts, themselves
involved in the changes at Dunoon, were as follows:

1 When other Clyde resorts maintained the Scottish traditional
shows, Dunoon introduced more of the 'big star acts'.   An accordian
player stated in Glasgow: 'I've played Dunoon since 1939, especially at the Old Cosy Corner on Dunoon front, then later at the Queen's
Hall opposite the pier, right up to 1972.   The Americans had wanted
changes - they couldn't understand the Glasgow jokes and cracks
about the 'maws' and 'paws' and the 'wanes', they wanted the sophisticated variety, a slick compere, and no lengthy jokes.'   There was
a clash of 'wants'.

2 Top of the bill used always to be a comic, and remained so elsewhere in Scotland;   less so in Dunoon after Proteus.   A retired
pianist said: 'Dunoon had American families with money, who preferred
to have a show modelled on the Sinatra package', so changes were
introduced accordingly;   however, locals preferred the traditional.

3 American Country music began to invade the music scene, which was
generally more welcome locally, because it was similar to the small
group playing of Scottish country dancing.

There was no doubt that the intrusion of the American type of entertainment had also upset many locals of the older generation who preferred the old 'ceilidh' (Scottish dance session).   In fact,
although it pleased the Cowal youths, as may be judged by the popular throngs, especially at the US-style cabarets at the Glenmorag
Hotel, none the less, they too still liked the old forms of music.
In other words, they wanted the best of both worlds.   The same was
true of the new humour.   On 'the other side', Billy Connelly, at
that time of international repute, had kept alive the long protracted jokes with a West of Scotland twist to them.   This approach was
still more popular locally, but the Americans did introduce more
diversification in the locality, as demonstrated above, especially
for the younger people.   It must also be added, that the SNP had

created a revival in Scottish lyrics, song and dance, which at that
time was strong, due to the immense increase in the SNP following in
1974.   This helped to minimise the American influence on the style
and content of some local shows in the years 1974-6.

With regard to sporting pastimes, an American influence was evident, as it was in the case of entertainment.   The new American
gymnasium at the Polaris Base was used at times by competing teams
from both sides of the Firth in which ball games were a feature,
which hitherto had almost no existence, particularly basketball.
Baseball was also played in the open field up at Black Park.
Yachting received a boost through the introductions of the American
Polaris Trophy and later the Poseidon Trophy, which although they
were unashamed 'tit-bits', to make the reality of missiles in the
locality more palliative, none the less, did attract yachtsmen, and
helped to keep the sea-sport alive in an area that had a long tradition in yachting.   The Americans also supported and ran dinghy
events.   In addition to this list of sports, either introduced or
encouraged by the USN presence, there was the enormous boost given
locally to the indoor game of pool.   The Cowal Pool Championship
probably endured because of the USN supportive influence.   There
was also the added interest given to the game of darts by the US
Petty Officer Dart Club.

The considerable influence here did not, however, bring in sports
which overshadowed the Cowal Highland Games nor local interest and
the support of shinty and football.   In addition, it being an area
where the population was disproportionately mature or elderly, the
impact was not as significant as it might otherwise have been.   As
I saw it, the effect was perhaps greatest with regard to sport in
the school yards and fields, where the American children were often
in large numbers.   But here, too, the 'fitba' madness was still
supreme.

The effects, however, with regard to golf, played at Strone,
Innellan, and particularly the Kirn course at the Cowal Golf Course,
were non-existent.   Golf, like football, is regarded in East Cowal
and Scotland as strictly 'our sport'.   The same was less true of
bowls at the various local greens.   The Americans may have given
out the golf trophies, as they did at the Cowal Highland Gathering,
in their gold braid uniforms, or at the championships on the greens,
and the golf links, but they were there to put on a show, not because
the games or golf owed anything to them.   What of the American
impact upon local clubs and associations?   Here the story is somewhat different, because the USN personnel and their dependants kept
very much to themselves, except perhaps in the case of the YMCA
where some locals did mix.

The YMCA (known locally as the 'Y') was set up to cater for the
USN personnel and their dependants, occupying a central position,
not far from Dunoon pier.   Here there was some merging of locals
with Americans.   Here there were more sophisticated table games,
films and a new-style emphasis given to family entertainment, rather
than events suited only for one particular age-group.   A joint

naval and local representative committee attempted to make the 'Y' a joint effort where people from the Base could be entertained with people from the locality.   It worked, but its contacts were limited, as in general appeared to be the interaction between locals and Americans.

In 1975, the Scottish-American Ladies Club was formed to extend the contact between Scots and Americans, but it had taken almost fourteen years for such a joint club to be created, and the initiative came from a Scottish local woman.   In addition, the club was only for women and consisted mainly of joint lunches.   As already noted, there was a high density of local clubs in Cowal.   Americans had their own at Ardnadam.   Certainly, youths were invited to the USN events at the Base, and certainly they were often at discos and suppers at Sandbank, but these were big events.   They were similar to any staged dance session or show, of an impersonal nature, in contrast with the clubs and associations where locals were engaged in joint pursuits.   USN personnel did nct generally participate in these.   For the young seamen of the mid-1970s Cowal was not their 'scene', they spent most of their time in Glasgow and on 'the other side'.

When the young seamen did frequent local haunts, they tended to do so at a cocktail bar at the top of Argyll Street and one or two public bars.   Over time, the drinks in these bars had changed to suit their tastes, and there were locals who had changed their 'pintas' and 'whisky tots' for the American 'Harvey Wallbanger'.   However, these were relatively few.   An American visitor observed in the Sunday Mail, 6 July 1975, that she had enjoyed Cowal, stating that the only place one could buy a 'Harvey Wallbanger' in Scotland was in Dunoon.   She spoke of an Argyll Street pub and of the service there, first the barmaid: 'The barmaid is from South Uist, but she can mix a "Black Russian" with one hand, a "Red Lion' with the other, and whistle Dixie at the same time.' (49)   In a Dunoon pub one can buy the usual Scotch, but it is possible to order the 'Sidecar', the 'Screwdriver', 'Gin Fizz', 'Bloody Mary', 'Tom Collins', the 'Fuzzy John', the 'Pink Lady' and the 'Pink Squirrel'. One of the reasons why there has not been much pub fighting between USN personnel and locals is that the Scots go to their traditional 'pub' without 'fancy wancy' drinks on the shelves, whereas the Americans drink in two or three bars where their tastes are catered for.

Having narrated the events related to the American invasion of Cowal in the context of impacts upon the cultural scape in terms of a clash of expectations and life-style, the effects of the McAlpine culture clash must now be considered.

As has already been stated, there was a low key reaction to the McAlpine intrusion, particularly because of the mode of impact, which, together with the overlap of the American impact, tended to confuse people.   There was also the 1974 year of two general elections, which preoccupied people until Christmas 1974.   Meanwhile, McAlpine navvies and technicians were moving in, and plans were well

advanced to create one of the UK's largest platform complexes at
Ardyne Point.   Some people had noticed them, and some felt uneasy,
especially at Toward.

Just as illegitimacy had jumped dramatically, shortly after the
USN Base was established, so too the illegitimacy rate doubled soon
after the advent of the incoming workers at Ardyne.   It jumped from
7.1 per cent in 1972 to 14.4 per cent in 1973, the second highest
figure since the 15.3 per cent rate in 1962, according to the Annual
Report of the RG (Scotland) for that year.   Looking at the Reports,
106-119 (HMSO publications), the figures are significant;   coming as
they do in the conjuncture of events shortly after the two major
impacts.   Before the major droves of navvies came in 1974, men were
filtering into the area month by month.

Just as the US navy had adversely affected the moral tone of
Presbyterian Cowal, so too did the navvy intrusion.   A former provost of Dunoon stated at the height of the McAlpine navvy influx,
'We have the oil men from Ardyne Point, and the vice girls are
moving in.   If there are the least signs of trouble or moral cor-
ruption, I will see that they are stamped out.'   The People on
20 July 1975 reported: 'Until now American sailors from the nearby
Holy Loch Polaris Base have been the top spenders in the Clyde
resort of Dunoon.   Now they're in Division Two.   The real big
league money men are those who work on oil platform construction at
Toward.'   'Irresponsibility and big money,' said a local resident
to me, 'spell vice - big vice.'   A well-respected local councillor
remarked,

> It's no use hiding our heads in the sand.   The vice-girls are
> coming back and we have heard reports of trouble with the taxis.
> When the American Base opened there was an invasion of vice-
> girls, but they were not allowed to settle, and were eventually
> cleared out.   Now they're creeping back in.   The money brings
> prosperity to the town, but it has its drawbacks.

The 'vice girls' were not quite the same as the girls who were
paid in dollars back in the 1960s.   Several Ardyne workers from
whom I gathered information explained, 'The boys are only interested
in rookies.'   When I asked what a 'rookie' was, they observed, 'a
rookie is a Third Division woman who is mature, eager and willing,
with no nonsense in her head'.   Kate Millet's term 'brute virility'
would best be applied to the attitude of some of the men. (50)
They did not compete with the Americans who were interested in
younger women ('jet set glamour' as a seaman put it to me).   The
sexual wants of the seamen did not clash with those of the navvies.
Most Ardyne navvies were mature married men interested only in the
stray adventure: 'a one-night stand m' boy', explained a navvy.
It was not the permissiveness of many of the incomers which bruta-
lised their heterosexual relationships, rather it was their male
arrogance and treatment of local women as so many objects - on a
level with a pint of beer after working at Ardyne, or with a rump
steak after working on the long night shifts in cold wet weather.

The stories of the McAlpine navvy escapades were legion in the
period, especially after Christmas 1974.   The methods by which men
managed to get women into their camp were a matter for considerable
local gossip.   The camp was a security location with the strictest
supervision, similar to that of any military camp.   But women were
driven into Ardyne camp in the boots of cars, and one on a truck.
'It makes for better chat at the Dunoon bus stop,' said an Innellan
woman.   'We used to talk about the weather, or the goins on of
"Coronation Street".'

Just as the Americans had affected the frequency and type of
deviancy and criminality locally, so too did the Ardyne work-force
in its turn.   Unlike the USN personnel, the Ardyne incomers were
not so easily distinguishable in the Sheriff Court reports of the
local press.   Sometimes, those who were convicted were identified
as residing at Ardyne Camp, less seldom as Ardyne workers.   However, it was significant that in 1973 after the 'go-ahead' for
McAlpine was given, the local crime figure rose significantly.
The convictions of local residents and of other Scots from 'the
other side' had risen appreciably.   The highest annual total since
1961 had been 73 non-USN non-motoring offences in 1971.   However,
the total non-USN offences between 1973 and 1975 were 112 (1973),
83 (1974), and 83 (1975). (51)   Records indicate that the number
of people 'of no fixed abode' who were guilty of local convictions
also went up in that period. (52)   Previously, there had been prostitutes coming into the town following the sailors, but in 1973-5,
the followers of the incomers tended to be mixed groups of older
women and 'mates' of the navvies, hoping for jobs at the site, or
for pound notes that might fall from their companions' more abundant
table.   These 'mates' wandered about the pier and the main streets.
Often they waited at the public houses for their friends to return
from Ardyne.   In 1974, there were eleven male confictions of people
of 'no fixed abode', and in 1975 there were eight.   In the previous
years from 1961, there had never been more than six in any one year.
'Spongers, that's what they are', said an Ardyne worker whom I met
on the boat on a journey across the Firth.

When criticisms of the McAlpine workers were rife in 1975, there
were only ten convictions of resident workers at Ardyne Camp (who
were guilty chiefly of breach of the peace). (53)   At this time
some local people blamed the Ardyne Camp personnel for almost every
misbehaviour or breakdown of law and order in Cowal.   Judging from
the convictions and observation, these accusations appeared to be
unfair.   The ten convictions, for example, represented only 8.6 per
cent of the total Sheriff convictions that year. (54)   It was the
Ardyne commuters who caused the trouble, throughout the McAlpine
venture, especially in 1973-4.

With regard to drugs, there did not appear to be any possession
of drugs amongst the navvies.   'Ye might pit a few pills in wi yer
booze to gee t a heave, but we fellers are in fur the chasers',
explained a McAlpine worker.

After the first conflicts there were fewer fights between the

navvies and the US seamen, because most of the navvies drank nearer
the pier and most USN men kept to the upper end of Argyll Street.
American cocktails did not appeal to the taste of men brought up in
the drinking habits of Clydesiders. There were pubs which catered
for one or other, but only a few publicans dared to cater for both,
such as the Argyll Bar, and it had to close down because of
breakages.

When I had lunch with the American officers in 1975 aboard the
Canopus*, the conversation turned almost immediately to the Ardyne
navvies. One senior officer remarked, 'the Ardyne worker has done
the Americans a power of good. The locals are now too annoyed
about the navvies to concern themselves about us.' Another officer
added, 'They're breaking up the joint, these hefty Irish guys.
Why, they're closing down the Argyll Bar because of them.' An
officer said, 'We've got our Shore Patrol to fix the flyers. The
McAlpine outfit has no control over their guys in town, and gee they
hit the town real hard.'

People locally were certainly turning their attention away from
the American presence, and complaining about the navvies, sprawled in
drunken stupor on pavements at noon, or making a nuisance of themselves on the ferries. These men were not the permanent core of
McAlpine workers, but tended to be the casual workers following the
job opportunities. People had been writing to the Glasgow Herald
about the rowdy, and often bawdy journeys between Dunoon and Gourock
in the summer of 1975 and residents called the ferry the 'booze
ship'.

A resident in the burgh pointed to a row of houses and said to a
Glasgow journalist:

That little row of houses there used to be filled with holiday-
makers in the summer, now we have a big crowd of American sailors
on the one side and a whole gang of McAlpine workers on the other
side. The singing and shouting sometimes goes on all night, and
there's a procession of young women arriving at all hours.
Anyone who comes here for holidays now is mad. Personally, I'd
move out like a shot if I could afford to. (55)

There was also the heavy drinking in the streets, as men wielded
bottles on the roadside. There was fighting at the Ardyne bus-
stop. Men urinated in house doorways and even execreted in stair-
ways of older buildings. One women put it this way, 'We used to
protest about dogs messing our doorways and gates, but now it's so-
called men.' When the USN created a nuisance, local residents
could always complain to the USN authorities, but now only a few
local policemen faced the formidable task of handling hundreds of
men from Ardyne.

They wandered about the town in navvy togs, often tired, weary
and hopelessly drunk, after having 'hit the town' following upon
doing a 'ghoster' (working through day and night without sleep), or
after having worked at 'a pour' for several weeks. 'A pour' was

* I was invited by the Chaplain and not by the Commander.

exacting work, when the flow of concrete had to pour continuously under constant supervision without a break for days on end.   The workers did extra long hours so that each shift would overlap the other to secure the maximum supervision and continuity of work. Most people in town knew when there was 'a pour', and as soon as it was over there was always a release of male exuberance in the local pubs with more fights and brawls, and hangers-on moving in.   The cultural scape was shaken.

Men were drinking on the ferries at 7a.m., as they returned to 'the other side' after a night-shift ar Ardyne: something that had never been seen before on Clyde ferries.   A journalist wrote about her crossing over the Firth in June 1975, describing a scene similar to that which I shared with others many times over two years.   She noticed that the summer pleasure ship was 'loaded to the gunn'ls with hefty chaps in working togs bound for the Ardyne oil rig development', she then added: 'a coffee cup goes flying over an old lady's tweedie lap.   "I used to like sailing across the Clyde", confided the woman later in the Ladies, "Now there's no pleasure in it at all.   You get elbowed out of the way and the bad language is so embarrassing."' (56)

People locally felt outraged that Dunoon was known as the 'beer town', and that their area was acquiring a bad name.   They had established certain forms of acceptable behaviour within Cowal which had no place for daytime drunkenness.   They had accepted certain modes of dress which were associated with holiday-making or tourism. The dirty togs and the dusty faces of hundreds of men moving through the streets of the old Victorian resort were incongruous.   There was a certain glamour attached to the large gleaming American cars, which were not as odd to people as were the large juggernauts, cranes, and workers' buses.   When cultural settings are disturbed by alien cultural forms which intrude upon the scene stresses are created.   The 'particularity' of life is affected and insecurity sets in.

It was noticeable that when navvies were the worse for drink they would poke fun at Americans.   Frequently in public places, especially at Dunoon pier, there was confrontation in the air.   I quite often saw a group of USN seamen move quickly in the opposite direction from a group of navvies; and I saw sailors on the ferry move downstairs in a huddle, when they spotted the navvies in the bar upstairs.   It was not surprising that a national newspaper stated that there was every possibility of a war between the men from Holy Loch and the men from Ardyne. (57)   People were cautious when they went out in the night.   'The old free and easy days are at an end', said one local mother.

The McAlpine men have a song, after the tune (more or less) of 'The Dublin Fusiliers', which has been sung throughout the civil engineering world from Argentina to Alaska.   It was chanted in the drinking haunts of the navvies in Dunoon.   Its words convey much of the 'cultural scape' in which the men live and work, and conveys a great deal of their spirit.

It begins with a monologue:

The crack was good in Cricklewood and you couldn't see the crown,
There were glasses flyin' and diddies crying - the boys were
goin' to town,
Oh, mother dear I'm over here, I'll ne'er will come back,
What keeps me 'er - the price o' beer, the biddies and the crack.

Then the verses:

It was down the glen came McAlpine's men with their shovels slung
behind them,
It was in the pub that they drank their sub or down in the spike
you'll find them.
We sweated blood and washed down mud with quarts and pints of
beer,
But now we're on the road again with McAlpine's Fuziliers.

I remember the day that the fellow O'Shea fell into a concrete
stair,
What Horseface said when he saw him dead wasn't what the rich
call prayers.
'I'm a navvy short', was his retort that reached unto my ears,
When the goin' is rough, oh, you must be tough with McAlpines
Fuziliers.

I've worked till the sweat near had me beat wi' washing, check
and pole,
At shutterin' jams up in the hydro dams or underneath the Thames
in a hole.
I've grafted hard and I got me card with many a ganger's fist
across my ears
If you value your life, don't join, by Christ, with McAlpine's
Fuziliers. (58)

The hard days and nights on the platform out in the basins in the
face of strong winds that swept up Loch Striven often amidst dangerous conditions which warranted the large wage, made huge demands
upon the men.   The hours were long (often the double shift), and
some men felt the need for release ashore, away from the basins,
dust and noise.   Like the USN crews, the McAlpine men were under
strain.   So, they 'hit the town' and had a 'fling'.   'Patsy of the
War Rigs', 'Spud was here', 'King Billy OK', were some of the
graffiti that registered their coming, at the bus-stop or toilet,
but in the pubs they had left behind them their songs, their
'cracks', and their 'Ardyne pound notes'.   Many locals remember
well the high atmosphere in those small Dunoon pubs with the
'rookies' and the McAlpine Fusiliers 'drinking hard' in the nights
of 1975-6.

It must be appreciated that the conditions for the navvies at
Ardyne were demanding.   Here the managers were fewer, the 'gangers'
many.   The pressures of keeping to the strictest work schedule to

prevent any slippage of the contract date for completion, made the 'gangers' petty press gang men keep their workers 'hard at it', whatever the conditions on the windswept shores of Ardyne.   When I asked for information, one of the staff at Ardyne told me over the phone that 'work not talk is the order of the day here.   And don't send me anything at the camp - the philistines will be sure to get hold of it!'   It was clear that only as a worker on the inside could I really appreciate fully the conditions of the men, and come to understand them more.   Difficulty of access cancelled this out. Moreover, my other inquiries ruled out my employment there.   As in the case of the military, I had to be satisfied with being on the outside, but so too were almost all residents, the impact on whom I wanted to study.   With them, I had more or less to look into the camp and the navvies from a distance.

It appeared to me that the navvies' lives were characterised by organisational independence, whereas those of USN men were characterised by organisational dependence.   R. Ryall, in his study of men working on four oil platforms, cites the close networks amongst the men and their supportive cliques. (59)   It is the clique which makes it possible for many of the men to survive.   Small groups move from one contractor to another and support each other, often following a 'ganger' to the best paid job at the time.   On the other hand, I would agree with A.J.M. Sykes, to whom I shall refer below in more detail, that many labourers are loners. (60)   During my time in Cowal, I often came across Ardyne navvies walking, or drinking, or travelling alone.   The military organisation contrasts with the organisational independence of the workers, because men are tied to their mates and peers from their joint training on their ships, tending to be more group-minded ('sticking together' more).

In general, with regard to the navvies, Sykes states that they often boast of their anti-social behaviour.   They usually view locals with suspicion.   A great many of the younger men have a glamorous view of their heavy drinking, their gambling and their fighting.   Sykes observes that they generally tend to despise men who save money, whilst many tend openly to flout the values of society.   I had discovered that these characteristics, identified by Sykes, were also to be found amongst hundreds of navvies employed at Ardyne.   One thing became very clear as the research advanced - the locals had little or no social contacts with the incomers.   Not one of the interviewees I contacted had had any recent conversation with any navvy.   'Here today and gone tomorrow' was very much the spirit whether at the camp or amongst the navvies who crossed each day by ferry.   Many of them went north to Aberdeen to seek bigger wages.   They were referred to as the 'Dunoon Mafia' by sociologists discussing the migrant oil workers at the March seminar of 1980 at Aberdeen University. (61)

What of the impact upon family, church, recreational pursuits and clubs locally?   These were considered in the case of the American impact.

Ardyne camp residents were largely resident, without family;

about 350 were there in 1974 when I arrived.   The majority of
workers came by ferry, and only a few families were resident in the
south-west, whilst some were in upper Kirn within the burgh.   In
addition, the men had long work hours, and very little time to
associate with local families.   The family impact was therefore
negligible in terms of influence.   In terms of effects, however,
the families of Cowal were shaken by the McAlpine presence.

Firstly, there were new hopes and expectations in the air - young
sons might not have to leave Cowal after all.   Some homes adopted
a more comfortable life-style, because some of the men had the good
fortune of procuring a job at Ardyne.   Other local men had the bad
fortune of being 'signed off', and having lost their former jobs,
felt alienated in a locality where neither the employers at Ardyne,
nor the employers of the locality would offer them any work.   Local
frustration and local jealousies within Dunoon's housing schemes
damaged working-class networks.   'Them big-headed lot doing damn
all for a fistful of money.   They were once along wi' us at the
Grammar school and in the queues at the exchange for the dole money,
but now they're the big-timers,' said an envious local.   'I've got
the biggest wage of my life,' said one of the local Ardyne employed
workers, 'but I've also got one of the biggest headaches too - my
neighbours just have not been the same since.   It's jealousy, I
suppose.   What with my new car and my wife's regular hairdos at the
hairdressers.'

The local churches were hardly affected, with the exception of
the RC parish.   The priests said Mass at camp every Sunday, and the
resident incomers, staying in Dunoon, did increase the numbers
appreciably at the RC church, but did not, however, join in parish
activities as the Americans did.   The husbands were far too busy at
Ardyne, and their wives were more retiring and shy of local involvement.   So, it could be said that, although there was a large number
of Catholic labourers at the camp and in the locality, their influence on parish life was peripheral.   It must be noted that the
McAlpine management had provided a special on-site Catholic chapel,
specially equipped with altar and a sanctuary, so that in itself was
indication enough that the number of Catholics was large.   The
local minister of the Church of Scotland did attempt to contact men
of Presbyterian conviction at the camp and had to discontinue, due
to the lack of numbers.

In terms of creating religious conflicts, the influence of the
navvies, as seen already, was considerable.   This created a situation that the locality had not known since the days, a hundred years
before, when the local Presbyterians blocked the exits to the pier
in an attempt to prevent people from 'the other side' coming ashore
on the Lord's day.   Perhaps the influx of Roman Catholic Irish or
Glasgow navvies in green helmets, travelling in green buses from the
pier to Ardyne*, revived the past in them, but as described already,

* Green has represented the Irish southener and the Catholics and
  has been associated with the Celtic football club at Parkhead,
  Glasgow.

it was probably the presence of the Orange Lodge, rather than any
eruption of latent opposition to the RC intruders, which created an
inflamatory situation, and also only affected a minority.

Clubs were not affected, neither were sporting pastimes.   The
Ardyne impact, however, did affect the men's drinking habits and
haunts.   There were men who not only avoided the pubs in Argyll
Street, but drank more at an earlier hour before the buses came in
from Ardyne.   Others drank at home, or out of either Dunoon or the
Innellan area.   For others, Saturday drinking was impossible,
because of the brawling and the crowding in the pubs.   When one
navvy put a stool through the huge mirror behind the bar in one of
the best pubs at the foot of Ferry Brae, the word went out and some
old faces disappeared.   Some locals, however, liked the changed
scene, because of the new influx of humour and often song, especially in the cold winter nights when once the pubs were quiet places,
'with a few old bores coming out with the same old stories and the
like', said a Dunoonite.

The McAlpine workers made up an organisation in which they were
independents, migrant workers with only the big money in mind.
Marginal people within the locality like their American counterparts, they tended to keep to themselves.   Like that of the military, the McAlpine organisation was a garrison within a world of
secrecy.   The organisation was watertight.   Although its workers
were not dependent as the USN personnel were, they had a rumbustious
mode of behaviour, which by no stretch of the imagination could
possibly attract people of Cowal.   As one man said to me, 'Ardyne
men could not care a tinker's damn about local people, they're not
here to make friends or to sell themselves, they're here to make
money.'   However, their instrumentalism and also their obvious
individualism did not clash as much with the shared ideals and
culture of the local people as did some of the USN incomers.

Having reviewed some of the main cultural stresses locally caused
by both the USN and McAlpine incomers, it will now be opportune to
conclude by assessing what the 525 interviewees had to say when I
called upon them at home in the autumn and winter of 1975-6.   The
interviewees chosen at random provided me with some insights linked
with the ethnography already presented.

Based upon responses of the 525 East Cowal residents, one is able
to identify four groupings amongst the interviewees:

1 191 who criticised the USN incomers, who were divided into:
111 persons who criticised the USN incomers more than once;
80 persons who criticised the USN incomers only once;
2 216 persons who criticised the Ardyne incomers more than once;
3 76 persons who criticised both sets of incomers more than once;
4 42 persons who did not criticise the incomers at any time.

Table 9.3 presents that data.   I calculated the above groupings by
noting the number of times the residents criticised the incomers,
but this did not include the negative responses regarding the
possible exodus of the incomers, which will be dealt with later.

TABLE 9.3 The three groupings of those who criticised the incomers compared with those who did not: their sex and their sector of residence

Sector of residence	Criticisms solely concerned with the USN incomers Frequencies						Criticisms solely concerned with the Ardyne incomers Frequencies						Criticisms with regard to both the USN and the Ardyne incomers					
	Nil		Once		Once+		Nil		Once		Once+		Nil		Once		Once+	
	n	%	n	%	n	%	n	%	n	%	n	%	n	%	n	%	n	%
n 97 NE of Dunoon — Male n 45	0	0.0	11	24.5	1	2.2	0	0.0	0	0.0	23	51.1	0	0.0	0	0.0	10	22.2
Female n 52	2	3.8	5	9.6	16	30.8	2	3.8	0	0.0	11	21.1	2	3.8	0	0.0	18	34.7
n 68 SW of Dunoon — Male n 28	0	0.0	0	0.0	4	14.2	0	0.0	0	0.0	24	85.8	0	0.0	0	0.0	0	0.0
Female n 40	4	10.0	4	10.0	9	22.5	4	10.0	0	0.0	23	57.5	4	10.0	0	0.0	0	0.0
n 360 Dunoon (Old Burgh) — Male n143	2	1.4	19	13.3	7	4.9	2	1.4	0	0.0	105	73.5	2	1.4	0	0.0	10	6.9
Female n217	34	15.7	41	18.8	74	34.1	34	15.7	0	0.0	30	13.8	34	15.7	0	0.0	38	17.5
n 525 Total — Male n216	2	0.9	30	13.9	12	5.5	2	0.9	0	0.0	152	70.4	2	0.9	0	0.0	20	9.3
Female n309	40	12.9	50	16.2	99	32.0	40	12.9	0	0.0	64	20.7	40	12.9	0	0.0	56	18.2

n = 191   n = 216   n = 76

There were one hundred and seven more women than men who were
solely critical of the USN incomers out of a total of 191 critics.
There were eighty-eight more men than women who were solely critical
of the McAlpine incomers, out of a total of 216 critics.   There was
a ratio of 3:5 women to men showing a greater difference in the case
of the former and 2:4 men to women in the case of the latter.   The
difference was more marked in respect of the women with regard to
USN incomers. (62)

As such, the actual responses of the 525 local residents did not
directly refer to the cultural scape as affected by the incomers,
but the responses, as will now be seen, did throw some light upon
what was happening within the cultural scape when taken into consideration with the ethnography and the episode of change as already
described.

Firstly, with regard to the 111 who criticised the USN incomers
more than once.   These divide into 99 women and twelve men.   Of
these 111, there were thirty-six persons who were most outspoken and
more vehement about their dislike for Americans.   Twenty-six were
women and ten were men.   The data as collated (at the Computer
Centre, University of Glasgow, 1980) shows that they were lower down
the socioeconomic scale, because 18 of the women and all of the men
had occupations which would be categorised as Registrar General's
social classes IV-V.   Twenty-five of the women and eight of the men
lived in council houses.   They were among the youngest of the
interviewees.   All of the women and men were under thirty.   The
data is in accordance with the view that the military mostly affects
lower socioeconomic groupings.   What also is clear is the fact that
not only were most of the critics of the USN incomers women, but
that the more antagonistic amongst the critics were also women.
Half of them were married.

The other 75 (73 women, 2 men) were not as ruthless in their
remarks;   they tended to be older, 73 (97.3 per cent) being between
30 and 59 years of age.   They simply criticised the incomers without ridiculing them, in contrast to the thirty-six persons above.
They were less distinguishable in terms of their socioeconomic
classification.

Remembering the points made earlier regarding local marriages,
the most emotionally loaded terms came from the men and women who
were not married.   Examples of their statements are as follows:
'These American bums ought to get the hell out of Dunoon';   'Scum,
I'd say they are - the bottom of the American barrel';   and
'Garbage, about the best name for these American louts.'   Perhaps
the younger men were peeved over the number of girls marrying or
dating American soliders.

As already noted, there was a very negative effect of enlisted
men in relation to women.   One nurse had said in 1974, when interviewed in the streets of the burgh, 'The young seamen think they are
God's gift to women and presume that we are just waiting to be
asked;   but many of us have learned from those local girls who have
been hurt.   I keep well away from them.'

What of the 216 who criticised the Ardyne incomers more than
once?   Firstly, there were thirty-nine women amongst them, who each
praised the American personnel in particular.   All of them were
women and were between thirty and thirty-nine years of age, owner
occupiers and, more important than all else, they each had contact
with the USN incomers.   Whereas those who criticised the USN incomers tended to be SNP supporters (93 out of 111, 83.7 per cent),
all of the thirty-nine were Tories.   The thirty-nine (7.4 per cent
of the 525) probably represented that small proportion of the local
population who mixed with the incomers, perhaps sharing interests
and time together gregariously.   Thirty-one of them were married,
and twenty-six of these had young children, not yet at school.
Having children at the local playgroups brought USN and local
mothers together, as was likely the case in this instance, because
of the remarks of a few of these mothers.   They were not young
mothers, being between 30 and 31 (the other eight were older: between 35 and 39 years of age).   There are a few points that must be
noted regarding these women, which relate to the ethnography.

As noted earlier, USN incomers mixed more with minority parishioners at local parish functions or services.   Apart from ten, who
were unsure of their religious denominational identity, the other
twenty-nine were adherents of eight different denominations.   In
contrast, all of the people who criticised the Americans were Presbyterians (there were 289 Presbyterians in the sample).

The thirty-nine had contact with USN personnel and in particular
with fourteen USN blacks.   One had the impression, based upon the
data, that many were family contacts and were free from racial
prejudice. (63)   Remembering that there were probably about 80
blacks at Base at that time, fourteen USN black contacts were proportionately more than might have been expected in a 6 per cent
sample.

At the outset, it must be said that the contact with the USN of
these thirty-nine women who had praise for them, and criticism for
the Ardyne incomers, represented only 7.4 per cent of the residents
interviewed.   The suggestion is that there was relatively little
contact with the USN incomers.   Most USN personnel kept to their
own naval groups, and within the security of their own corporateness.

In their replies the thirty-nine residents indicated that they
were in touch with at least 104 American households.   They were
mostly those of officers or POs.   As indicated by the data, most of
the contacts, 282 - 90.9 per cent, were made with the same persons
during the past week and past year.   The majority of contacts were
with the officers and their families;   contact with the enlisted was
clearly less evident.   Of the thirty-nine women, thirty-one were
wives, twenty-four of whom had pre-school children.   As one might
expect, the highest proportion in contact with the USN incomers was
in the north-east of Dunoon and least to the south-west, the latter
being farthest away from the USN Base.   Those with pre-school
children spoke of their meeting with USN parents at the playgroup

sessions, and as shown by the data, thirty out of the thirty-nine had contact with USN children.

None of the thirty-nine were Presbyterian. (64)   They belonged to a wide variety of denominations.   The minority churches locally had more contact with the USN incomers on a prish basis.   The Americans hardly affected the club life of the locality, but there was a very involved minority of the incomers who did associate and work with minority church groups.   There was one particular Baptist woman in the south-west who had contact with eleven American fami-lies through her religious ties with the Baptist fellowship.   The high proportion of blacks (considering the low number at Base in 1975-6), was due also to the contact made by two other Baptists and a RC.   They both spoke of their church links with them.

In addition to these thirty-nine there were another 51 persons who were well disposed towards the USN incomers, and badly disposed towards the Ardyne incomers.   Like the thirty-nine, they were within the 216 grouping.   Firstly, there were eight men and four women who had daughters married to USN incomers.   They were criti-cal of the Ardyne incomers, and in their conversations were making invidious comparisons between the USN and Ardyne strangers.   The Americans they generally described as 'civil' and the navvies as 'uncouth', 'rough', 'not fitting in', or the like.   Secondly, there were the thirty-nine who had corresponded with the USN.

Of these thirty-nine there were twenty-eight fathers and four mothers, who were corresponding with Americans who had once been at Holy Loch. (65)   All of them were parents.   As noted earlier, in terms of marriage, there were indications that some women admired the American wives.   As already noted, thirty-one of the thirty-nine women who had spoken with USN incomers were wives.   But, the above also shows that as many as twenty-eight fathers also were cor-responding with ex-Polaris Holy Loch families.   Twenty-five of them indicated that they were writing jointly with their wives - letters, in other words, from couples.   In addition, there were letters from couples to single American personnel, who had once been their lodgers (in my sample there was only one household with a USN lodger - lodgers had decreased since the 1960s.

It is interesting that amongst the 216 persons who had criticised the Ardyne incomers more than once, there were 90 who had either had contact with the USN incomers currently at Holy Loch, or were writ-ing to former contacts who had left the locality, or who had daughters married to USN personnel.   Ties with the incomers were therefore evident amongst 17.1 per cent of the interviewees.   These represent probably that slice of the local population upon whom the USN had had the greatest positive effects.   The ties were familial, one way or another, and largely with the officers, suggesting that positive good effects were mainly those of the officer caste and their dependants.

Any possible cultural long-term impacts upon their way of life depended upon the degree of contact.   The good relations might well

have been diluted by wider and more negative USN societal impacts
such as the growth of drug addiction. Good relations were largely
confined to those of minority church people at cultural levels. In
the contact made between senior officers and the influential families, the link was almost always of a diplomatic, almost public
relations nature. Only a handful of influentials were probably on
familiar everyday terms with the outsiders. In addition, the ties
were very restrictive. Once the Americans left after completing
their duty, the locals with whom they interacted did not seem to extend their friendship to other Americans.

What of the Ardyne intruders and their impact upon the 216, who
had been criticised by them more than once? As has been noted
already, the men had stronger feelings in this instance than they
had regarding the American outsiders. As indicated by the details
of Table 9.3, there were at least twice as many men as women who
criticised the Ardyne workers more than once out of the 216 critics.

The men had been put out by the incoming navvies, in their drinking haunts, and by the abrasive effects they had upon the men in
terms of religion. The toilet graffiti indicated that local men
were expressing their protests on walls, although they were a
minority. The large number of men in the sample, however, who were
critical of the navvies may very well indicate that many males
locally were affected by the navvies at both the lower and higher
socioeconomic levels. In terms of the cultural scape, the customary behaviour and routines of life in Cowal appeared to be more
generally affected across class boundaries.

The men and women who criticised the Ardyne incomers were from
higher socioeconomic groupings than they were in the case of those
who criticised the USN incomers. As already noted, there was a
growing antagonism for the Ardyne project amongst those who ran
local businesses, who were joined for totally different reasons by
those who were skilled and in manual employment. The latter wanted
to be employed at Ardyne, the former had successfully blocked them
once they saw the drain of skilled men moving out to Ardyne Point.
In addition, there were many who had been pleased that they were
enjoying life away from the heavy industries of 'the other side' to
settle in quiet Cowal, which was romantically called 'the gateway to
the Highlands'. The trucks, the navvies and the rising concrete
legs of the platforms were seen by many interviewees as the threat
of an expanding industrial take-over. Such fear was ill-founded as
it turned out, for when the landscape and the traditions of any
locality are altered in any way by industrialists, local rumour
turns the most exaggerated forebodings into threatening certainties.
50 of the 216 who criticised the Ardyne incomers expressed fears
that the locality might become an industrial extension of 'the other
side'. (66)

What of the 76 who criticised both the USN and Ardyne incomers? (67) Their number (14.5 per cent) compared with that of
the sole critics of the USN personnel (36.4 per cent), or with the sole
critics of the Ardyne incomers (41.1 per cent), shows that the com-

bined presence of the USN and McAlpine incomers mattered less than
the single aggravation felt by the two main groupings already referred to above.   The 76 people were blander in their criticisms.
The women were more heterogeneous than the men.   I had noticed that
those who were only critical of the USN tended to originate more
from the 'outscape' than those who criticised the Ardyne incomers.
With the 76, origin from the 'outscape' was less evident regarding
both women and men.   It appeared that the 76 tended to be the incomers, who had simply wanted peace and quiet.   They expressed as
much.   35.7 per cent of the women, in contradistinction to the men,
represented the drifting women in their middle years, who were
single and crossed the Firth to find peace in accommodation that was
left them by recently deceased relatives. (68)

There were forty women who did not criticise the incomers at any
time during the interviews. (69)   I was struck by the fact that
they tended to be older than those who did criticise the incomers,
that they were often more isolated retired women and housewives in
the burgh.   They were also primarily from the locality.   They
appeared to be oblivious of the recent incomers.   I have already
spoken of the anomaly of people in the midst of change, who are not
aware of it.

When it came to determining the origin of the interviewees, I was
struck by the number who originated from the 'outscape'.   It seemed
that many had been married into local families, and many others had
been evacuees during the Second World War.   Dunoon and locality was
not only a place for strangers in transit, or on tour, or on holiday, it appeared to be inhabited by many settlers from the outscape.   Many explained that they had come on holidays and fallen in
love with the place, deciding to buy, rent for a time, and then
settle down amongst the hills of Cowal.   These people quickly identified with the area, and were more critical of the recent naval and
navvy incomers than the local natives, as my data demonstrates.
Some of the people, when asked where they were born, refused to
answer.   I felt that they did not want to reveal their outside
origins.   Many giving it, would quickly add, 'But, I've been here
for years, I'm a local now.'   (The natives tended to state with
great pride that they were the 'real locals'.)

I had expected that the criticism of the American children would
have been significant, but out of 455 responses, only 62 had stated
that they were more badly behaved than the local children (and only
two that the Ardyne children were worse). (70)   In fact, the USN
children were held in high regard: 51 said that they were better
behaved than local children; and 340 that they were as well behaved
as the local kids. (71)   In fact, when I was in the area, a 17-
year-old American girl had been elected Grammar School Captain.   In
addition, the building of the larger Primary School at Sandbank and
of a new RC school in Dunoon, to make more room for the bulge in US
school pupils, had defused the earlier heated debate over the over-
crowding in the primary schools.

What of the views of the residents with regard to the possible

exodus of the intruders?   In fact, most of the interviewees chose
not to indicate their feelings.   There was, however, a large negative response to the possible exit of the Ardyne workers, travelling
to Dunoon and back on the Gourock ferries, and also a less dramatic
negative response related to the USN wives.   With regard to the
possible exit of the navvies travelling from Gourock (37.1 per cent)
195 of the 525 interviewees were either 'glad' or 'overjoyed'.
With regard to the possible exit of the American wives, there were
101, who said that they would be 'glad', in contradistinction to 72,
who said that they would be 'sad'. (72)

As was seen, there was considerable local concern about the
tourist image of the locality.   The rough, tough navvies who
crowded the ferries were a talking point locally.   But the 101 who
said that they would be glad when the US wives moved out presented a
surprisingly high negative comment from a locality in which the
wives had been involved in local charity and general welfare.   One
man may have explained the feelings of a cruel segment of the 101
persons: 'American ladies get under ma skin; they're like a lot o'
busybodies interferin wi' oor folk, tryin' tae cut a figure, tryin'
tae get intae the local press fur do-goodery and aw that.   We
dinnae need their US subs, and we dinnae need their candy charity.'

In concluding this chapter, it can be said that in cultural
terms, the American and Ardyne worker impacts had had a disruptive
effect mainly in their quest for 'wine, women and song'.   The alien
nature of the men from nearer or wider outscapes also entailed culture clashes because the wants, expectations, fears, prejudices, and
habits of people of an outside scape were transferred to that of a
foreign local scape, where life tended to be localistic, and limited
by its own wants, expectations, fears, prejudices and habits.   The
male sexism of the incomers was an obtrusive negative factor in each
case.   The incoming American seamen appeared to have an effect upon
the illegitimacy rate and certainly upon the heterosexual behaviour
of the youths.   Ardyne workers' impact was less.   The high rate of
illegitimacy which took place in the wake of the Ardyne intrusion
would have probably been related to the involvement of older outside
women who came over to the local pubs and haunts of the navvies.

The increase in deviancy in the form of soft drugs was one USN
effect not shared by the impact of the Ardyne workers.   The overt
drunken behaviour of navvies in the streets, morning and afternoon,
was one particular effect of the navvy presence which affected the
tone of the area in a way which the American invasion never did.
The institutions of the family, of law and order, and of religion,
had each in turn come under the impact of alien patterns of behaviour and outscape values.   All of which took place within an over-
lay of complex effects and surprises in a situation of increasing
uncertainty.   One wonders how the local way of life and the cultural scape could survive the multiple impacts upon them, especially
when crime soared in 1973-4.

There is a sense in which the very nature of the USN and McAlpine
organisations made the total obliteration of a local cultural scape

a virtual impossibility.   Firstly, the Americans were highly dependent members of an organisation which could not afford to be perme-
able.   Its walls were those of a garrison.   Its cultural scape
could truly be described as a 'Little America', a cultural colony
living its own life with its own goals within an alien local scape.
Only the hedonistic wants of the younger enlisted men, in particular, drew the men out of their naval shell, often to plunder the
locality.   The American dependants did live amongst the locals, but
with little contact, and where it existed the families were off
within two years, to yet another round of ephemeral relationships
somewhere else on the globe.   The American Naval Department also
made doubly sure through its monitoring political and civilian machinery that abrasive cultural impacts were cushioned.   How badly
this worked at times has been obvious.

Secondly, the McAlpine workforce was not only in Cowal for a
short period, it was made up of men who were detached from the local
scene.   The organisation like that of the USN Base was not perme-
able and tended to be a world unto itself, which shunned local
involvement and was cosmopolitan in terms of values and outscape
contacts.   Almost all its workers were migrants so that a nomadic
mentality dominated the droves of workers on the ferries, the buses
and on the pavement of parochial Cowal.

The interviews highlighted the above observations, and the
greater criticism by the local women of the USN incomers and that by
the local men of the McAlpine incomers served particularly to show
more cogently the main effects upon the sexes and their cultural
scapes.

It was clear that the conjuncture of both the navvy and navy
impacts upon the cultural scape had shaken the local scene.   Court
convictions rose rapidly in number from late 1972 and remained well
above average till mid-1974.   Almost by way of symbolising the
general misbehaviour and the general unrest, two youths (one from
the burgh and one from Sandbank) in 1972 assaulted the Dunoon
provost.   The people were shocked.   The youths were called for
trial at the Sheriff Court in November 1972 on the eve of what has
probably been East Cowal's worst period of street unrest and
breaches of the peace during the stressful period from November
1972 to March 1974.

Part Four

CONCLUSION

Chapter 10

PUTTING TOGETHER
THE PICTURE

I always say to our people go and dig the truth out and it will
be our truth, because the truth is always partial and so are we.
(Tony Garnett) (1)

The conjuncture of events in East Cowal between 1961 and 1976 were
particularly drastic, perhaps unique because they brought together
the impacts of increasing militarisation, industrialisation and
bureaucratisation within a peripheral area whose total population
including incomers was approximately 16,808.   The study was therefore able to examine these developments at local levels not only
contemporaneously, but to some extent comparatively within the limitations of time.   The importance of assessing the process and episodes of impact was appreciated throughout the research.

Firstly, by way of recapitulation, there were, broadly speaking,
certain identifiable phases with regard to each of the impacts which
were as follows:

1 Initial shock: November 1960-March 1961; this included the
period just before and just after the establishment of the Polaris
Base and was initiated by Harold Macmillan's statement as divulged
on 5 November 1960.

2 Period of spin-offs, April 1961-February 1963: this period extended after the establishment of the USN Base until the end of the
immediate repercussions when they levelled off.

3 Period of routinisation and uneasy co-existence,which commenced
in March 1963: it began once the USN Base had become part of the
configuration of life locally and once a pattern of coexistence had
begun.   When I left, in February 1976, the period had not yet run
its course due to the recurring unease and uneven routines, and
periodic unrest or protests against the Base.

There were three phases to the McAlpine project:

1 Initial shock of McAlpine's project, as happened between November

1972, when the local people first heard of the project, and March 1974 when McAlpine managed to extend his site on the Cowal shores.

2 Period of spin-offs from March 1974-March 1975: the site could now cater for the building of six platforms at one time, and not for 400 workers, but for at least a thousand men.   The scheme was then described as 'the rape of Ardyne in the national interest' in the issue of the Dunoon Observer on 23 March 1974.

3 Period of routinisation commenced in March 1975, when the work-force was at its maximum, and more or less established.   In the initial period McAlpine established the site;   in the secondary, McAlpine extended the site;   and in the third, McAlpine's workforce settled down to steady production and the winning of orders for platforms.

There were two phases of the Strathclyde impact which took place before my departure in February 1976:

1 Initial shock: from the Wheatley Report, October 1969, when administrative changes were to be arranged till finalised in May 1975.

2 Period of spin-offs from May 1975, when rates rose phenomenally in the locality, when there was confusion over the number, boun-daries, and types of community councils, and perplexity over the jurisdiction of the Region's centre and the District's centre. People did not know where they were, especially the aged, as they sought advice.   Lochgilphead, the District HQ, could be reached by occasional buses and by car, and it was miles away, and expensive and inconvenient to visit.   People had to write, or phone - if they could afford it - when they had a District problem. As regards the eventual adaptation period, I was never there to see it happen.   I left when people were witnessing the spin-offs in the immediate period after implementation.   The scheme had not yet fully established itself.

The effects of these impacts upon the local scapes are listed in Table 10.1.

TABLE 10.1

The effects upon the ecological scape

The USN impact	The McAlpine impact	The Strathclyde impact
1 The USN impact	2 The McAlpine impact	3 The Strathclyde impact
1.1 The nesting assembly associated with environmental features of the landscape and seascape remained much the same, and attempts were made to make the ships part of the tourist loch attractions. The ships and submarines were out of sight for most people in the burgh and the south-west. Access to the Holy Loch and sailing was not forbidden, although the movement was impaired.	2.1 The nesting assembly was altered by the creation of a new hill. It had an inhibiting effect for some Toward folk because the familiar open aspect was altered. For others, the well-landscaped hill did not spoil the local scene. The McAlpine platform-building site was out of sight for most people in the burgh, the north-east, and also for Innellan people, and most other parts of the south-west. Three miles of shore were now out of bounds.	3.1 The nesting assembly – no effects identified.
1.2 The quality of the setting was affected by the noise from vessels. The presence of the vessels did not alter people's views generally about the beauty of the locality. With regard to the hazard of radiation there were no explicit fears, but at least 20 per cent of the 525 interviewees had found the Base 'worrying'. 300 mentioned 'the healthy sea air'.	2.2 The quality of the setting was affected by the noise from the site and the roads leading to it from Dunoon along the shore. The McAlpine site however did not alter people's views generally about the beauty of the locality.	3.2 The quality of the setting was not altered in Dunoon District, except that the main road in Dunoon which Strathclyde Roads Dept could not manage to resurface for months, remained an ugly sight – the tarmac laid was peeling off the surface onto shoes and car tyres.

1.3   In the long-term there was hope that the ships and submarines would move out.
In the meantime, there were some who lived in the 'inscape of yesterday' who did not appear to notice the Polaris Base. 42 persons did not mention the Polaris Base at any time out of the 525 interviewed at their homes, and spoke as if the USN Base was non-existent. They contrasted with the others who appeared to be well aware of the presence of the USN Base.

2.3   In the long-term there was hope that the site would close down, and that afterwards McAlpine would build a marina in the area. There were some who were living in the 'inscape of tomorrow' with dreams of a new Ardyne. There were others who lived in the past in the 'inscape of yesterday', speaking as if there had been no influx of navvies, and apparently unconscious of their presence and of the Ardyne complex.

3.3   In the long-term there were fears that Glasgow would alter the locality's environment, because roads and tourism would come under the administration of in insensitive urban planners, and industrialisation take place in the environs. Inverkip Tower on 'the other side' was an ever-present ugly symbol of what the planners on the other side could do to the beautiful Firth of Clyde.

The effects upon the economic scape

1   The USN impact
1.1   Goods in the form of Scottish souvenirs and mementos increased in the shops, as also did tartan material. There was an increase in the sale of alcohol and spirits and petrol. So, shopkeepers, etc. gained but some also suffered. American luxury goods were sold at discount prices, as was food at USN PX exclusive stores. There was also increased buying on 'the other side' by USN personnel and dependants.

2   The McAlpine impact
2.1   Goods: there was an increase in the sale of alcohol throughout the week. So, publicans profited. One pub closed, however, through damages.
Petrol increased locally because the garage owners made up the leeway caused by loss of staff to Ardyne. Big wages for mechanics were paid to keep them from going to Ardyne.

3   The Strathclyde impact
3.1   Goods: no effects were identified.

1.2 Services: public transport ceased, there was an increase in taxis, probably seven-fold. Housing Accommodation had a high priority for married USN personnel in particular. Rents soared. There were gains for some landlords, but higher rents for locals. Hospital Services were strained, especially the maternity unit with an increase of young families from the USA. Local patients did not suffer, but NHS subscribers were concerned about the free medicine for USN personnel and dependants. Locals could not enter their PX stores, but Americans could enter the Dunoon hospital. Education: USN used local schools. Rotation at base created a disorganised school programme with uneven influx of pupils during the school year.

1.3 Employment: there was no impact except that a handful of employees were local.

2.2 Services: public transport was not used, but was affected by drivers leaving for better wages at Ardyne. Housing Accommodation had a high priority. Houses were bought, rather than rented by McAlpine for the firm's employees. Hotels were also bought, especially in the south-west. House prices soared. Hospital Services: no effects identified. Education: none were identified.

2.3 Employment: there was a significant impact. There was a disparity in wages between the local unskilled man at Ardyne and those who were employed locally, e.g. skilled workers and mechanics, also bus drivers and local tradesmen.

3.2 Services: there was a massive rise in the rates once Strathclyde was created - rates were to rise by 30 per cent in three years. Housing Accommodation was not immediately affected, because the old County Council building programme was to be conserved, expectations of higher rate of house building did not then materialise. House loans were made more available for some. Hospital Services: none were identified. Education: none were identified. Amongst other services, that of the local police force was improved considerably: 6 new policemen and 4 wardens were allocated to the area.

3.3 Employment: none were identified.

232 Chapter 10

Employees left local employers. 'Run-down' services. Old employers' ties were severed and resulted. Some laid off. These were unable to return to their former bosses. Those who were turned away from Ardyne (after SNP MP had intervened on behalf of local employers) were envious of those employed at Ardyne.

1.4 Tourism: 12.2 per cent of the travellers on the ferries who were interviewed stated that the USN personnel had ill effects upon Dunoon and/or locality. 18.2 per cent stated that both the USN and Ardyne workers had a bad effect upon Dunoon and/or locality. The majority of these stated that the worse effect of the USN was on Dunoon.

The effects upon the political scape

1 The USN impact
1.1 As a political issue Polaris was dead during the autumn General Election of 1974. The SNP Manifesto was against retention of Polaris, but the campaigners did not quote this, there being a fear that they might alienate

3.4 Tourism: to be an outside responsibility within the Region. Many locals were sceptical about Glasgow's ability to publicise the attractions of the locality.

2.4 Tourism: 45.9 per cent of the travellers on the ferries stated that the Ardyne personnel had ill effects upon Dunoon and/or locality. Many praised the warmth and the hospitality of the people. Most agreed that Ardyne workers had a particularly bad effect upon Dunoon.

2 The McAlpine impact
2.1 As a political issue oil was central at the autumn election of 1974. Ardyne was caught up in the general debate. The SNP MP made much of the issue of England not planning realistically, and the rush of industrialists and

3 The Strathclyde impact
3.1 As a political issue regionalisation was very much an SNP bugbear. The party wanted the National Assembly to become the central administration machinery in an independent Scotland. The

some of the local influentials who clearly had always supported the Polaris Base.

1.2 The 'status quo' in terms of local controls and power was reinforced by the USN senior staff. The local Town Council members were courted by the Polaris captains and the Polaris Commander.

1.3 Outscape political conflict was brought into the locality regarding the black American issue. It affected youth locally, but was a bigger problem for senior staff at the Polaris Base. It was to cause problems later ashore with the riot. The riot had been triggered off by conflict over girls rather than by a political issue, but latent feelings about black power did surface.

engineers to create sites without regard for local need. Too many were created, so people had suffered needlessly.

2.2 The 'status quo' in terms of local controls and power was not reinforced by the Ardyne venture. The County Council was contacted, but it was soon to be disestablished, as also the Dunoon Town Council. The latter was by-passed, and Town Councillors were not consulted, and the SNP MP took on a central role in negotiations with management at Ardyne.

2.3 Outscape political conflicts in Ulster were raised within the locality as issues by the navvies. Some locals were involved, probably because of the presence of the Orange Lodge. Local tolerance had been a feature, but with Ardyne workers coming into the area, together with the establishment of the Lodge, friction arose. As the toilet graffiti showed, a great deal of hostility between groups was triggered off.

local SNP M made much of the issue, and many locals took sides leading to further political divisions between Tories and SNP electors.

3.2 The 'status quo' in terms of local controls and power was altered dramatically. An elected Town Council - 'the local parliament' - was completely destroyed after a century of rule locally. The County Council also went, but most locals had little time for the County Councillors at Lochgilphead, which, in fact, became the District HQ. Dunoon lost out badly.

3.3 Outscape political conflicts associated with the Labour and Tory confrontations in Glasgow had consequences locally, because the SNP and Tory electors feared that the Labour hold at that time on city politics might alter the scene locally, where local councillors tended not to be elected on any party ticket and where the people were generally anti-Labour. Local elections took on a new dimension after Strathclyde, caught up as they were with the politics of the city of Glasgow and of other industrial cities of 'the other side'.

The effects upon the cultural scape

1 The USN impact
1.1 Customary behavioural patterns were affected. Younger girls under sixteen years of age dated sailors. Greater sexual permissiveness was commented upon in the press. The national press cited the local trend. At first the illegitimacy rate doubled. Over time the sailors found their way to 'the other side', where they had access to prostitutes, which removed much of the stress locally. Deviancy in the form of drug addiction also increased locally. The Americans added to the breaches of the peace and to careless driving in the area. Fighting over local girls created conflicts between local men and USN personnel which erupted into a major naval riot and also had racial undertones.

2 The McAlpine impact
2.1 Customary behavioural patterns had suffered hardly any impact, apart from the occasional fight with local or USN men. The illegitimacy rate also rose dramatically not long after the navvies came, but it appeared that the women involved were from 'the other side', who accompanied the men together with a growing number of persons who were of 'no fixed abode'. The navvies were responsible for breaches of the peace and for drunken behaviour.

3 The Strathclyde impact
3.1 Customary behavioural patterns: none were identified.

1.2 Effects upon family life varied between those who had an American son-in-law, or enjoyed contact with the USN personnel and dependants, or those who looked upon the USN personnel as a sexual threat to their daughters, and those who could not stand their sense of superiority, Americans emphasised the status of the family and believed in it as an institution. Locals did sometimes admire the stability of USN marriages. Wives locally were impressed with the US wives' freedom.

2.2 Effects upon family life were not dramatic in terms of influence, but some families had an altered pattern because the young sons did not have to leave Dunoon because Ardyne now offered some of them employment. Jealousies between families followed upon the changed life-style of homes where men and a few women had been employed at Ardyne. Longer hours and weekend work disturbed some.

3.2 Effects upon family life: none were identified.

1.3 Effects upon religion were such that the US orshippers associated with the parishioners of the minority churches rather than with the Presbyterians. The Baptists and Roman Catholics had more contact than most. Of all the 90 interviewed who had either a daughter married to a USN mariner, or who were corresponding with USN incomers who had left the area, or who had been currently in contact with American incomers locally, none were Presbyterian.

2.3 Effects upon religion in terms of parish involvement were almost non-existent. With regard to religious conflict, there was some evidence of abrasive encounters, as shown by the toilet graffiti.

3.3 Effects upon religion: none were identified.

1.4 Effects on entertainment and sporting pastimes were felt upon the stage, but this did not alter the Scot's preference for traditional Scottish humour and Scottish music and dance. The American influence on local sporting pastimes was more apparent. But shinty, football and golf were still very much the local preferences.

1.5 Effects on clubs and associations was less obvious. Only the YMCA and the Scottish-American Ladies Club appeared to be jointly sponsored by the locals and the incomers.

1.6 Effects on drinking habits were not widespread, because the Scots preferred their own drinks. Some Dunoon pubs catered for the USN incomers. The Americans tended to keep to one in particular at the top of Argyll street.

2.4 Effects on entertainment and sporting pastimes: none were identified.

2.5 Effects on clubs and associations: none were identified.

2.6 Effects on drinking habits were evident amongst the men in Dunoon, who shifted their time and place of drinking to avoid confrontations with the Ardyne navvies. Some pubs, however, were jollier because of the navvies, who helped to bring good cheer to them in the dull winter nights.

3.4 Effects on entertainment and sporting pastimes: none were identified.

3.5 Effects on clubs and associations: none were identified.

3.6 Effects on drinking habits: none

Note: General effects on people:

Approximately 36* per cent more
women (interviewed in the 6 per
cent sample) than male residents
criticised the USN personnel.
They tended to be from lower
socioeconomic groupings. They
were amongst the youngest and
least married of the under-
thirties.

In contrast, 415 girls had
married USN personnel between
1961 and 1973.

Approximately 40* per cent more male
(interviewed in the 6 per cent
sample) than women residents criticised the Ardyne workers. They were
from both the lower and higher
socioeconomic groupings.

Although the issue of Strathclyde
had caused divisions before (and
at first during implementation),
people became more united when
they were disturbed by the changes.
These affected them more than did
the impacts of the USN and
McAlpine workers.

* Percentage taken as a proportion out of the n of males and females, including the 191, 216 and 76
groupings as in Table 9.3.

In terms of a possible synthesis several components appear to
be crucial.

THE FIRST COMPONENT WAS THE INTRUSION OF THE OUTSCAPE ON THE LOCAL
SCAPE

The three impacts exemplified the strategy of militartists, industrialists, and bureaucrats, whose tactics followed the same lines
of action.   They were all carried out in the name of the higher or
common good.   They all created local division, or ambivalence, with
regard to their schemes.   They all promised local benefits.   They
were all characterised by 'a show' of democratic free discussion, or
even open protest, but 'de facto' negotiated by secrecy and 'in
camera'.   At the same time, they were all supremely autocratic
acts, whose deliberations were of intrigue, and whose priorities
were those of self-interest in the outscape, whatever the costs to
the local scape, which they exploited, regardless.   Surprise and
alacrity were the key to their success, but only after a pre-phase
was created, in which the divisions could take place.   Once people
were divided over the issue(s) involved, the plans could be implemented.   When the plans were devised and thought up in the wider
outscape, as the Polaris invasion was, the scheme was bound to be
more clandestine, more unpredictable, and fraught with uncertainty.

THE SECOND COMPONENT WAS THE EPISODE OF CHANGE WHICH ACCOMPANIED
EACH IMPACT

Initial shock created confusion, and totally unpredictable periods
in which what was really happening was eclipsed by the local concern
with less significant implications.   Once the spin-offs took place,
the local people were preoccupied with the spin-offs, and overlooked
the long-term effects, or the intent of the strategy in the first
instance.   There were some who gained and some who lost out as
spin-offs affected people diversely.   Divisions increased.   For
example, the Ardyne impact was welcomed by the local workers, and
decried by many local employers who lost them to Ardyne.

THE THIRD COMPONENT IS CONCERNED WITH THE TEMPORAL DIMENSION AND THE
CONJUNCTURE OF EVENTS WITHIN THE PERIOD UNDER FOCUS

Figure 10.1 presents the three impacts within this frame of refer
ence.   The three phases of each of the three impacts are set out,
running in parallel lines.   They are separately drawn in this way
for clearer identification;   in fact, they should be understood to
come together and create overlays.   With their conjuncture, the
people had to contend with all three· at the same time, and in the
same locality.   It is evident that the period of the greatest uncertainty was between November 1972 and March 1974.   As can be seen
from the diagram, there were then three converging impacts, two of
which were initial, and the third in the phase of uneasy adjustment.
It was as though people were moving through a maze, and the further

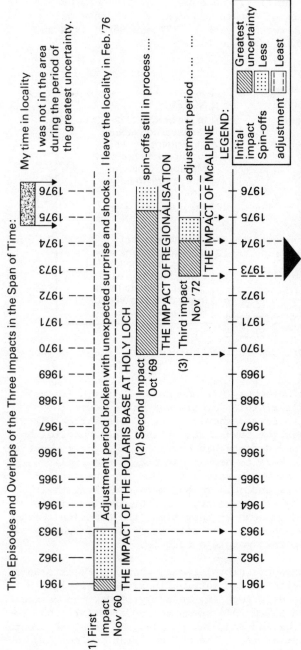

The Episodes and Overlaps of the Three Impacts in the Span of Time:

My time in locality

I was not in the area during the period of the greatest uncertainty.

I leave the locality in Feb.'76

1) First Impact Nov '60

Adjustment period broken with unexpected surprise and shocks ...

THE IMPACT OF THE POLARIS BASE AT HOLY LOCH

(2) Second Impact Oct '69

spin-offs still in process .....

THE IMPACT OF REGIONALISATION

adjustment period ....

(3) Third impact Nov '72

THE IMPACT OF McALPINE

LEGEND:

Initial impact
Spin-offs
adjustment

Greatest uncertainty
Less
Least

Between November 1972 and March 1974 there was a conjuncture of 2 initial impacts and a period of uneasy adjustment to the USN invasion. Between Jan. and Dec.1973, when the pressures upon the locality were at their height the non-motoring offences reached their peak at 130 (the mean for the period 1961-Feb 1976 was approx. 75) and the motoring offences reached their peak of 295 (the mean for the period 1961-Feb. 1976 was approx. 202). These figures indicate the considerable local unrest that existed in the period.

FIGURE 10.1   The overlap of impact episodes and the levels of disturbed routines

they went in the passage of time, the more uncertain they became. The unexpected conjuncture of events crowded in upon them discon- certingly in the period between November 1972 and March 1974 and local crime shot to its highest (see Figure 10.2).

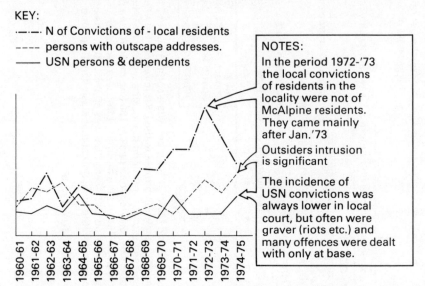

KEY:
—·—·— N of Convictions of - local residents
- - - - persons with outscape addresses.
———— USN persons & dependents

NOTES:
In the period 1972-'73 the local convictions of residents in the locality were not of McAlpine residents. They came mainly after Jan.'73

Outsiders intrusion is significant

The incidence of USN convictions was always lower in local court, but often were graver (riots etc.) and many offences were dealt with only at base.

FIGURE 10.2   Sheriff Court convictions between 1961 and 1975 (non-motoring offences)

In the period between November 1972 and March 1974 (inclusive) the USN effects were still visible: there was unrest over the influx of US children into local schools; the US riots took place, and there was protest over the over-usage of the local hospital by USN incomers.   The Ardyne incomers had begun to make their negative impact; the exodus of workers to Ardyne had begun, and public services were suffering, as buses were withdrawn for the lack of local drivers; as plumbers and joiners and mechanics left their jobs to seek the better wages at Ardyne.   The Strathclyde implemen- tation in May 1975 looked ominous at that time: the Damocles sword had dropped upon local autonomy.   The cold steel of bureaucracy began at once to cut deep into people's budgets.

If one compares the days of initial shock, when the Polaris Base was announced, and the national and international publicity given to the demonstrations at the Holy Loch in the early 1960s, the period between November 1972 and March 1974 seems to register far less pro- test.   However, apart from the Sandbank people, the local residents had not joined the demonstrators.   The CND movement had not touched them, and led by the Town Council of Dunoon many local people appeared at first to welcome the USN.   Some were more concerned about the invading 'beatniks' and the damage that they were doing to the tourist trade.   The people of the local scape appeared, throughout the USN intrusion, to have been able to detach themselves from the issues discussed on 'the other side'.   Only when their personal lives were affected, did they collectively demonstrate concern.   In the episode of change, consciousness is dulled, and when one impact after another takes place, it is difficult to adjust and take an objective look.

Returning to the temporal dimension, it was clear throughout my period in the locality, that there was hope that in time the USN submarines and vessels would pull out, and that the navvies would leave the locality for good.   That hope anchored them in the turmoil, and many said so to me, often referring to the day when the submarines and the navvies would move out.

THE FOURTH COMPONENT HAS TO DO WITH THE DIMENSIONS OF THE FAMILIAR

I referred early in this book to 'particularity', which refers to the familiar micro dimensions of a setting and its local routines.

The familiar skyline and seascape in Cowal remained much the same for most local residents for most of the time, except for those around Holy Loch and around Ardyne.   Familiar sounds and sights for many around these spots were affected by the impacts of the alien invasions.

What had once been a peaceful area, became particularly stressful between November 1972 and March 1974, judging by the appearances in the Sheriff Court of sailors, navvies and locals in breach of the peace, and later a growing number of youths convicted of drug abuse.

It is not therefore surprising that hundreds of locals criticised the incomers during my interviews in the locality.

THE FIFTH COMPONENT HAS TO DO WITH THE DIMENSION OF THE SOCIAL INSCAPE

One focuses here upon the shared views of people which sediment over time, as people share and discuss the same routines or the local round of life.   It is therefore experiential, and is of a different order from sharing reported details about events beyond the local scape.   It has two elements: experience of the phenomena, and also shared views about it which form the basis of a 'social inscape'.

The reason why I interviewed people during the research was to tap their experience and views.   Local views may converge, and the shared experience of living through impacts being to indicate common plight and stress, or shared benefits.   Obviously, when people communicate their plight and stress with others in the same milieu their singular experience takes on a plural social dimension.

THE SIXTH COMPONENT HAS TO DO WITH THE SUBJECTIVE DIMENSION

Although this is not a psychological study, and although I have
already stated that I am not studying the singular inscape experience 'per se', none the less I became aware that some people were
consciously or unconsciously escapist, or unaware of what was
happening in East Cowal.   They presented an anomaly locally.

As noted, Ogburn spoke of 'selective forgetting'.   There were
clearly some who forgot the days of CND protest, or cut out the
realities that were too threatening for them.   Whether these were
conscious or unconscious processes, I could not tell, but having
talked with 803 local people in the interview situation, and lived
locally, I had come across people who appeared to be cut off from
the realities.

Many were living in the present, but because of the complex over-
lay of the three impacts, there were necessarily lags in people's
perception and awareness of what was happening.   There were lags
between those for whom the impacts meant many things, and for whom
there were felt effects which varied and contrasted by reason of the
diverse social circumstances of each.

There were also those who were living for tomorrow, when the
locality could be restored to its former status as 'gem of the
Costa Clyde'.   They appeared to be living in hope, and spoke of
Ardyne 'tomorrow' with its marina, and of the locality as thronged
with visitors, and not a US sailor in sight.   The navvies have
gone, but Ardyne is now a derelict site.

Chapter 11

POSTSCRIPT

Many events have taken place since I walked on to the gangway of the
Gourock ferry at Dunoon Pier in February, 1976 and left Cowal, after
the completion of my local studies. However, the people of the
locality, at the time of writing this book, still continue to be
under siege. Although McAlpine has left behind the scarred sea-
scapes at Ardyne, and disillusioned people with their empty dreams,
Kilmory Castle still casts its bleak shadow from the outscape of
Lochgilphead upon the now empty Council Chambers at Castle House,
Dunoon. On the horizon across the Firth the bureaucracy of Strathclyde still looms up from 'the other side', as the Glasgow City
Chambers strengthens the metropolis's regional administrative hold
upon the historic terrain of Argyll. On Holy Loch, the gull-pale
hull of the depot ship and its black squadron of ballistic submarines still remind the local residents that the locality is a
strategic outpost of the USA. The base's deployment and strike
action of the squadron is controlled in the outscape, beyond the
UK. The uneasy coexistence of the local residents and the naval
incomers is still punctuated with surprises and recurrent impacts.

The people of Sandbank by Holy Loch found in September 1981 that
their homes were literally surrounded by US naval installations, as
the USN moved into yet another 50-acre plot which they had leased
clandestinely. The people of the village felt 'claustrophobic' and
hemmed in on all sides. (1) In protest the Sandbankers wrote
directly to President Reagan and not to the Prime Minister of the
UK. They had attempted to protest to the PM over the American
intrusion years before but without avail. They said in their
statement to President Reagan:

> Over the years our village life has been numbed by the sprouting
> growth of the American complex - housing, private car parking,
> offices (even the foreshore taken when land ran out), ample
> building for leisure and entertainment, etc., all for exclusive
> American use. All this crammed into the bounds of a rural com-
> munity of under 400 homes and 1200 population, 50 per cent of
> whom are elderly.

We see our roads in little better condition, than they were 20
years ago.   Land for District Council housing is now at a pre-
mium.   There is no public amenity space in the village.   No
public car park - but the US Navy has 500 car parking spaces, exclusive to themselves within the village.

It had been firmly promised that there would be the minimum of
shore installations.

Today, the reality is very different.   For example, this unit
of 50 acres would almost complete the encirclement of our
village.   The whole community is getting a general 'claustrophobic' foreboding and our people say that enough is enough.   We
thus appeal to you, President Reagan, to very firmly put on the
brake. (2)

The episode indicates that the oblique dealings of the USN
authorities endure and the locality still continues to be plundered
by forces in the outscape.   Curiously, the pillage which the area
has suffered throughout history is replicated again and again.

The ecological hazards and threat also remain.   The national
press reported that a USN Poseidon ballistic missile on 2 November
1981 had dropped into the Holy Loch, as it slipped from the depot
ship's crane into the water.   The Dunoon Observer reported on 21
November: 'Claims that a missile dropped into the Holy Loch from
the USS Holland during loading operations were refuted yesterday by
the US Navy.' (3)   Mr Duncan Campbell of the New Statesman observed, 'Everything the US Navy has been saying has been a greater set
of lies than ever before.' (4)   The claim, which could be substan-
tiated, was that the operator of the crane was drunk, doped, or
both. (5)   Evidence was cited that there was a 50 per cent chance
of the missile exploding.   The experts were divided, but concerned.

The Dunoon people and the villagers especially of Sandbank,
Kilmun and Strone were shocked by the incident, but not by the indifference of the House of Commons.

The response within the House of Commons to the accident was no
different from that of the 1960s.   When Mr George Foulkes MP drew
the Prime Minister's attention to the incident, Mrs Thatcher said
'there had been no danger in the incident'. (6)   Parliament then
turned its attention to the business of the House.

In an area often shrouded in mists and fog, mystification continues to settle around the ominous turtlelike base and the ten submarines of the US 14th Squadron.   It obscures the uglier realities.
Deceit and uncertainty prevail, as is well expressed by a Cowal
woman in the following letter to the Dunoon Observer on 5 December
1981.

Two weeks ago there was an accident on a nuclear submarine in the
Holy Loch; that is a fact, but we only found out about it in a
round-about way.   Although the whole of this area was in peril,

we did not know anything about it.   How many more accidents will
happen without our knowing? (7)

There is no knowing what twists the US presence will take.   When
this account was about to go into print, in March 1983, a Dunoonite
wrote to me:

> The women of Greenham Common will find as we have found that
> whatever their protest, or the strength of their arguments, what-
> ever their public support, cruise missiles will be installed.
> The democratic structure of this nation is a hoax.   The UK is
> ruled by the USA.   No electorate can alter that, and no Parlia-
> ment can control the situation.

Strong words, but set in the context of the Polaris affair they
cannot simply be brushed aside as groundless and exaggerated.   The
impact of the centre on the periphery in terms of plans and schemes,
whether bureaucratic or industrial, also poses crucial questions
about the rights of people and the ethics, if any, which influence
politicians.

NOTES

1 SETTING THE SCENE

1 K. Mannheim, Ideology and Utopia, London, Routledge & Kegan Paul, 1936 (1960 edition), p. 175.
2 Dunoon Observer and Argyllshire Standard, 4 March 1961.
3 Ibid., 11 March 1961.
4 D.E. Plowman et al., 'Local Social Status in England and Wales', in Sociological Review, 1962, X, no. 2; P. Collison, The Cutteslowe Walls, London, Faber & Faber, 1963; I. Emmet, A North Wales Parish, London, Routledge & Kegan Paul, 1964; R. Glass (ed.), London: Aspects of Change, London, McGibbon & Kee, 1964; H.H. Jennings, Societies in the Making, London, Routledge & Kegan Paul, 1962; J. Littlejohn, Westrigg, London, Routledge & Kegan Paul, 1964; J. Spencer, Stress and Release in an Urban Estate, London, Tavistock, 1964; W.M. Williams, A West Country Village - Ashworthy, London, Routledge & Kegan Paul, 1963; P. Willmott, The Evolution of a Community, London, Routledge & Kegan Paul, 1963; N. Elias and J.L. Scotson, The Established and the Outsiders, London, F. Cass, 1965; R. Frankenberg, Communities in Britain, Harmondsworth, Pelican, 1966.
5 See C. Bell and H. Newby, The Sociology of Community, London, Frank Cass, 1974; C. Bell and H. Newby, Community Studies, London, Allen & Unwin, 1971; M.R. Stein, The Eclipse of Community, Princeton University Press, 1972 edn; E. Poplin, Communities: A Survey of Theories and Methods of Research, New York, Macmillan, 1972; M. Stacey, Tradition and Change: A Study of Banbury, Oxford University Press, 1960; D.W. Minar and S. Greer, The Concept of Community, London, Butterworth, 1969; G.A. Hillery, Jnr, 'Definitions of Community: Areas of Agreement', Rural Sociology, 1955, 20, pp. 111-23; G.A. Hillery, Jnr, Societies: Evolutionary and Comparative Perspectives, Englewood Cliffs, N.J., Prentice-Hall, 1963; G.A. Hillery, Jnr, Communal Organizations: A Study of Local Societies, University of Chicago Press, 1968; R. Konig, The Community, London, Routledge & Kegan Paul, 1968; G. Salaman, Community and Occupation, Cambridge University Press, 1974; R. Nisbet, The Social Philosophers, London, Heinemann, 1973.

6 Consult the bibliography attached to the SSRC Report to the
   North Sea Oil Panel, The Planning Exchange, Glasgow, 31 May
   1977; R. Moore, 'Northern Notes Towards a Sociology of Oil',
   Scottish Journal of Sociology, November 1978, vol. 3, no. 1;
   J.J. Rodger, 'Inauthentic Politics and the Public Inquiry
   System', Scottish Journal of Sociology, November 1978, vol. 3,
   no. 1, pp. 103-27; J.D. House, 'Oil Companies in Aberdeen: the
   Strategy of Incorporation', Scottish Journal of Sociology,
   November 1978, vol. 3, no. 1; M. Grieco, 'Social Consequences of
   Rapid Industrial Developments in Sparsely Populated Areas',
   Aberdeen University, 1976, unpublished ms; A.P. Cohen, 'Oil and
   the Cultural Account: Reflections on a Shetland Community',
   Scottish Journal of Sociology, November 1978, vol. 3, no. 1,
   pp. 124-41.
7 A. Toffler, Future Shock, London, Pan, 1970.
8 Webster's Third New International Dictionary, W. Benton.
9 Ibid.
10 W.F. Ogburn, Theories of Social Change, New York, B.W. Huebach,
    1922, see pp. 145-6 and 150-93.
11 Ibid.   See also G. McFarlane, 'Shetlander Identity: Change and
    Conflict', ms cited in the RNSOP.   See T. Steel, The Life and
    Death of St. Kilda, Glasgow, Collins, 1975.   The unpublished
    ms, 'Way of Life Seminars', Edinburgh University, 1979, were
    found to be most helpful when I was formulating my ideas.
12 See T. Cox, Stress, London, Macmillan, 1978 and H.M. Proshansky et
    al. (eds), Environmental Psychology, Holt, Rinehart & Winston,
    1970, especially p. 410ff and R.W. Kates, Experiencing the
    Environment as Hazard.
13 See F. Braudel, Écrits Sur l'Histoire, Paris, Flammarion, 1969,
    as cited by A.S. Smith, Social Change, London, Longman, 1976.
14 Toffler, op. cit., ch. 4.
15 E.C. Zeeman, Catastrophe Theory: Collected Papers, 1972-1977,
    Reading, Mass., Addison-Wesley.   See also D. Postley,
    Catastrophe Theory, Glasgow, Fontana, 1980.
16 M. Stacey, 'The Myth of Community Studies', British Journal of
    Sociology, June 1969, pp. 134-47.
17 J.R. Gusfield, Community, Oxford, Basil Blackwell, 1971.
18 P. Sztompka, System and Function, New York, Academic Press,
    1974, see pp. 111-23.
19 G.A. Hillery, op. cit., 1955.
20 E. Gellner, 'Concepts and Society', ch. 7 in Sociological Theory
    and Philosophical Analysis, eds D. Emmet and A. MacIntyre,
    London, Macmillan, 1970.
21 R.L. Warren, 'Toward a Reformulation of Community Theory', Human
    Organization, 1956, 15, no. 2, Summer.
22 A.J. Vidich and J. Bensman, 'Small Town', in Mass Society,
    Princetown University Press, 1958.
23 Stacey, op. cit., 1969, p. 145.
24 See W. Outhwaite, Understanding Social Life, Allen & Unwin,
    1975, for a discussion of 'form'.
25 P. and B. Berger, Sociology: A Biographical Approach, Harmonds-
    worth, Penguin, 1976.
26 See W.A.M. Peters, G.M. Hopkins, Oxford University Press, 1948
    and W.H.C. Gardner, Gerard Manley Hopkins, Harmondsworth,

Penguin, 1953, and Duns Scotus, Opus Oxoniense and the Sentences
of Peter Lombard, c. 1301.

27 G.D. Suttles, The Social Construction of Communities, Chicago
University Press, 1974, pp. 4-5.

28 Ibid., p. 7.

29 R. MacIver, as presented in R.L. Warren (ed.), Perspectives on
the American Community, Chicago, McNally, 1966.

30 Smith, A., op. cit., pp. 20-3.

31 N.J. Smelser, 'Towards a Theory of Modernisation', in A. and E.
Etzioni (eds), Social Change, New York, Basic Books, 1964.   See
also N.J. Smelser, 'The Modernization of Social Relations', in
M. Weiner (ed.), Modernization, New York, Basic Books, 1966.

32 J. Bensman et al., Reflections on Community Studies, New York,
Harper & Row, 1971, p. i.

2 THE MAKINGS OF NEW DUNOON

1 R. Konig, The Community (trans. E. Fitzgerald), London, Routledge & Kegan Paul, 1968, p. 7.

2 J.E. and R. Inglis, Handy Guide to Dunoon, Dunoon, Inglis, 1883.

3 T. Dunlop, Notes on Dunoon and Neighbourhood, Glasgow,
R. McKenzie, 1885, p. 8.

4 The blockade at the pier to the 'Sunday Breakers' is commented
upon in the issues of the Dunoon press of the 1870s.

5 K. Marx, The Eighteenth Brumaire of Louis Bonaparte, Moscow,
Foreign Language Publishing House, 1852, p. 5, published 1954.
See also the following for discussions on the historical dimen-
sions of settlement studies: R. Long, The Community, London,
Routledge & Kegan Paul, 1968, p. 76; W.E.S. Form and D.C.
Miller, Industry, Labour and Community, New York, Harper
Brothers, 1980, p. 51; A.S. Vidich and J. Bensman, Small Town
in Mass Society, Princeton University Press, 1958; R.A. Nisbet,
'Moral Values and the Community', Industrial Review of Community
Development, 1960, no. 5, pp. 77-85; C.M. Arensberg and S.T.
Kimball, Culture and Community, New York, Harcourt, Brace,
Jovanovich, 1965; Avenshez and Kimball, 'A Community Study:
Retrospect and Prospect', American Journal of Sociology, 1967-8,
vol. 73, pp. 691-705; D. Martindale, Institutions, Organisa-
tions and Mass Society, Boston, Houghton Mifflin, 1966, pp.
198-9; P. Cohen, Modern Social Theory, Lond, Heinemann, 1968,
see p. 151; E.H. Carr, What is History?, New York, Knopf, 1962;
H.S. Hughes, 'The Historian and the Social Scientist', American
Historical Review, 1960, vol. 66, pp. 20-96; H.S. Hughes, 'His-
tory, the Humanities and Anthropological Change', Current Anthr
Anthropology, April 1963, vol. 4, pp. 140-5; H.S. Hughes, His-
tory as an Art and as a Science, New York, Harper & Row, 1964;
C. Degler, 'The Sociologist as Historian: A Look at Reisman,
Whyte and Mills', American Quarterly, Winter 1963, vol. 15, pp.
483-97; B. Moore, Jnr, Political Power and Social Change: Six
Studies, Cambridge, Mass., Harvard University Press, 1958;
R. Bierstedt, 'The functions of Anthropological Methods in
Sociology', American Journal of Sociology, January 1948, vol.
54, pp. 22-30; M. Stacey, Tradition and Change: A Study of

Banbury, Oxford University Press, 1960; Stacey, 'The Myth of
Community Studies', British Journal of Sociology, June 1969,
pp. 134-47; M.R. Stein, The Eclipse of Community, Princeton
University Press, 1960; M.R. Stein et al., Reflections on
Community Studies, Princeton University Press, 1971, ch. 6;
R. Frankenberg, Communities in Britain, Harmondsworth, Penguin,
1966.

6 Konig, op. cit., p. 76.

7 Stein, op. cit., 1971 edn, pp. 275-6.

8 See Rev. M.M. MacKay, The New Statistical Account of Scotland
Vol. VII, Edinburgh and London, William Blackwood & Sons, 1845,
p. 569.   See also G.C. Smith, Argyll, in Third Statistical
Account, C.M. MacDonald (ed.), Glasgow, Collins, 1961, p. 333.
For a comprehensive study of the derivation of 'Dunoon', see A.
McLean, Dunoon Observer and Argyllshire Standard, 1970, where
other derivations are considered in scholarly fashion.

9 MacKay, op. cit., p. 568.

10 1st Statistical Account of Scotland, Renfrew, Argyll, vol. 2,
p. 48.   Drawn up from the communications of the ministers of
different parishes, 1791, Edinburgh, Sir John Sinclair.

11 See Dunoon Observer and Argyllshire Standard Centenary Issue,
27 March 1971; Major A.J.M. Bennett, solicitor, gave a talk on
Dunoon on the evening of 18 January 1923, which was reprinted in
the 1971 issue which referred to the ferry road.

12 See both Statistical Account (1791) and Dunoon Observer and
Argyllshire Standard, March 1971.

13 A. Webster, Account of the Number of People in Scotland 1755,
published 1921, p. 29.

14 1st Statistical Account of Scotland 1791, op. cit., p. 385.

15 Dunoon Observer and Argyllshire Standard Centenary Issue,
27 March 1971.

16 McKay, op. cit., pp 595ff.

17 Ibid., pp. 594-5.

18 Ibid.

19 Ibid., p. 598.

20 Ibid., pp. 598-600.

21 Ibid., p. 593.

22 1st Statistical Account, p. 389.

23 Ibid., p. 391.

24 Ibid., p. 392.

25 Ibid., pp. 30-1.

26 Ibid., p. 388.

27 A.G. Frank, Sociology of Development and Underdevelopment of
Sociology, London, Pluto Press, 1971; A.G. Frank, Capitalism
and Underdevelopment in Latin America, New York, Monthly Review
Press, 1967.

28 H. Hamilton, The Industrial Revolution in Scotland, Oxford,
Clarendon Press, 1932, pp. 1ff.

29 E. Shevsky and W. Bell, Social Area Analysis, Stanford Univer-
sity Press, California, 1955; B.J. Berry and P.H. Rees, 'The
Factorial Ecology of Calcutta', American Journal of Sociology,
April 1969, 74, pp. 445-91.

30 M.M. MacKay, Memoirs of James Ewing, Esq., Glasgow, James
Mackelbrose, 1866, p. 95.

31 See J. House, Down the Clyde, Edinburgh and Glasgow, W. & R. Chambers Ltd, 1959.
32 MacKay, op. cit., 1866, p. 96.
33 M. Lindsay, Clyde Waters, London, Robert Hale, 1958.
34 MacKay, op. cit., 1845, p. 627.
35 Ibid., p. 621.
36 Lindsay, op. cit., p. 75.
37 A.J.S. Patterson, The Victorian Summer of Clyde Steamers 1864-1888, Newton Abbot, David & Charles, 1972, p. 179.
38 MacKay, op. cit., 1845, p. 612.
39 Lindsay, op. cit., p. 75.
40 Patterson, op. cit., p. 197.
41 Ibid., p. 114.
42 Ibid., p. 197.
43 Ibid.
44 1st Statistical Account, p. 385.
45 MacKay, op. cit., 1845, pp. 628-9.
46 Frankenberg, op. cit.
47 House, op. cit., p. 112.
48 See ibid.
49 Ibid., p. 110.
50 Lindsay, op. cit., p. 83.
51 Ibid., p. 89.
52 Ibid.
53 G.C. Smith, op. cit., p. 339.
54 Ibid., p. 339.
55 Ibid., pp. 338-9.
56 Ibid., p. 339.
57 Ibid.
58 R.G. Returns 1914-1946 (HMSO).
59 Census 1961, Argyll (HMSO).
60 G.C. Smith, op. cit., p. 338.
61 R.G. Returns, 1911-1961 (HMSO).
62 MacKay, op. cit., 1845, p. 602.
63 Ibid.
64 G.C. Smith, op. cit., p. 334.
65 Ibid., p. 339.
66 Ibid., p. 625.
67 Ibid., p. 609.
68 MacKay, op. cit., 1845, p. 613.
69 F. Tönnies, Community and Association, London, Routledge & Kegan Paul, 1887, 1955 edn.
70 Electoral Rolls 1930-61 at Register House, Edinburgh. See also the discussion of 'private-regarding'/'public-regarding' attitudes in J.Q. Wilson, 'Planning and Politics: Citizen Participation in Urban Renewal', Journal of America, Institute of Planning, XXXIX, 1963, no. 4, pp. 242-9.
71 G.C. Smith, op. cit., p. 330.
72 See Dunoon Observer and Argyllshire Standard Centenary Issue, 1971.
73 See A. McLean's articles in the Dunoon Observer and Argyllshire Standard in the 1970s and the Centenary Issue of 1971.
   A. McLean, a Dunoon lawyer, researched the town's records and reviewed court cases of the Dunoonites versus the new grandees

in the late nineteenth century.   He produced a pamphlet, published by W. Inglis of the Dunoon Observer, on the derivation of
the name of the town, and was most familiar with Dunoon's history, especially the litigations.

74   In local history such as that of Lindsay, op. cit.;   House, op.
cit.;   cited also by Local Tourist Brochures over the years and
cited in Inveraray Court Records.   See also T. Dunlop, Notes on
Dunoon and Neighbourhood, Rutherglan, R. MacKenzie, 1885, p. 7;
and Jack House, Dunoon, Dunoon Town Council, 1968, p. 10.

75   G.C. Smith, op. cit., pp. 333ff and Dunoon Observer and Argyllshire Standard, 27 March 1971.

76   G.C. Smith, op. cit., p. 334.

77   Ibid., p. 337.

78   Ibid.

79   Ibid., p. 341.

80   E. Durkheim, The Division of Labour (trans. George Simpson),
Chicago, Free Press, 1893, 1960 edn.

81   The practice continues.   A new hostel has been built for these
pupils in upper Kirn.   The pupils come from many scattered
areas of the West, both from the Isles and rural areas of
Argyllshire.

82   See Censuses (HMSO) up to 1931 inclusive.

83   G.C. Smith, op. cit., p. 335.

84   See adverts and church notices in the holiday brochures at
Dunoon Library.

85   G.C. Smith, op. cit., p. 59.

86   Ibid.

87   See Dunoon Observer and Argyllshire Standard, Centenary Issue,
1971.

88   As a transit point northwards and stopping place it had always
been immersed in events outside the locality in political terms.

89   G.C. Smith, op. cit., p. 335.

90   Shevsky and Bell, op. cit..

91   See Smith's account in the Third Statistical Account, op. cit.

92   R. Redfield, A Maya Village, Washington D.C., Carnegie Institu-
tion of Washington Publications, 1934, p. 448;   R. Redfield, The
Folk Culture of Yukatan, University of Chicago Press, 1941;
J.F. Embree, Suye Mura: A Japanese Village, University of
Chicago Press, 1939;   C.P. Loomis and J.A. Beegle, Rural Social
Systems, Englewood Cliffs, N.J., Prentice-Hall, 1950;
G. Hillery, Jnr, 'Villages, Cities and Total Institutions',
American Sociology Review, 1958, 28, pp. 779-91;   G. Hillery,
Jnr, Communal Organizations: A Study of Local Societies, Univer-
sity of Chicago Press, 1968.

93   Dunoon Observer and Argyllshire Standard, 6 April 1960.

94   Ibid.

95   G.C. Smith, op. cit., p. 14.

3   THE MILITARY INVASION

1   C. Wolf, Garrison Community, Connecticut, Greenwood Publications, 1969, p. 66.

2   The Survey of International Affairs, Oxford University Press,
1970, pp. 132 and 164.

3   Parliamentary Debates (Hansard), Vol. 627: House of Commons
    Official Report: Session 1959-1960, p. 279.
4   Ibid., vol. 629, p. 37.
5   See 'Man-Environment Relationships', in D. Canter and
    P. Stringer, Environmental Interaction, Surrey University Press,
    1975.
6   Dunoon Observer and Argyllshire Standard, 5 November 1960.
7   Ibid.
8   J. House, Dunoon, Dunoon Town Council, 1968, p. 5.
9   Hansard, op. cit., see Column 333.
10 Ibid., see Column 337.
11 Ibid., see Column 340.
12 Ibid., see Column 343.
13 Ibid., Debate on 2 November 1960.
14 Ibid., see Column 375.
15 Ibid., see Column 306.
16 Ibid., see Column 444.
17 Ibid., see Column 777.
18 Ibid., see Column 837.
19 Ibid., see Columsn 830-2.
20 Ibid., cited by Mr Davies MP, on 16 December 1960 in the House
    of Commons, see Column 746.
21 Quoted by ex-marchers living in Yorkshire and in Glasgow whom I
    interviewed concerning their marching experiences in the early
    1960s whilst I was carrying out my research programme.
22 Dunoon Observer and Argyllshire Standard, op. cit.
23 Ibid.
24 Ibid., 12 November 1960.
25 Ibid.
26 Ibid., 10 December 1960.
27 Ibid.
28 Ibid., 17 December 1960.
29 Ibid., 25 February 1961;   see CND attempts to block the USS
    Proteus.
30 Ibid., 30 December 1961.
31 Ibid., see issues of December 1961 and June 1962.
32 A. Vagts, A History of Militarism, New York, Meridian Books,
    1959.
33 M.D. Feld, 'Professionalism and Politicalisation: Notes on the
    Military and Civil Control', in M.R. Van Gils (ed.), The Renewed
    Role of the Military, Rotterdam University Press, 1971, pp. 269-
    71.
34 A senior officer at the Polaris Base was my informant regarding
    this ratio.
35 M.D. Feld, 'The Military Self-Image in a Technical Environment',
    in M. Janowitz (ed.), The New Military Changing Pattern of
    Organisation, New York, Russell Sage Foundation, 1964, 1971.
36 D.R. Segal and M.W. Segal, 'Models of Civil-Military Relations
    at the Elite Level', in The Perceived Role of the Military,
    Rotterdam University Press, 1971.
37 Ibid.
38 P.H. Partridge, 'Education for the Profession of Arms',
    Canberra Papers on Strategy and Defence, no. 5;   R.A. Preston,
    'Military Academics in a Changing World. Possible Consequences

of the Student Protest Movement', in <u>The Perceived Role of the
Military</u>, p. 14.

39 K. Lang, <u>Military Institutions and the Sociology of War</u>, New
York, Russell Sage Foundation, 1972; S.P. Huntingdon, <u>The
Soldier and the State: The Theory and Politics of Civil Military
Relations</u>, Cambridge, Mass., Harvard University Press, 1957.

40 B. Abrahamsson, <u>Military Professionalisation and Political
Power</u>, New York, Russell Sage Foundation, 1972, p. 15.

41 H.L. Willensky, 'The Professionalisation of Everyone?', <u>American
Journal of Sociology</u>, 1964, 57, no. 2, pp. 137-58.

42 A. Etzioni, <u>A Comparative Analysis of Complex Organisations</u>,
Chicago, Free Press, 1961, pp. 14ff.

43 C.C. Moskos, <u>The American Enlisted Man</u>, New York, Sage, 1970,
p. 47.

44 J. Van Doorn, 'The Officer Corps: A Fusion of Profession and
Organisation', <u>Archives Européenes de Sociologie</u>, 1965, 6, pp.
262-82.

45 A. De Tocqueville, <u>Democracy in America</u>, New York, Vintage
Paperback Edition, published 1954, vol. II, pp. 286ff.

46 S.A. Stouffer et al., <u>The American Soldier</u>, Princeton University
Press, 1949, vol. I, pp. 371-2.

47 Moskos, op. cit., p. 45.

48 Ibid., p. 68.

49 Ibid., p. 69.

50 M.D. Feld, 'Professionalisation and Politicalisation ...', op.
cit., pp. 273 and 275.

51 Moskos, op. cit., and National Opinion Research Center, 1964,
published 1966, University of Chicago.

52 D.J. Carrison, <u>The United States Navy</u>, New York, Praeger Lib.
of US Government Department and Agencies, 1966.

53 US Department of Defense, <u>Selected Manpower Statistics</u>, 1968, 37.

54 Moskos, op. cit.

55 S.P. Huntingdon, <u>The Soldier and the State</u>, Cambridge, Mass.,
Harvard University Press, 1957.

56 A. Vagts, op. cit., chs 9 and 12.

57 M. Janowitz, <u>The Professional Soldier</u>, Chicago, Free Press,
1960, ch. 12 in particular.

58 T.W. Adorno et al., <u>The Authoritarian Personality</u>, New York,
Harper, 1950; M. Rokeach, <u>The Open and Closed Mind</u>, New York,
Basic Books, 1960; K. Roghman, <u>Dogmatismus and Authoritiaris-
mus</u>, Meisenheim am Glan, Hain, 1966; W. Eckhart, 'The Factor of
Militarism', <u>Journal of Peace Research</u>, Oslo, 1969, 2, pp. 123-
33.

59 Moskos, op. cit., p. 47.

60 J.P. Thomas, 'The Mobility of Non-Commissioned Officers', in <u>The
Perceived Role of the Military</u>, op. cit., p. 155. Thomas does
not present the applications as adapted by the researcher in the
text.

61 Moskos, op. cit., pp. 64ff.

62 M. De Fleur, 'Occupational Roles as Portrayed on TV', <u>Public
Opinion</u>, Spring 1964, 28, pp. 57-74.

63 See R.W. Hodge et al., 'Occupational Prestige in US: 1952-1963',
<u>American Journal of Sociology</u>, 1964, 70, pp. 286-302.

64 K. Lang, <u>The Military Institutions and the Sociology</u> of War,
New York, Sage, 1972, p. 66.

65 Moskos, op. cit., p. 76.
66 S.A. Richardson, 'Organisational Contrasts on British and American Ships', ASQ, 1956, vol. 1, p. 168.
67 Moskos, op. cit., 1970, pp. 50-1.
68 Moskos, op. cit.
69 Ibid.
70 Ibid., pp. 90 and 183.
71 Ibid., p. 122.
72 Ibid., p. 146.
73 J.E. King, 'Civil Affairs: The Future Prospects of Military Responsibility', American Paper, 1958, No. 3, Bethseda, Maryland Operations Research Office, June 1958 Staff Paper.
74 M.D. Havron, 'Non-Conventional Educational Requirements for the Military, in The Perceived Role of the Military, op. cit., p. 315.
75 K. Von Clausewitz, On War (trans. J.J. Graham, rev. edn, 3 vols), London, Routledge & Kegan Paul, 1949.
76 K. Marx and F. Engels, as quoted and cited in Guerilla Warfare and Marxism, ed. W.J. Pomeroy, New York, International Publishing Co., 1968, pp. 63 and 66.
77 D.B. Bobrow, 'Adaptive Politics, Social Learning and Military Institutions', in The Perceived Role of the Military , op. cit., pp. 296-7.
78 C.W. Mills, The Power Elite, New York, Oxford University Press, 1956.
79 Carrison, op. cit.
80 Ibid.
81 Ibid.
82 Ibid.
83 Ibid., pp. 76-7.
84 See FBM Facts, Washington Official USN Information Brochure sent to me by Dept of Navy.
85 Carrison, op. cit., p. 79.
86 M. Janowitz, 'The Emergent Military', vol. I of Public Opinion and The Military Establishment, ed. C.C. Moskos, New York, Research Progress Series, 1970, p. 258.
87 Lang, op. cit., p. 137.
88 M. Janowitz, The Community Press in an Urban Setting, Chicago, Free Press, 1952; R. Konig, The Community (trans E. Fitzgerald) London, Routledge & Kegan Paul, 1968, p. 147; B. Berelson, 'What Missing the Newspaper Means', in P.F. Lazarsfeld and F.M. Stanton (eds), Communication Research, New York, Harper, 1948-9; E. Katz and P. Lazarsfeld, Personal Influence, Chicago, Free Press, 1955; L. Ivirsky (ed.), Your Newspaper, New York, Macmillan, 1947; W. Albig, Modern Public Opinion, New York, McGraw-Hill, 1956; N.E. Long, 'The Local Community as an Ecology of Games', American Journal of Sociology, LXIV, November 1958, pp. 251-61.   See J. Samuels, 'Pareto' on Policy, New York, Elsevier Scientific Publishing Co., citing Pareto 'Treatise on General Sociology', The Mind and Society, 1974, 1963 print.
89 See Dunoon Observer and Argyllshire Standard, Saturday, 3 April 1971, statement of Provost Harper.

4 THE INDUSTRIAL INTRUSION

1 D.L. Johnson, 'On Development', in D.L. Johnson and André Gunder
   Frank (eds), Dependence and Underdevelopment, New York, Anchor
   Books, 1972.   Doubleday, p. 272.
2 A.J. Vidich and J. Bensman, Small Town in Mass Society, Princeton University Press, 1958.
3 Op. cit., 1968 edn, p. XVIII.
4 See J.D. Cockcroft and A. Gunder Frank, in Johnson and Frank,
   op. cit., p. 63.
5 W. Lippman, Public Opinion, New York, Harcourt & Brace, 1922,
   1944 edn.
6 C.M. Arensberg and S.T. Kimball, 'Community Study: Retrospect
   and Prospect', American Journal of Sociology, 1967-8, vol. 73,
   no. 6, pp. 691-705.
7 See 'The Scottish Ruling Class' by J.P. Scott and M.D. Hughes,
   in Scottish Class in Scottish Society, ed. A.A. MacLaren,
   London, Routledge & Kegan Paul, 1973; also, 'Finance, Capital
   and the Upper Class: Some Devolutionary Prospects', in Socialist
   Perspectives for Scotland, ed. G. Brown, Edinburgh University
   Student Publication.
8 H. Conroy, Scottish Daily Record, 11 February 1976, p. 1.
9 A. McBarnet, 'Industry Missing North Sea Boat', Glasgow Herald,
   8 August 1975.
10 G. Salaman, Community and Occupation, Cambridge University
   Press, 1974.
11 R.E. Pahl and J.T. Winkler; see contributions in Elites and
   Power in British Society, eds P. Stanworth and A. Giddens,
   Cambridge University Press, 1974.
12 See J.P. Scott and M.D. Hughes, 'The Scottish Ruling Class', in
   Scottish Class in Scottish Society, ed. A.A. MacLaren, London,
   Routledge & Kegan Paul, 1973, for further details and
   A. McBarnet, op. cit.
13 Ibid.
14 Ibid.
15 A. McBarnet, 'The North Sea Oil Story', Scottish Journal of
   Sociology, 1978, vol. 3, no. 1.
16 Ibid.
17 Ibid.
18 Dunoon Observer and Argyllshire Standard, 'Onlooker', 16 September 1972.
19 Ibid., 4 November 1972.
20 Ibid., 9 December 1972.
21 Ibid.
22 Ibid., 10 March 1973.
23 Ibid., 3 November 1973.
24 Ibid., 10 November 1973.
25 Ibid., 17 November 1973.
26 Ibid.
27 Ibid., 19 January 1974.
28 Ibid.
29 Ibid., 9 February 1974.
30 Ibid., 16 March 1974.
31 Ibid.

32   Ibid., 23 March 1974.
33   Ibid.
34   Ibid., 6 April 1974.
35   Ibid., 4 May 1974.
36   Ibid., 1 June 1974.
37   Ibid., 30 November 1974.
38   Ibid.; see letters in issue of 22 June 1974.
39   Ibid.
40   Some locals when talking with me about the navvies spoke of them
     as 'wreckers' and at least two referred to the 'Sabbath
     breakers' in the same conversation.   They likened them to the
     unwanted 'Godless' types whom their ancestors had blocked at the
     pier.
41   Guardian, 29 April 1972.
42   See, for example, the issue of Dunoon Observer for 15 June 1974.
43   Ibid.
44   Consult the SSRC Report to the North Sea Oil Panel (RNSOP), the
     Planning Exchange, Glasgow, 31 May 1977.
45   Report to the North Sea Oil Panel (RNSOP), 31 May 1979, Section
     2.3.
46   R. Moore, 'Northern Notes Towards a Sociology of Oil', Scottish
     Journal of Sociology, November 1978, vol. 3, no. 1; also
     R. Moore, The Social Impact of Oil, London, Routledge & Kegan
     Paul, 1982.
47   W. Lippman, op. cit.
48   J.J. Rodger, 'Inauthentic Politics and the Public Inquiry
     System', Scottish Journal of Sociology, November 1978, vol. 3,
     no. 1, pp. 103-27.
49   Moore, op. cit., 1978;   I. Carter, 'The Highlands of Scotland as
     an Underdeveloped Region', in De Kadt and Williams, Sociology of
     Development, 1976, and 'The Peasantry of N E Scotland', Journal
     of Peasant Studies, 1976, vol. 3, no. 2, pp. 151-91.
50   See RNSOP, op. cit., Section 2.3.3;   and Mark Shield, Social
     Impact Assessment: An Analytical Bibliography, National Techni-
     cal Information Service, US Dept of Commerce, 1974.
51   J.D. House, 'Oil Companies in Aberdeen: the Strategy of Incor-
     poration', Scottish Journal of Sociology, November 1978, vol. 3,
     no. 1.
52   M. Grieco, 'Social Consequences of Rapid Industrial Developments
     in Sparsely Populated Areas', Aberdeen University, unpublished
     ms, 1976.
53   RNSOP, op. cit.
54   Ibid., Section 2.4.1.
55   A.P. Cohen, 'Oil and the Cultural Account: Reflections on a
     Shetland Community', Scottish Journal of Sociology, November
     1978, vol. 3, no. 1, pp. 124-41;   also A.P. Cohen, Belonging,
     Manchester University Press, 1982.
56   Ibid., see pp. 130ff.   See also 'The Same but Different',
57   Sociological Review, 26 (3), 1978
     See Cohen's article in Scottish Journal of Sociology, op. cit.
58   G. McFarlane, 'Shetlander Identity: Change and Conflict', ms
     cited in the RNSOP.
59   See T. Steel, The Life and Death of St. Kilda, Glasgow, Collins,
     1975.

60 Unpublished ms, Way of Life Seminars, Edinburgh University, 1979.
61 G.D. Suttles, The Social Construction of Communities, Chicago University Press, 1974, pp. 170-1 and ch. 7.
62 Ibid., p. 41.
63 J.R. Gusfield, Community: a Critical Response, Oxford, Blackwell, 1975, p. 28.
64 See ibid. for a discussion of Franklin Gidding's (1922) concept of 'consciousness of kind'.
65 See Suttles, op. cit., pp. 248-50.
66 M. Janowitz, The Community Press in an Urban Setting, University of Chicago Press, 1952.
67 Way of Life Seminars, op. cit.
68 Cohen, op. cit., see p. 133 particularly.
69 See unpublished ms of J. Ennew, 'Self Image and Identity in the Hebrides', Cambridge University, May 1979.
70 See local Tory handouts for the autumn general election of 1974.
71 R.S. Lynd and H.M. Lynd, Middleton in Transition, New York, Harcourt & Brace, 1937, p. 62.
72 See MacCormick handout for SNP campaign in election period of 1974, SNP HQ, Argyll.
73 D. Taylor, 'The Social Impact of Oil', in G. Brown (ed.), The Red Paper on Scotland, Edinburgh Student Publications Board, 1975; M. Broady, 'David and Goliath in Scottish Rural Development', Community Development Journal, 1975, vol. 10, no. 2; A. Varwell, 'The Highlands and Islands Communities', in M. Broady (ed.), Marginal Regions, London, Bedford Square Press, 1973; J.J. Rodger, 'Inauthentic Politics and the Public Inquiry System', Scottish Journal of Sociology, 1978, vol. 3, no. 1, pp. 103-27
74 A. Etzioni, The Active Society, New York, Free Press, 1968, p. 619.
75 J. Habermas, 'The Public Sphere: An Encyclopaedia Article', New German Critique, 1974, no. 3, Fall.
76 A. McBarnet, op. cit., p. 46.

5 THE BUREAUCRATIC TAKE-OVER

1 Quoted by R. Michels, Political Parties, New York, Dover Publications, 1959.
2 G.C. Smith, Third Statistical Account, 1961, p. 60.
3 Ibid.
4 Ibid.   See also Centenary Issue of the Dunoon Observer and Argyllshire Standard.
5 T. Roszak, Man Made Futures, London, Hutchinson Educational, 1970, p. 71.
6 M. Harloe, Swindon: A Town in Transition, London, Heinemann, 1975, p. 233.
7 K. Hudson, An Awkward Size for a Town, Newton Abbot, David Charles, 1967.
8 See Dunoon Observer and Argyllshire Standard, 1 November 1969.
9 Ibid., see issues of October 1969-May 1970.
10 Ibid., 8 December 1969.

11 Ibid., 17 January 1970.
12 Ibid., 16 March 1970.
13 Ibid.
14 Ibid., 20 February 1971.
15 Ibid.
16 Ibid.
17 Ibid.
18 Ibid., 13 March 1971.
19 Ibid., 24 April 1971.
20 Ibid., 29 April 1972.
21 Ibid., 13 May 1972.
22 Ibid.
23 Ibid., 26 August 1972.
24 Ibid., 16 September 1972.
25 Ibid., 11 November 1972.
26 Ibid., 3 March 1973.
27 Ibid., 16 February 1974.
28 Ibid., 9 March 1974.   SNP win with a majority of 3,388 over the
    Tories.
29 Ibid., 16 March 1974.
30 Ibid., 30 March 1974.
31 Ibid., 6 April 1974.
32 Ibid., 27 April 1974.
33 Ibid., 11 May 1974.
34 Ibid., 18 May 1974.
35 Ibid., 31 August 1974.
36 Ibid., 16 November 1974.
37 Ibid., 23 November 1974.
38 Ibid.
39 Ibid., 21 December 1974.
40 The Town Council was in disarray.   The Dunoon Observer reported
    on 18 January 1975 that it was split over the issue of whether
    or not the Cowal area should be in with the Inverclyde District
    of Strathclyde rather than with Lochgilphead in the District of
    Argyll and Bute.   A Mr Cullen put forward a motion: 'That this
    Council, in the interests of Dunoon and Cowal make the strongest
    representations to the Local Government Boundary Commission for
    Scotland to have Dunoon and Cowal reinstated in the Inverclyde
    District of Strathclyde.'   Mr Cullen made the points that (1)
    no member of Dunoon had been appointed a convener;   (2) more
    workers travel daily from Renfrewshire to work at Ardyne than
    there are locals employed there, and if they were in the Inver-
    clyde District, he was sure the authority there would build
    houses here for these workers.   Judge Harper, however, stated
    'that it could not be said that Dunoon had a community of inter-
    est with Greenock.   Their main interest was tourism and Green-
    ock's was the opposite to that.'   He moved that Dunoon and
    Cowal be joined with Rothesay and Bute as a separate District
    and that the Boundary Commission be informed of their wishes.
    His motion was carried, but in the end Cowal was tied with
    Argyll and Bute under Lochgilphead.
41 A. Toffler, Future Shock, London, Pan, 1970.   Toffler bases
    much of his analysis of modern society under stress through
    change, upon the overload of information which is a feature of

modernity.   The complexities of reorganisation, added to the
impacts of the Polaris Base and the McAlpine project, created
such an overload of change, which brought with it the new dimensions of life and new modes of coping with life locally.
Stress was inevitable, and as noted lags developed in a situation of uneven change.   Toffler also states that much of modern
stress is due to such lags, citing Ogburn.

6   ENVIRONMENTAL HAZARDS

1   Dunoon Observer and Argyllshire Standard, 17 December 1960.
2   K.H. Wolff, 'Surrender and Community Study', in Reflections on
    Community Studies, eds D.J. Vidich and J. Bensman, New York,
    Harper & Row, 1971, pp. 239-40.
3   R.G. Baker, 'On the Nature of the Environment', in Environmental
    Psychology, eds H.M. Proshansky, W.H. Ittelson and L.G. Rivlin,
    New York, Holt, Rinehart & Winston, 1970, pp. 15ff.
4   R.M. Downs, 'The Role of Perception in Modern Geography', Uni-
    versity of Bristol, Dept of Geography, Summer Paper Series,
    1968, A 11, pp. 1-20;   D. Stea and R.M. Downs, 'From the Outside
    Looking In at the Inside Looking Out', Environment and Behaviour,
    1970, 2, pp. 3-12;   F.W. Shemyakin, 'On the Psychology of Space
    Representations', as cited from his 1940 paper by B.G. Ananyev
    et al. (eds), Psychological Science in the USSR, vol. 1,
    Washington Office of Technical Services, 1960;   also, 'Orienta-
    tions in Space', in ibid., Report No. 62, 11.83
5   G.G. Giarchi, PhD Thesis, 'Between McAlpine and Polaris', Glas-
    gow University, in which the cognitive maps of the local people
    are discussed, 1980, pp. 265-70 and Appendix 9.2.   See also
    G.D. Suttles, The Social Construction of Communities, Chicago
    University Press, 1972, see pp. 22, 25, 32-3, 41, 56-7.
6   P. Berger and T. Luckmann, The Social Construction of Reality,
    London, Penguin, 1966.   See index for references to 'sedimenta-
    tion'.
7   Giarchi, op. cit.
8   Dunoon Observer and Argyllshire Standard, 6 March 1971.
9   R.W. Kates, 'Experiencing the Environment as Hazard', in Envir-
    onmental Psychology, 2nd edn, eds H. Proshansky, W.H. Ittelson
    and L.G. Rivlin, New York, Holt, Rinehart & Winston, 1976,
    p. 404;   Dunoon Observer and Argyllshire Standard, 26 July
    1975;   Dunoon Observer and Argyllshire Standard, 1 March 1975.
10 The article was by Jack House, Evening Times, Glasgow, 2 March
    1976.   Findings of research (SSRC), PhD Thesis, Giarchi, op.
11 cit., Appendix 9.5.
11 Ibid.
12 Photographs showing the Polaris Base, or depot ship on greeting
    cards produced by Dennis Production, Scarborough.
13 See Appendix 9.3 of Giarchi, op. cit.   See also p. 280.
14 Dunoon Observer and Argyllshire Standard, 1 March 1975.
15 See Giarchi, op. cit., pp. 561-90.
16 Dunoon Observer and Argyllshire Standard, 26 July 1975.
17 Ibid.
18 J. House, Evening Times, Glasgow, 2 March 1976.

19 The local people have talked about this situation as proof that
    no one can be trusted outside the locality; as one local put it
    to me: 'If they can't go to the trouble of providing a road
    sign to our town, how can one hope for any constructive help
    from the powers that be at Strathclyde.'

7 A PLUNDERED ECONOMY

1   S. Giner, Sociology, London, Martin Robertson, 1972, p. 266.
2   Dunoon Observer and Argyllshire Standard; see issues of the
    autumn 1960.
3   Ibid., 16 April 1960.
4   Ibid., 2 November 1963.
5   Ibid., 19 November 1960.
6   Ibid., 12 December 1960.
7   Ibid., 15 April 1961.
8   Ibid., 30 March 1963.
9   Ibid. No appropriate concern for local creditors was expressed
    by the official communique.
10 Ibid., 9 March 1963.
11 See Evaluation Rolls, Register House, Edinburgh, 1958-9 and
    1961-2.
12 Ibid.
13 The US officers often boasted that American money subsidised
    Dunoon and the locality.
14 Dunoon Observer and Argyllshire Standard, 28 September 1967.
15 Ibid., 15 February 1969.
16 Ibid., 8 March 1969.
17 Ibid., 6 February,1971.
18 Ibid., 23 September 1972.
19 Ibid., 20 July 1974.
20 Evening Times, Glasgow, 21 January 1975, p. 5.
21 J. Fryer and G. Rosie, Sunday Times, 7 March 1976.
22 See Sunday Times, accompanying article to the above.
23 Ibid.
24 The 'single buoy mooring' had been devised. It basically con-
    sisted of a floating pipe to which a discharging tanker could be
    moored. There was a huge programme of alternative methods put
    forward, which have since been dropped. The costs of building
    concrete gravity structures were regarded as extreme. All
    sorts of inventions received attention in an attempt to cut out
    such enormous expenditure for platform-building.
25 Rosemary Long, Evening Times, 19 January 1976, an article on
    Ardyne. The journalist lived locally.
26 Ibid.
27 Rosemary Long, Evening Times, Glasgow, 2 June 1975, an article.
28 Ibid., 23 January 1975.
29 Dunoon Observer and Argyllshire Standard, 1 March 1975.
30 Ibid., 25 May 1975.
31 Ibid., 2 November 1975.
32 G.G. Giarchi, 'Between McAlpine and Polaris', unpublished PhD
    Thesis, Glasgow University, Appendix 8.
33 Ibid.

34 Ibid., see Appendix 9.5.

35 Ibid.

36 Ibid., see Appendix 9.3 and 9.5 and pp. 324-5.

37 Dunoon Observer and Argyllshire Standard, 30 November 1968.

38 Ibid.

39 Ibid., 26 August 1978.

40 Ibid., 11 September 1975.

41 Ibid., 24 January 1976.

42 There were no new public buildings, apart from the indoor swimming pool on the East Bay, since the Americans arrived. If anything, according to many local people, things had deteriorated. One of the biggest complaints was the condition of the roads. A local wrote a poem in the Dunoon Observer and Argyllshire Standard to express his dissatisfaction on the 8 February 1975. It ran as follows:

'Ode to Roads in Dunoon'

> You may travel east, you may travel west,
> But, there is a town to beat the rest,
> With roads to make McAdam swoon.
> Where is this place?   It is Dunoon.
>
> Who made these ditches and numerous holes?
> Gas?   Electricity?   Hydro-Boards or Moles?
> From Gourock to Skye, Glasgow to Troon,
> You won't find roads like those in Dunoon.
>
> There are so many ditches, trenches and holes,
> That drivers are asking, 'Why pay the tolls?'
> And they would be all over the moon,
> If something was done about the roads in Dunoon.
>
> Don't get me wrong, I'm no moaner,
> And wouldn't like to be labelled a 'groaner';
> But, I'm sure that my end will come soon,
> If something isn't done about the roads in Dunoon.
> M.T.S. (Dunoon)

Those who supported the move to Strathclyde alluded to the state of the roads under the older regime, and hoped that somehow things would be better under Glasgow and Lochgilphead. Ann Melville in 1975 saw little hope of any improvement. Local residents became quite fatalistic after the American let-down after the promised naval boom (see the postscript to this study for further proof of the negative effects of that promised boom which was never to be).

8 A POLITICAL BABEL

1 J.D.B. Miller, The Nature of Politics, Harmondsworth, Pelican, 1962, p. 14.

2 Dunoon Observer and Argyllshire Standard, 3 December 1960.

3 Ibid.
4 R.L. Warren, The Community in America, Chicago, Rand McNally, 1963.
5 Ibid., p. 151.
6 As reported by B. Wilson in the Glasgow Herald on the occasion of the annual CND protest rally in 1977.
7 See the Dunoon Observer and Argyllshire Standard, 2 June 1973, for a local citation of the Foreign Policy Document of the Labour party.
8 Ibid.
9 J. Habermas, 'The Public Sphere', as referred to earlier.
10 SNP Manifesto, Scotland's Future, Edinburgh, SNP Manor House, August 1974.
11 Scotsman, 4 October 1974.
12 S. Lukes, 'Political Ritual of Social Integration', in Sociology, 1975, vol. 9, no. 2.
13 Dunoon Observer and Argyllshire Standard, 22 May 1971. In this issue it was stated, 'Despite reports from the Pentagon last month that development of Poseidon missiles might be indefinitely postponed ... a US naval spokesman confirmed last Sunday that the USS James Madison was being loaded with Poseidon missiles from the depot ship Canopus. He added that the agreement of the British government for their deployment from the Holy Loch, not expected until late summer, had been recently given. The James Madison is the first of the 31 submarines out of the American fleet of 41 to be converted to carry the larger weapon.' Locals knew of the deployment of the missile when the Pentagon protested it would postpone deployment. A local man told me that people at Sandbank and Kilmun spoke of some new missile when no one knew in the UK of the existence of Poseidon.

Concern locally increased over the presence of Poseidon. There had been a fire aboard the Canopus on 5 December 1970, when the local residents became acutely concerned because the fire was within 90ft of the main Polaris and Poseidon missile store as reported in the local press on 2 January 1971. The concern created a revival amongst the followers of Mrs Robertson at Sandbank and Mr Smith (CND) at Inverchaolin. One of the biggest demonstrations followed in March and the BBC team for the programme '24 Hours' spent several days working on a programme concerned with the Polaris Base, which had been 'dead news' for some years.
14 D. Fairhill, 'The Cosy American Connection', Manchester Guardian, 29 September 1981, p. 17.
15 D.R. Segal and M.W. Segal, 'Modes of Military and Civil Relations at the Elite Level', in Perceived Role of the Military, Rotterdam University Press, 1971, pp. 283-4.
16 D. Sutton, 'The Military Mission Against Off-Base Discrimination', in C.C. Moskos (ed.), Public Opinion and the Military Establishment, California, Sage, 1971, pp. 162ff.
17 P.Y. Hammond, 'Effects of Structure on Policy, Public Administration, 1958, 18, pp. 175-9. Also 'A Functional Analysis of Defense Dept. Decision-Making in the MacNamara Administration', American Political Science Review, 1968, 62, pp. 57, 59ff.

Also, <u>Organising for Defense</u>, New York, Princeton University Press, 1961.

18 'The Negro in the Armed Forces', Government Printing Office, Washington D.C., pp. 169-224 (mimeograph).

19 C.W. Mills, <u>The Power Elite</u>, New York, Oxford University Press, 1956, p. 195.

20 J.M. Swomley, Jnr, <u>The Military Establishment</u>, Boston, Beacon Press, 1964, pp. 250ff.

21 Sutton, op. cit., pp. 168-9.

22 Ibid., p. 170.

23 Senator Stennis, a Chairman of the Armed Services Committee, has commented: 'the executive department does not have the final say as to what shall be considered "fitness and efficiency" entitling an officer to promotion: the final power rests with the Senate'. See Sutton, op. cit.

24 See <u>Army Times</u>, September 1963, USA, p. 1. Also cf. Sutton, op. cit., who states: 'Inconsistent "Defense Directives" are on record.'

25 G.C. Homans, 'The Small Warship', <u>American Sociological Review</u>, 1964, 11, pp. 294-300; P.L. Berkman, 'Life Aboard an Armed Ship', <u>American Journal of Sociology</u>, 1964, 51, pp. 300-87; L.A. Zurcher, Jnr, 'The Sailor Aboard Ship: A Study of Role Behaviour in a Total Institution', <u>Social Forces</u>, 1965, 43, pp. 389-99; R.W. Little, 'Buddy Relations and Combat Performance', in M. Janowitz (ed.), <u>The New Military: Changing Patterns of Organisation</u>, New York, Russell Sage Foundation, 1964, pp. 195-223.

26 <u>Dunoon Observer and Argyllshire Standard</u>, 30 November 1974.

27 A. McBarnet, 'The North Sea Oil Story', <u>Scottish Journal of Sociology</u>, 1978, vol. 3, no. 1, p. 45.

28 M. Drummon, R. Bryer et al., <u>Ardyne Tomorrow: An Outline For Discussion</u>, Southampton, Inland and Waterside Planners, 1975, p. 6.

29 Ibid., p. 17.

30 See 'Community Councils: Some Alternatives for Community Council Schemes in Scotland' (HMSO); see also terms of Section 51(1) of the Local Government (Scotland) Act, 1973. Asaadvertised in the local press, Community Councils in Argyll and Bute (see for example issue of 5 April 1975, <u>Dunoon Observer</u>): 'The main role of Community Councils will be to ascertain, co-ordinate, and express to Strathclyde Region and Argyll and Bute District Councils and other public bodies the views of the community about matters for which those authorities and bodies are responsible.'

The remit was therefore enormous, but the actual power of the councils were minimal because they simply had powers to express public opinion. Their remit was enormous because they had to express it at District and at regional HQ levels within tight schedules in which committees at both levels, besides those of other public bodies, might clash or come too close together on the calendar of events.

They also had to raise their own funds, subsidised by the new

authority.   They were also caught in the double-bind situation
of having the role 'of organising action with the community', so
whenever such action involved them in confrontation over an
authority issue, they the authorities with regard to the amounts
of money given to subsidise their funds.

There was also the problem of identifying boundaries, whether
of:

1 the 'neighbourhood type' of between 2,000-15,000 persons in
urban settings, or of between 'under a hundred people to several
thousand in rural settings; or of

2 the 'locality type' of 'several neighbourhoods', ranging in
size 'in urban districts from about 10,000 to about 50,000',
while in 'mainly rural districts' varying 'from about 5,000 to
(in a few cases) over 25,000'.

In the Cowal area there was endless confusion in the process
of determining the Community Councils following upon such vague
guidelines with regard to dispersed settlements in particular.
Draft schemes were supposed to be in at Lochgilphead by the 10
February 1976.   They were delayed due to endless local debate
over what was the 'neighbourhood'.

31 See G.G. Giarchi, 'Between McAlpine and Polaris', unpublished
PhD Thesis, Glasgow University, 1980, Appendix 1, pp. 473-97.
32 Ibid., Appendix 9, pp. 620, 622 and 636.
33 R. Taylor, 'Ach Him A Kent His Faither', Scottish Journal of
Youth and Community Work, 1976, vol. 4, no. 1, Edinburgh:
Board for Information on Youth and Community Service.
34 See Giarchi, op. cit., pp. 618-19.

9 CULTURE CLASHES

1 H. Brody, Inishkillane, Harmondsworth, Penguin, 1973, p. 8.
2 P. Berger and T. Luckmann, The Social Construction of Reality,
Harmondsworth, Penguin, 1966.
3 R. Feinberg, 'Schneider's Symbolic Culture Theory', Current
Anthropology, University of Chicago Press, September 1979.
4 Brody, op. cit.
5 W.F. Ogburn, Social Change, New York, Heubsch, 1922.
6 Brody, op. cit., p. 43.
7 C.C. Moskos, The American Enlisted Man, New York, Sage, 1970.
8 Dunoon Observer and Argyllshire Standard, 9 September 1961.
9 Cited in Dunoon Observer on 20 January 1962.
10 Ibid., 27 January 1962.
11 Ibid., 7 April 1962.
12 Ibid.
13 Ibid., 14 April 1962.
14 Ibid., 5 May 1962.
15 Ibid., 16 June, 1962.
16 Ibid.; the poem appeared in a May issue, 1963.
17 See K. Millet, Sexual Politics, London, Rupert Hart-Davis,
1969, for a discussion of sexual exploitation.

18 See also J. Mitchell, Woman's Estate, Harmondsworth, Penguin,
    1971, for a discussion of male dominance.
19 N. Mailer, Why Are We in Vietnam?, London, Weidenfeld &
    Nicolson, 1969; D. Ponicsan, Cinderella Liberty, London, Sphere
    Books, 1974.
20 See W. Caudhill, 'American Soldiers in a Japanese Community', un-
    published ms, and see G.G. Giarchi, 'An Organization Study of
    the US Navy', MA dissertation, Sociology Dept, Leeds University,
    1974.
21 Cited by Moskos, op. cit.
22 D. Wecter, When Johnny Comes Marching Home, Cambridge, Mass.,
    Houghton Mifflin, 1944, p. 332.
23 This was especially the case in the summer holiday periods.
    See Moskos, op. cit., for a commentary on the enlisted culture.
24 For a discussion of the American servicemen and their liberal
    attitudes abroad, see Wecter, op. cit.
25 Dunoon Observer and Argyllshire Standard, 29 June 1963.
26 Ibid., 19 October 1963.
27 Ibid., 26 October 1963.
28 Ibid., 21 March 1964.
29 Census 1971 Argyll, County Local Authority Areas (HMSO) see
    Tables.
30 Brody, op. cit.
31 Dunoon Observer and Argyllshire Standard, 10 November 1973.
32 Ibid., see 'local Echoes', 3 October 1973; ibid., 10 November
    1973; ibid., 27 October 1973; see also letter of Mr Wyatt,
    'The Safety Valve'.
33 Daily Telegraph, 16 October 1973, 'Black Power Inquiry After US
    Ratings Charged'.
34 Moskos, op. cit., p. 123.
35 Ibid.
36 See Daily Record, Thursday, 10 October 1974, 'Taunt in Pub That
    Started a Riot'.
37 See Sun, Monday, 1 December 1975.
38 This was reported in January 1977, in the Sunday Express. See
    also, Sunday Post, 6 March 1977, Sunday Times, 23 January 1977,
    Sunday Mail, 23 January 1977.
39 Daily Record, 1 May 1977, p. 1.
40 See Giarchi, 'Between McAlpine and Polaris', unpublished PhD
    Thesis, Glasgow University, 1980, Appendix 5.
41 Wolf, op. cit.
42 See Giarchi, op. cit., 1974. The appendices present a full
    statement of military privileges and full discussion of naval
    privileges. These are also available in the handout given to
    the naval arrivals by the US Naval Activities United Kingdom
    Detachment, Holy Loch, as already referred to.
43 C.C. Moskos, op. cit.
44 Ibid., p. 146.
45 Ibid., pp. 153-4.
46 A.J. Vidich and J. Bensman, Small Town in Mass Society, New
    York, Doubleday, 1960; E. Chinoy, Automobile Workers and The
    American Dream, Boston, Beacon Press, 1965; H.J. Gans, The
    Levittowners, New York, Parthenon Books, 1965.
47 R. Nauta, 'Armed Forces and Ideology', in The Perceived Role of

the Military, ed. M.R. Van Gills, Rotterdam University Press, 1971, pp. 282-3.

48 See Giarchi, op. cit., 1980, p. 397.

49 Sunday Mail, 6 July 1975, 'You've Never Lived Till You've Tried a Harvey Wallbanger'.

50 Millet, op. cit., pp. 33-8.

51 See Giarchi, op. cit., 1980, Tables 1 and 2, Appendix 5.

52 Ibid.

53 Ibid., Table 3, Appendix 5.

54 Ibid.

55 Evening Times, Glasgow, 2 June 1975, Rosemary Long.

56 Ibid., 2 June, 1975.

57 The People, 20 July 1975.

58 Heard in Dunoon in the winter of 1975.

59 R. Ryall, 1980: 'Cliques Within the Multi-National Migrant Oil Workforce - Instruments of Survival', unpublished ms, Aberdeen University, presented at the March 1980 Seminar, Sociology Department.

60 Strathclyde University lectures of Professor Sykes. See also Sykes, 'Navvies' Work Attitudes', Sociology, 1969, vol. 3, no. 1, pp. 21-35 and 'Navvies, Their Social Relations', Sociology, vol. 3, no. 2, pp. 157-72.

61 Reference made to the 'Dunoon Mafia' at the Aberdeen Conference by researchers in N.E. Scotland: Aberdeen, March 1980 SSRC/ North Sea Oil Panel.   Peter Taylor, G. Philip, and Alan Hutton reported on Sullom Voe: 'There's a lot of people from Dunoon working up here.   They call them the Dunoon Mafia', p. 24 of University handout, Seminar on Migrant Labour in the North Sea Oil Industry.

62 See Giarchi, op. cit., 1980, Appendix 9, pp.620ff

63 Ibid., see questions 7-12 inclusive, pp. 614ff.

64 Ibid., p. 631.

65 Ibid., p. 615.

66 Ibid., p. 433.

67 Ibid., Appendix 9, p. 629.

68 Ibid.

69 Ibid., p. 631.

70 Ibid., p. 615.

71 Ibid.

72 Ibid., pp. 637-8.

10 PUTTING TOGETHER THE PICTURE

1   T. Garnet, as cited in the Radio Times, 15-26 April 1978, p. 35 (Garnet - drama product to 'Law and Order' BBC Documentary).

11 POSTSCRIPT

1   See Dunoon Observer and Argyllshire Advertiser, 26 September 1981.

2   Ibid.

3   Ibid., 21 November 1981.

4   Ibid.
5   Ibid., 'Missile Inquiry', 12 December 1981.
6   Ibid.
7   Ibid., 5 December 1981.

SUBJECT INDEX

AUTHOR INDEX